# The Rebirth of Latin American Christianity

# The Rebirth of Latin American Christianity

TODD HARTCH

OXFORD

UNIVERSITY PRESS

# OXFORD
UNIVERSITY PRESS

Oxford University Press is a department of the University of Oxford.
It furthers the University's objective of excellence in research, scholarship,
and education by publishing worldwide.

Oxford   New York
Auckland   Cape Town   Dar es Salaam   Hong Kong   Karachi
Kuala Lumpur   Madrid   Melbourne   Mexico City   Nairobi
New Delhi   Shanghai   Taipei   Toronto

With offices in
Argentina   Austria   Brazil   Chile   Czech Republic   France   Greece
Guatemala   Hungary   Italy   Japan   Poland   Portugal   Singapore
South Korea   Switzerland   Thailand   Turkey   Ukraine   Vietnam

Published in the United States of America by
Oxford University Press
198 Madison Avenue, New York, NY 10016

CIP data is on file at the LOC

9780199844593
9780199843138 (pbk.)

1  3  5  7  9  8  6  4  2

Printed in the United States of America
on acid-free paper

*For Trevor*

# Contents

# Acknowledgments

LAMIN SANNEH AND Jon Bonk encouraged me to write this book, and I am glad they did. It has been a great privilege to work with them and the other scholars associated with Oxford Studies in World Christianity.

At Eastern Kentucky University, my colleagues in the history department have created an environment that supports and appreciates scholarship, no easy task at a regional comprehensive institution that focuses on teaching. Special thanks go to my chair, Chris Taylor, and dean, John Wade, for giving me a course release in the spring of 2011 that enabled me to write the first few chapters. Bob Houston, Marianella Machado, Scott Hunt, Carroll Hale, Marilyn Maturani, Cat Stearn, Ronald Gainer, Mike Austin, and Steve Barracca have contributed to an interdisciplinary culture of intellectual exchange at EKU that has aided my work immensely. I also give thanks for my students, especially those in my undergraduate course on Latin American Christianity in 2011 and my graduate course on World Christianity in 2013, who heard much of this material in draft form and gave me important new ideas to consider. I have taught at several institutions, but I have to say that EKU students are my favorites.

I could not have completed this project without the support of my wife, Kathline. Her care, reassurance, and example, day in and day out, made it possible for me to finish the manuscript with a minimum of stress. Trevor, Peter, Evelyn, Greg, Tim, John, Sue, Cal, and Missy gave me crucial encouragement at various points in the writing process. At Oxford University Press, Theo Calderara and two anonymous readers provided valuable advice that enabled me to tighten and clarify my work. Finally, Bill Peatman deserves credit for introducing me to the complex world of Latin American religion on a trip to the Yucatán in 1987. That experience raised questions that I have been trying to answer ever since.

# Abbreviations

| | |
|---|---|
| ASJ | Associaçâo do Senhor Jesus, Association of the Lord Jesus |
| BGEA | Billy Graham Evangelistic Association |
| CCR | Catholic Charismatic Renewal |
| CEB | Comunidad eclesial de base, base ecclesial community |
| CELAM | Consejo Episcopal Latinoamericano, Latin American Episcopal Council (Conference) |
| CLADE | Conferencia Latinoamericana De Evangelización, Latin American Evangelization Conference |
| CLAI | Consejo Latinoamericano de Iglesias, Latin American Council of Churches |
| COMIBAM | Congreso Misionero Iberoamericano, Ibero-American Missionary Congress |
| COMLA | Congreso Misionero Latinoamericano, Latin American Missionary Congress |
| CONELA | Confraternidad Evangélica Latinoamericana, Latin American Evangelical Fraternity |
| COPACHI | Comité de Cooperación para la Paz en Chile, Committee for Cooperation for Peace in Chile |
| CNBB | Conferência Nacional dos Bispos do Brasil, National Conference of Brazilian Bishops |
| CPT | Comissão Pastoral da Terra, Pastoral Land Commission of Brazil |
| ECCLA | Encuentro Carismático Católico Latino Americano, Latin American Catholic Charismatic Conference |
| EOC | Economy of Communion (Focolare) |
| EZLN | Ejército Zapatista de Liberación Nacional, Zapatista Army of National Liberation |

| | |
|---|---|
| FEINE | Federación Evangélica Indigena Nacional del Ecuador, National Evangelical Indigenous Federation of Ecuador |
| IURD | Igreja Universal do Reino de Deus, Universal Church of the Kingdom of God |
| LAM | Latin America Mission |
| LPA | Luis Palau Association |
| MEB | Movimento de Educação de Base, Basic Education Movement |
| NEM | New Ecclesial Movement |
| OAP | Ondas de Amor y Paz, Waves of Love and Peace |
| SIL | Summer Institute of Linguistics (Wycliffe Bible Translators) |
| SINE | Sistema Integral de Evangelización, Systemic Integral New Evangelization |
| SVC | Sodalitium Vitae Christianae, Sodality of Christian Life |
| UNEC | Unión Nacional de Estudiantes Católicos, National Union of Catholic Students |

# Introducing the Oxford Series

## LAMIN SANNEH

AMONG THE MANY breathtaking developments since World War II and in the subsequent post-colonial years, few are more striking than the worldwide resurgence of Christianity. Christianity has become, or is fast becoming, the principal religion of the peoples of the world. Primal societies that once stood well outside the main orbit of the faith have become major centers of practice, while Europe and North America, once considered the religion's bastions, are in noticeable recession. We seem to be in the middle of massive cultural shifts and realignments whose implications are only now beginning to become clear. Aware that Europe's energies at the time were absorbed in war, Archbishop William Temple presciently observed in 1944 that this global spread of the religion was "the new fact of our time." An impressive picture now emerges revealing Christianity's stunningly diverse profile: the growing numbers and the geographical scope of the religion's growth, the cross-cultural patterns of encounter, the variety and diversity of cultures affected, the structural and anti-structural nature of the changes involved, the kaleidoscope of cultures often manifesting familiar and unfamiliar variations on the canon, the wide spectrum of theological views and ecclesiastical traditions represented, the ideas of authority and styles of leadership that have been developed, the process of acute indigenization that fosters liturgical renewal, and the production of new religious art, music, hymns, songs, and prayers.

These unprecedented developments cast a revealing light on the serial nature of Christian origins, expansion, and subsequent attrition. They fit into the cycles of retreat and advance, of contraction and expansion, and of waning and awakening that have characterized the religion since its birth, though they are now revealed to us with particular force. The pattern of contrasting development is occurring simultaneously in various societies across the world. The religion is now in the twilight of its Western phase and at the beginning of its formative non-Western impact. Christianity has not ceased to be a Western religion, but its future as a world religion is now being formed and shaped at the hands and in the minds of its non-Western adherents. Rather than a cause for unsettling gloom, for Christians this new situation is a reason for guarded hope.

Today students of the subject can stand in the middle of the recession of Christianity in its accustomed heartland while witnessing its resurgence in areas long considered receding missionary lands. In 1950, some 80 percent of the world's Christians lived in the northern hemisphere in Europe and North America. By 2005 the vast majority of Christians lived in the southern hemisphere—in Asia, Africa, and Latin America. In 1900, at the outset of colonial rule, there were fewer than 9 million Christians in Africa, of whom the vast majority were Ethiopian Orthodox or Coptic. In 1960, at the end of the colonial period, the number of Christians had increased to about 60 million, with Catholics and Protestants making up 50 million, and the other 10 million divided between the Ethiopian Orthodox and Coptic Churches. By 2005, the African Christian population had increased to roughly 393 million, which is almost 50 percent of Africa's population.

It is estimated that there are just over 2 billion Christians worldwide, making Christianity among the world's fastest growing religions. In terms of the languages and ethnic groups affected, as well as the variety of churches and movements involved, Christianity is also the most diverse and pluralist religion in the world. More people pray and worship in more languages and with more different styles of worship in Christianity than in any other religion. Well over 2,000 of the world's languages are embraced by Christianity through Bible translation, prayer, liturgy, hymns, and literature. More than 90 percent of these languages have a grammar and a dictionary only because the Western missionary movement provided them, thus pioneering the largest, most diverse, and most vigorous movement of cultural renewal in history. At the same time, the post-Western Christian resurgence is occurring in societies already characterized by currents of indigenous religious pluralism. In addition to firsthand familiarity with at least one other religion, most new Christians speak at the minimum two languages. This massive diversity represents a Christianity quite different from the religion a Christian in the secular West has been accustomed to, but it is now the reality.

Increasingly and in growing numbers, Third World churches are appearing in the towns and cities of the West, while Third World missionaries are also arriving to serve in churches in Europe and North America—the beginning of the re-evangelization of a secularized West by orthodox Christians of former missionized countries. It is sobering to reflect on the implications and political impact of such a sharp cultural encounter. The empty churches of the West are being filled with mounting numbers of non-Western Christians whose orthodox religious views will pose a radical challenge to the secular liberal status quo, while institutions of liberal theological education are busy redefining themselves to preempt a cultural collision with the post-Western Christian resurgence. Orthodox Christian groups in the West are meanwhile positioning themselves to effect a complex strategic alliance with the new resurgence.

Mainline denominations have already felt the force of this shift. In the Roman Catholic Church the structural adjustment of Vatican II has allowed the new winds of change to sweep through the church (if at times it has been impeded), producing movements in several different directions and across the world. The New Catholic Catechism reflects the change in language, mood, and style, and the rapid creation of bishops and cardinals in the non-Western church, accompanied by a steady stream of papal encyclicals, testifies to the fresh momentum of post-Western Christianity. The papacy has not been only an observer of the change but also an active promoter of it, and, in the particular case of Pius XII, the source of a well-tempered preparation for it. Similarly, churches and denominations involved in the Protestant ecumenical movement have felt jostled in unexpected, uncomfortable ways by the sudden entrance into their ranks of new Third World churches. The worldwide Anglican Communion has been reeling under pressure from the organized and concerted Third World reaction to the consecration and installation of a practicing gay bishop by the Episcopal Church USA. The other Protestant churches with sizable Third World memberships have paused to reflect on the implications for them of such a culture clash. Not since the Reformation has there been such a shakeup of authority in the Western church, with unprecedented implications for the West's cultural preeminence.

In the meantime, the number of mainline Protestant missionaries is decreasing while evangelical missionary numbers are growing steadily, complemented by a rising tide of African, Asian, and other Third World missionaries, including more than 10,000 from South Korea alone. In 1950, Christians in South Korea numbered barely half a million; today there are some 13 million, and they are among the most prosperous and mobile of people anywhere. It is likely that churches in South Korea rather than churches in the West will play a key role on the new Christian frontier about to open in China, which might well become a dominant axis of the religion, with hard-to-imagine implications for the rest of the world.

These facts and developments afford a unique opportunity and challenge for cross-cultural study of the asymmetry of the turnover and serial impact of Christianity, where a dip here is followed by a bounce there. The intersection of the path of decline in the West with the upward swing of momentum of post-Western Christianity makes the subject a compelling and deeply rewarding one for comparative study and critical reflection.

The new reality brought about by the shift in Christianity's center of gravity from the northern to the southern hemisphere provides the context for the volumes in this series, which are designed to bring the fruits of new research and reflection to the attention of the educated, non-specialist reader. The first volume offers a panoramic survey of the field, exploring the nature and scope of Christianity's worldwide multicultural impact. The agents, methods, and means of expansion are investigated closely to clarify the pattern and forms as well as issues of appropriation and inculturation. The cultural understandings that allowed the religion to take root in diverse settings under vastly different historical and political circumstances are assessed to determine how they shaped the reception of Christianity. Similarly, Christianity's intercontinental range as well as its encounter with other religions, including Islam, elicited challenges for the religion in the course of its worldwide expansion. These challenges are also examined.

The subsequent volumes will be devoted to specific themes and regions within the general subject of Christianity's development as a world religion. While each volume is conceived and written individually, together the volumes are united in their focus on post-Western developments in Christianity and in the elaborations, variations, continuities, and divergences with the originating Western forms of the religion.

# The Rebirth of Latin American Christianity

# Introduction

OVER THE LAST century Christianity has experienced marked numerical growth, even as Europe, its homeland for the previous millennium, has become increasingly secular. The world Christian population has increased from 600 million to over 2 billion, with the most rapid growth occurring in Africa, Latin America, and Asia. In fact, "we are currently living through one of the transforming moments in the history of religion worldwide," as, in both numbers and intensity, Christianity is shifting from the global North to the global South, from Europe and North America to Africa, Asia, and Latin America. Africa, which was home to only 9 million Christians in 1900 but hosts 360 million today, and Latin America, with more than 480 million Christians, are becoming the new centers of Christianity, while "the era of Western Christianity has passed within our lifetimes."[1]

The rapid growth of Christianity in Africa was the last thing that most academics had expected.[2] Decolonization was supposed to bring secularization, or perhaps a return to traditional African religions, as Christianity departed along with the colonial overlords. Instead, the rate of Christian growth increased, with, for example, 16,000 Africans converting *every day* by 1985.[3] Similarly, the communist takeover of China in 1949 was presumed to be the death knell for the Chinese churches. Western missionaries did have to leave, but, despite persecution, Christianity expanded, growing from fewer than 1 million believers in 1949 to between 15 and 75 million today.[4] An even more radical story can be found in Korea, which had only a handful of Christians in 1900 but is now one of the missionary powerhouses of the twenty-first century, with millions of Christians sponsoring over 10,000 missionaries in 2002.[5]

Latin America is part of this southward shift of Christianity, but its story and its role in the transformation of world Christianity are different from those of Africa and Asia. Although it is located mostly in the southern hemisphere, Latin America, unlike Asia and Africa, is neither newly Christian nor truly "non-Western." After 500 years of Christianity, the region hosts a spectrum of religious beliefs and practices, from tangentially Christian indigenous religion, to folk Catholicism, to the institutional Catholic Church, to more recent phenomena such as Protestantism and liberation theology. Predominantly Catholic since its conquest and colonization by Spain and Portugal in the fifteenth and sixteenth centuries, Latin America is still largely Catholic today, but the religious continuity in the region masks great changes that have taken place in the past six decades. In fact, it would be fair to say that Latin American Christianity has been transformed dramatically in the years since 1950. The change has not been as obvious as it has been in other regions because the transformation has not been, as in Africa and Asia, the sudden and massive growth of a new faith. It has been rather a simultaneous fragmentation and revitalization that threatened, awakened, and ultimately brought to greater maturity a dormant and at times parochial religion. The vibrant panoply of Christianity can be seen in a few "snapshots" of Latin American religious life over the last several decades.

The first takes us to an island in the Solentiname archipelago of Lake Nicaragua in the 1970s, during the brutal dictatorship of Anastasio Somoza. Every Sunday, instead of a sermon, the priest and poet Ernesto Cardenal conducted a Bible study of the day's Gospel reading using the simple Protestant *Dios Llega al Hombre* (*Good News*) translation. Participants, mostly campesinos from the islands with little education, some of them illiterate, simply commented on their understanding of the text in question. Cardenal asked questions and made comments from time to time, but in general he tried to stay in the background. In one of these Bible studies, in response to Mary's song of praise, the Magnificat, where she says of God, "He pulls down the mighty from their thrones and raises up the humble/He fills the hungry with good things and he leaves the rich with nothing," Cardenal asked what King Herod would have said if he had heard Mary's words. One woman replied, "That she was a communist." A man added that such a comment would have been correct because Mary really was a communist. They then interpreted Mary's words as referring to a coming revolution. "We are just barely beginning to see the liberation she announces," they concluded.[6]

A different strain of Christianity can be seen in Garanhuns, in northeastern Brazil, where a woman named Dona Joanina was intrigued by a new group that had started at her local Catholic church in the 1990s. The group devoted itself to singing, prayer, and lively personal testimonies, all conducted in a manner that made some parishioners believe it was a Protestant incursion that had somehow been allowed to fester in their church. Still attracted by the life she saw in the meetings and convinced that it could not truly be Protestant if it was taking place in a Catholic church, Joanina started attending. Although her parish priests, proponents of liberation theology, looked down on the Charismatic group, it prospered and continued to attract adherents. Years later, Joanina had become a steadfast member of the group and led their decision to start a day care facility for street children.[7]

Still another form of Christianity is found in southern Mexico. When sociologist Enrique Marroquín set out to study religion in the indigenous villages of Oaxaca in the early 1990s, he found not some idealized form of indigenous religion but rather a very complex situation. In the typical village, he said, one encountered the old ways and the new ways utterly intertwined. The traditional cargo system, in which men slowly moved their way up the positions of the civil-religious hierarchy over the course of a lifetime, still operated and still sponsored feasts for the village's patron saint, while Protestant villagers dismissed these activities as worthless and rejected the alcohol involved in such celebrations. Shamans still went to sacred caves, yet young people, returning from migrations to the cities, found such activities backward and unappealing. Atheists confronted members of the Catholic Cursillo renewal movement, who in turn rejected traditional indigenous religion but supported the institutional version of the faith. Feminists and liberationists locked horns with traditionalists and conservatives.[8]

Each of these snapshots raises particular issues that will reappear throughout this book. The rise of Pentecostalism introduced a form of spirituality that was especially suited to urban areas, while a variety of new movements within the Catholic Church emphasized the agency of lay Catholics. But the dominant theme of our story is the relationship between Catholicism and Protestantism. At times, there has been bloody conflict, especially for early converts to Protestantism in the countryside. But in recent decades, despite continuing episodes of violence in places such as Chiapas, the relationship has proved surprisingly fruitful, even if neither side usually admits it. Protestants in Latin America used the region's Catholic culture as a sort of "pre-evangelism" that had already introduced the Trinity and many other Christian concepts. It was thus four centuries of Catholicism that prepared the way for the stunning rise of Protestantism in the twentieth century. At the same time, Protestants often provided a valuable service by breaking the religious monopoly held by indigenous religion in rural villages. Once they had done so, it was not just Protestants who benefited but institutional and theological forms of Catholicism as well.

There has been a strange symbiosis between these two expressions of Christianity, as our snapshots illuminate. Note that (1) Cardenal's revolutionary Christianity relied upon a simple and poetic Protestant translation of the Bible, (2) Protestantism had become so widespread and attractive in Brazil that Joanina joined the Charismatic group at her church specifically because it seemed to be a Catholic version of what she found attractive in Protestantism, and (3) most of the conflict in Marroquin's villages was between Catholic groups who sparred with each other in the space created, no doubt, by the original Protestant converts. In other words, the importance of Latin American Protestantism was not just its rapid growth; rather, Protestantism had a profound influence on Catholicism itself. The rivalry between the two forms of Christianity was not a zero-sum game but has been mutually beneficial.

More specifically, the snapshots reveal the dynamism and complexity of Christianity in contemporary Latin America. The discussion in Cardenal's Bible study challenges some preconceptions about Christianity in Latin America. Here was a Catholic Church thoroughly engaged with the poor, reading a Protestant Bible, and hoping for a political revolution. Clearly the orientation and practice of at least some Catholics had changed since the days when Catholicism was most often associated with the status quo. It was clear from Marroquin's research that indigenous Mexicans were living in the midst of an extremely complicated religious drama, where the Protestant-Catholic and progressive-conservative dynamics were only two of many axes of religious tension. The Protestant-Catholic dichotomy was the most obvious, but equally real were divisions between different streams of Catholicism and between different Protestant churches. And finally, while scholars usually see liberation theology and the progressive church as antithetical to the more evangelical impulses of the Charismatic movement, Joanina's experience in Brazil shows that the two can in fact be combined. Where Marroquin's experience emphasized difference and division, Joanina's made clear that this was not the whole story—that different groups and movements could not only get along but even, at times, merge.

## 500 Years of Latin American Christianity

Recent developments in Latin America have, in some ways, precipitated a return to Christianity's dynamic missionary beginnings in the region. In the early decades of colonial rule, Christianity was driven by both evangelization and social concern. Zealous Franciscans, convinced that the end times were near, brought Catholicism, often through mass baptisms, to millions of indigenous Mexicans in the decades after the conquest. Behind them and spreading to almost all the areas of the new Spanish and Portuguese colonies in the Americas came Dominicans, Augustinians, and Jesuits, often learning and preaching in the indigenous languages. Also of particular note was Mexico's College of Santiago Tlatelolco, founded in 1536, in which Franciscans taught the sons of the indigenous nobility in both Latin and Nahuatl, the Aztec language. In Michoacán in central Mexico, Franciscan Vasco de Quiroga (d. 1565) built up a missionary utopia in which the native Purepecha people produced various crafts, worked a six-hour day, and participated in democratic local government.

In South America, the Jesuits not only brought hundreds of thousands of souls into the church but also created massive indigenous republics, entire Catholic societies in which Guaraní and other indigenous languages were spoken. These missions incurred the jealousy of Spanish and Portuguese landowners, who coveted the labor of the mission Indians, but for the native peoples themselves life in the missions was generally quite attractive. The Jesuits designed societies in which private property was balanced by communal land and in which work on an individual's own land or craft was balanced by service to the common good. Throughout all was infused a Catholic ethic of work, charity, and beauty. Particularly impressive were church buildings built by the Guarani, full of statues and paintings by local artists, with Masses sung by indigenous choirs accompanied by trained indigenous musicians. Because of raids by slavers from Sao Paulo, the missions also trained their own militias. In 1641 the combined militias of what is now Paraguay defeated a Sao Paulo slaving expedition that numbered at least 2,000 and thereby saved thousands of Catholic Indians from enslavement.[9]

Finally, Bartolomé de Las Casas (d. 1566), a Dominican priest who had been a slaveowner, but who experienced a profound change of heart, spoke out for the indigenous Americans. In his *A Brief Account of the Destruction of the Indies* and in personal intercession before the Spanish throne, he denounced the atrocities and injustices committed by Spaniards in the conquest of the New World. His advocacy played a large role in the crown's change of policy toward indigenous communities in the "New Laws" of 1542, which prohibited the enslavement of Indians and spelled out certain indigenous rights. Although the laws were resisted by landowners and weakened by the crown, they did improve the lives of some Indians and therefore marked an important milestone in Spanish-indigenous relations.[10]

This was certainly not the whole story of early colonial Catholicism. Secular priests (those not members of religious orders) generally lacked the missionary zeal of their religious colleagues and in many cases fought against their innovations. Spanish and Portuguese migrants and their descendants displayed a wide variety of religious attitudes—from intense Catholic piety, to superstitious credulity, to veiled atheism. The Catholicism of cities and towns, therefore, rarely reached the heights of passion achieved by the early Franciscans or the comprehensive catholicity of the Jesuits' thoroughly Christian indigenous societies or the clear moral stance voiced by las Casas. It was not that there were no pious priests or lay Catholics in the cities, or that those cities ignored Catholicism, or that they were places of irredeemable hatred for the indigenous. These settlements were simply much more complicated. In the early years they contained conquistadors focused on gold and glory, and in the later period merchants focused on achieving the same goals by different means. They contained African slaves with no knowledge of Christianity and colonial officials for whom the church was, at least for many of them, either a rival or a means of social control. Alongside these social groups were churches, convents, seminaries, and schools, filled with Catholics of various orientations, some of deep faith and some Catholic in only the most superficial sense.

Gradually the missionary and justice-oriented aspects of colonial Catholicism faded. This was in part a natural process, as the millenarian Franciscans, for instance, were replaced by a more practical generation, less prone to dream of the second coming of Christ and more inclined toward maintenance of what the visionary generation had achieved. The Jesuits, however, were attacked from outside. Unlike the Franciscans, the Jesuits continued their indigenous missionary activity well into the eighteenth century, not only maintaining their large indigenous republics but also expanding into new areas in the interior of South America. Spanish and Portuguese monarchs, however, coveted Jesuit wealth and objected to Jesuit independence. Therefore, the Portuguese expelled the Jesuits from their empire in 1759 and the Spanish followed suit in 1767. With the partial exception of the remote missions of Chiquitos and Mojos in present-day Bolivia, the missions gradually collapsed, prey to despoiling by non-indigenous colonists, traders, and large landowners.[11]

By the mid-eighteenth century Latin America was thus home to a broad religious spectrum. Almost everyone was theoretically Catholic, but this apparent uniformity masked a diversity of belief and practice. At one extreme were indigenous groups that had limited contact with the church. Such groups might consider themselves Catholic because their ancestors had been baptized, and they might have a church building in their village, but they knew little about Catholic doctrine and, without priests in their villages, could not go to Mass or confession even if they wanted to. In practice, they continued to offer sacrifices to local deities as their ancestors had done before them, to live in a sacred geography of holy caves and mountains, and to believe in a pantheon that incorporated the members of the Trinity, Catholic saints, and ancestral deities and spirits.[12]

On the other end of the spectrum was the sort of institutional, cosmopolitan Catholicism that was found in cities like Mexico City, Lima, or Buenos Aires, or at least in certain neighborhoods of those cities. This was a religion of priests, bishops, and nuns, of theology and doctrine, of the Mass and the other sacraments. This was a religion aware of its place in a global church, of the pope in Rome and bishops around the world, aware that the Americas were a new frontier for an ancient religion. This was a religion proud at once of its place in the universal church and of its roots that were growing deeper and deeper in the soil of the New World.

Sor Juana Inés de la Cruz (1651–95) provides a startling example of this cosmopolitan Catholicism. As a nun in Mexico City, Sor Juana devoted herself to study and writing and produced a body of work, including poetry, drama, and theology, that made her one of the greatest writers, if not the greatest writer, of colonial Latin America. Her writing was full of scriptural quotations in Latin and references to church fathers such as Augustine and John Chrysostom and to theologians such as Thomas Aquinas and Brazilian Jesuit Antonio Vieira.[13] Her social world of nuns, priests, bishops, and viceroys—with whom she interacted regularly—and her intellectual world of scripture, theology, and contemporary Catholic thought meant that, although she spent most of her days in a convent, her life reflected the breadth and depth of the institutional Catholicism that flourished in the major cities.

Between these two poles existed a wide range of beliefs and practices that could be characterized broadly as "folk Catholicism." In a vast swath of the Latin American population saints assumed prominence. Priests and the Mass were known, but often more important were lay associations that sponsored festivals and served as mutual aid societies. In popular neighborhoods of large cities and in smaller cities, towns, and villages, there could be limited contact with priests, so lay Catholics developed their own traditions and devotions. They might be aware of the local bishop and the pope, but such figures were distant in comparison to the lay brotherhoods that infused much of their religious life. In the same way, they might understand intellectually that there was a Trinity of Father, Son, and Holy Spirit, but the saints often seemed closer and more likely to bring aid.

This short sketch of the religious spectrum in colonial Latin America is, of necessity, reductive. The point is not to isolate or to enshrine the three forms—indigenous, folk, and institutional—but rather to emphasize that religiosity was much more complex than a short generalization can capture. In one sense, colonial Latin America was indeed Catholic. From northern Mexico to the tip of South America, almost everybody was somehow connected to the Catholic Church. At the same time, assuming that people who considered themselves Catholic therefore believed the same things or practiced their religion in the same way would be greatly mistaken. A shaman seeking guidance in the holy cave of his ancestors and Sor Juana writing about theology were simply in different spiritual worlds. A Brazilian peasant making a pilgrimage to the shrine of a local saint might have a certain amount of respect for both the shaman and the nun, but in his religion he differed significantly from both. Colonial Latin America was indeed "Catholic," but that word covered an extremely wide variety of religious beliefs and practices.

Independence added another level of complexity. When Spanish American nations broke away from the mother country in the 1820s, they faced some daunting challenges. They had to write constitutions and to create new national governments; they had to craft new identities distinct from that of their Iberian colonizers; they had to defend themselves from European powers and to prevent themselves from being recolonized by France or Great Britain; they had to develop their economies after years of warfare; and they had to build some sense of national unity after battles for independence that were as much civil wars as anti-imperial struggles. That last issue, national unity, became Latin America's greatest struggle in the decades after independence. In most cases two groups of elites with (theoretically at least) irreconcilable differences fought for control of the new nations. On one side were liberals who believed in individual rights and free markets and who saw the United States and revolutionary France as political models; heirs of the Enlightenment, they saw Catholicism and especially clericalism as dragging down their nations. On the other side were conservatives who honored Catholic and Hispanic tradition and who had a corporate view of society in which various groups had their own privileges; these conservatives tended to believe in monarchy and even envisioned a European prince in the role.[14]

The long struggle between liberals and conservatives, which was resolved mostly in favor of the liberals, had profound consequences for religion. Once in power, liberals generally disestablished the Catholic Church and often went after its property, forcing it to sell its large estates. Liberals also tended to allow freedom of religion and the work of Protestant missionaries, who were seen as a counterweight to the Catholic clergy's power. Consequently, although liberalism itself petered out in the last quarter of the nineteenth century, as liberals in power turned into positivists skeptical of freedom and democracy, it left a lasting impact on the region's religious landscape. The Catholic Church entered the twentieth century weakened by the loss of much of its wealth, but freed from many long-standing entanglements with the state. Protestantism, still considered exotic and foreign, nevertheless spread across the region as a minority religion often connected to liberalism or immigrant groups.

Thus, by the beginning of the twentieth century, the Catholic Church was in a difficult but not desperate position. Despite its political weakness and its new Protestant religious rivals, it was still a major cultural, moral, and even political power, but what its role in society would be was unclear. Could it return to its previous position of power and influence, sponsored by the state and playing a dominant religious and cultural role? Many members of the hierarchy thought that it could, and thus was launched what has been called the "New Christendom" project. The goal was to create a thoroughly Catholic society in which the institutional church worked closely with a sympathetic and supportive state.

Meanwhile, the quickening of the process now referred to as globalization meant that Rome and the Vatican could more easily monitor and influence the national churches. The Colegio Pio Latino-Americano, founded in Rome in 1859 to train Latin American priests, played an increasingly important role in tying clerics more closely to the Vatican. In 1869 forty

Latin American bishops participated in the First Vatican Council, and in 1899 the Colegio hosted fifty-three bishops for the Latin American Plenary Council. With Vatican I defining the dogma of papal infallibility and with the Plenary Council calling specifically for each national church to train some of its priests at the Colegio Pio Latino-Americano, these two gatherings tied the Latin American church to the Vatican and specifically to the pope more closely than it had been since the early colonial period. Although some historians have faulted, with reason, the Plenary Council for ignoring the "whole rich conciliar and synodal tradition of Latin America," this new relationship with Rome reconnected Latin America to the global Catholic Church, a connection that came to fruition sixty years later with the Latin American participation in the Second Vatican Council and in subsequent efforts at reform. In the short run, however, this "Romanization" (as it is often called) could often *disconnect* the Romanized priests and bishops from the still vibrant folk Catholicism of their dioceses.[15]

The New Christendom project and the Romanization process merged in attempts to emphasize religious instruction in local parishes and to start more Catholic schools for the same purpose. Religious orders from Europe (and a few from the United States) came to the region to staff these new schools and both reintroduced a more doctrinal approach to Catholicism, which Rome was advocating, and contributed to the re-Christianization of society. Catholic Action, an organization that attempted to catechize and mobilize lay Catholics in various sectors of society, came to the region in the 1920s and 1930s. Despite these efforts, the New Christendom never materialized, as several major developments altered the face of Latin America between 1875 and 1950.

One major change for the region was the rise of the United States as a global industrial and military power, which was brought forcefully to the region's attention by repeated interventions of the US Marines in Central America and the Caribbean, by the Spanish-American War of 1898, and by the building of the Panama Canal in the next decade. After dispatching Spain easily in the Spanish-American War, the United States seized Puerto Rico and the Philippines and, through a forced amendment to the Cuban constitution that virtually mandated American intervention in Cuba, turned Cuba into a de facto colony. In Panama, Teddy Roosevelt's "big stick" guaranteed Panamanian independence from Colombia and then American control of an enormous strip of land across the isthmus; American ingenuity then accomplished a remarkable canal. The United States had become the powerful actor in the hemisphere.

The change for Latin America was not simply that, as American investment streamed into region, the Marines often followed, especially in weak Central American nations. In retrospect, even more significant than the military role of the new hegemon was the entrance of the individualistic, market-based *culture* of the Americans. For those accustomed to traditional—and in Latin America traditional meant *Catholic*—ways of life, the regimented, moralistic, and impersonal approach of the American companies operating in the region contrasted sharply with traditional patron-client relationships. Sometimes the Americans consciously undermined Catholic belief and practices, such as when they encouraged Protestant churches and Protestant-influenced institutions such as the Boy Scouts and the Young Men's Christian Association. But the challenge to Catholicism and traditional culture came more often through labor regulations and incentives.[16] The Americans were successful and powerful, but they seemed to many Latin Americans to be missing something essential. Uruguayan writer José Enrique Rodó, for instance, found the northerners pragmatic and efficient, but lamented that their "fervent pursuit of well-being" had "no object beyond itself."[17] Similarly, Nicaraguan poet Ruben Dario concluded a poem addressed to President Roosevelt, and by extension to all Americans, by asserting, "And though you have everything, you are lacking one thing: God!"[18]

Other challenges to Catholicism came in the form of the related phenomena of urbanization and industrialization. Capital cities like Lima and Buenos Aires had long been significantly larger than other cities in their nations. In the twentieth century the comparative wealth of these cities, the beginnings of industrialization, better roads, and growing railroad networks attracted people from the countryside. As industrialization intensified toward the middle of the twentieth century, this trend became even more pronounced. The concentration of people in cities might have been expected to make the job of the church easier, but in practice urban living posed several barriers to religious life, especially for the majority of migrants who came to the city with minimal funds. They often settled in makeshift dwellings on the outskirts of cities in new neighborhoods without city services. The Catholic hierarchy rarely took much initiative to reach these squatter settlements, so most new urban residents had little contact with the institutional church. This need not have been a major problem, for many of the villages from which they came had lacked priests as well. The difference was that back in those villages, they had practiced a religion dependent on community, tradition, and geography. In their new homes they had neither priests nor community. Instead, thrown among migrants from various parts of their nations and struggling to survive in dangerous and unstable environments, they often felt anonymous and unmoored. They no longer had their shaman or their sacred cave; they had left behind their lay brotherhoods and patron saints; and the institutional church had not replaced these forms of religion with a church or a priest. In short, for many Latin Americans the journey to the city was also a journey away from their traditional religious practices.

As challenging as American influence and urbanization were for the Catholic Church, two other rivals were starting to pose a more direct threat. First, Protestantism, which had been mostly the province of liberals and immigrants in the nineteenth century, was finding willing adherents in exactly those places—the new and impoverished fringes of cities—where the Catholic Church had little institutional presence. It was evident that Protestantism, able as it was to accept married men with little training as pastors, had become a dangerous competitor. It was almost as if urbanization had wiped away centuries of Catholic history and created a new environment in which motivated Protestants could compete for souls without any of the usual barriers they had previously encountered. When prelates denounced Protestantism as an American plot, their fears were exaggerated but understandable, since Protestantism was flourishing in a situation created in many cases by American capital, American culture, and American industry.

Second, and perhaps even more worrisome to the church, was radical politics in general and Marxism in particular. The Mexican Revolution (1910–20), although ultimately hospitable to big business, had its radical aspects. As enshrined in the Constitution of 1917, the new Mexican state was not merely secular but actually anti-religious in many respects. For instance, the constitution outlawed any Catholic role in primary or secondary education, forbade churches and religious organizations from owning any land, prohibited outdoor religious services of any type, and forbade priests or religious periodicals to comment on politics. When President Plutarco Elias Calles began to enforce these constitutional strictures he faced the wrath of millions of Catholics and the revolt of thousands of peasants in the Cristero Rebellion (1927–29). Even after American ambassador Dwight Morrow helped to resolve the conflict, religious tensions remained high throughout the 1930s, as church and state attempted to work out a new modus vivendi, in part because, despite the state's softening approach toward the church, anti-religious laws remained on the books and their principles remained enshrined in the Constitution.

Before 1920 activists in Argentina and Mexico had started communist parties. Elsewhere in the region socialist and anarchist organizations proliferated in the early decades of the century, with communist parties arriving in Brazil, Chile, and Peru in the 1920s. Marxist intellectuals such as Peruvian writer José Carlos Mariategui and Mexican painter Diego Rivera gave the movement a prominence and public role beyond that implied by its relatively small number of official adherents. For Catholic officials, this rise of Marxism was perhaps the most worrisome of all the changes taking place in the region, for Marxism posed both an ideological and a political threat to Catholicism. As a materialist philosophy, it was, of course, diametrically opposed to Christian theism. Before the Russian Revolution, Marxism was an ideological rival for the church; after the Revolution, which created a powerful and repressive state with a special animus toward Christianity, the danger posed by Marxism seemed much more acute. Having seen the troubles caused by the more moderate Mexican Revolution, there was little doubt in the minds of senior clerics that a Marxist triumph anywhere in Latin America would put the church in an untenable position.

In addition to these external challenges, Catholicism also faced internal problems. As early as 1940, Chilean Jesuit Alberto Hurtado was asking, "Is Chile a Catholic Country?" He feared that, because of a shortage of priests that was especially severe in the countryside, millions of Chileans were living without the sacraments. In what sense, he wanted to know, could it be said that Chile was Catholic, if her people could not practice the most basic elements of the religion? In fact, why was a supposedly Catholic country not producing anywhere near the number of priests that it needed? American Maryknoll priest John Considine extended Hurtado's concerns to the rest of Latin America with *Call for 40,000*, in which he wrote that the region was suffering the devastating consequences of having a shortage of 40,000 priests and religious. Finally, in 1953 Catholic Action hosted a conference in Chimbote, Ecuador, to assess the state of Catholicism in the region. The conclusions were not reassuring. Most Latin Americans, the delegates concluded, were nominal Catholics who did not practice their faith. The priest shortage, poor catechesis, Protestantism, Marxism, and freemasonry received varying degrees of blame, but the general picture was clear: Latin American Catholicism was in crisis and something had to change if it was to be the sort of personal, social, and cultural force that the delegates wanted it to be.[19]

The Vatican took note of the looming crisis. Here was, theoretically at least, the most Catholic region of the world, suddenly on the brink of disaster. For an institution steeped in history, it was difficult not to think of the loss of the Eastern churches in 1054 or of the loss of northern European churches during the Reformation. To lose Latin America, unthinkable in 1900, appeared to be a distinct possibility. In response, Pope Pius XII took two major actions. He called for all the bishops of the region to meet in Rio de Janeiro in 1955 and he asked Catholics around the world to help Latin America. At the Rio de Janeiro meeting, the Latin American bishops formed the Consejo Episcopal Latinoamericano (CELAM, Latin American Episcopal Council), the first regional bishops' conference in any part of the world, an organization designed to allow the bishops to work together to confront the many challenges in their region. To facilitate greater aid for the region, in 1958 Pius created the Pontifical Commission for Latin America.[20] The next pope, John XXIII, was even more concerned about Latin America. Throughout his papacy (1958–63) he called the European nations, Canada, and the United States to pay special attention to Latin America and to provide material and spiritual aid. In 1961 he went so far as to ask American religious congregations to send 10 percent of their personnel to Latin America in the next decade.[21]

## Vatican II

Vatican II, which met for three months in the fall of each year from 1962 to 1965, also had a profound influence on the Catholic Church in Latin America. In fact, the council had a greater impact on Latin America than on any other region of the world. When John XXIII announced in 1959 that he would be calling an ecumenical council, it was not immediately clear what would be on the agenda other than the somewhat vague idea of *aggiornamento*, or updating. Brazilian bishop Helder Camara argued that poverty and economic development were the central issues facing the church and the world, but in general the approximately 600 Latin American bishops and 300 *periti* (theological advisors) attended more as pupils than as teachers, despite making up the largest regional bloc. While European cardinals handled most of the preparatory work for the council and European bishops were the most visible group in the council hall, behind the scenes the Latin American bishops were experiencing the council as a kind of epiphany.[22]

CELAM had had little impact on the region thus far. It was the council that made CELAM into a strong voice for the Latin American bishops and thereby transformed the Latin American Church in the coming decade. The 2,400 bishops and hundreds of *periti* at each council session created an atmosphere of intellectual ferment that served as a graduate school of theology for many of the Latin American bishops. Morning and evening, whenever the council was not in session, bishops and their advisors met in various informal and formal settings for lectures, discussions, and simple conversations, all of which introduced the Latin Americans to their colleagues from around the world and to the latest theological and political ideas.

The council also gave CELAM the chance to hold its annual meeting in Rome in conjunction with the council. Although these yearly meetings would have happened anyway, whether the council had been meeting or not, the special location and atmosphere of the council added a sense of gravity and possibility. Helder Camara, auxiliary bishop of Rio de Janeiro, and Manuel Larraín, bishop of Talca, Chile, played key roles in pushing CELAM to come together, to consider matters of regional importance, and to support issues of common concern on the floor of the council. In 1965, at Larraín's suggestion, CELAM agreed to hold its own major meeting to bring the teachings and attitudes of the council to Latin America. This event, the Second General Conference of CELAM in Medellín, Colombia, in 1968, and its successor, the Third General Conference in Puebla, Mexico, in 1979, would have a significant impact on the church (as we will see in detail in Chapter 3).[23]

Finally, the documents produced by the council had a profound influence on the Latin American bishops, on the upcoming Medellín conference, and then on the church in the region. Of the sixteen council documents, most important for Latin America was *Gaudium et Spes*, the Pastoral Constitution on the Church in the Modern World, which made clear that the church had the duty of working for peace and justice. The second most influential document was *Lumen Gentium*, which defined the nature and mission of the church in a way that put special emphasis on the role of lay (non-clergy) Catholics. The laity was part of "the new People of God" who exercised a "common priesthood" and had a solemn duty to spread the faith, to build the "domestic church" in their families, and "to work for the sanctification of the whole world from within as a leaven." This latter commission, the sanctification of the world, gave the laity the "principal role" in the transformation of society and thus emphasized, as the church had rarely done since the first century, their utterly pivotal role. The priests, bishops, and religious all had their specific tasks, but it was lay Catholics who stood on the front lines of the church's efforts. The call for them "to expend all their energy for the growth of the church and its continuous sanctification" made clear that everyday Catholics, no less than the clergy, must show total commitment to the work of God. For the Latin America laity, the picture of the church as the People of God proved especially empowering.[24]

A bit of a shock came for Latin America in the council document on ecumenism, *Unitatis Redintegratio*. In a region where Catholics called Protestant churches "sects" and where Protestants viewed Catholicism as a glorified form of idolatry, relations between Protestants and Catholics had long been difficult. The council, however, clarified that those born into Protestant communities could not logically be blamed for schism. In fact, the church embraced them as "separated brethren" and fellow Christians because "men who believe in Christ and have been truly baptized are in communion with the Catholic Church, even though this communion is imperfect." Protestant bodies possessed many elements of grace and other "truly Christian endowments." With the ultimate goal of restoring unity among all Christians, Catholics should dialogue with Protestants and could cooperate with them in social projects, even in prayer.[25] Another document affirmed that religious freedom was not just a policy that the Catholic Church could affirm in certain situations but was actually a human right based on the dignity of the human person. In fact, religious freedom was the most important and most fundamental human right and one that should be protected by every government and embraced by every Catholic.[26] It took decades for these concepts to filter down to average Catholics, but they had revolutionary implications for Latin American Christianity: from the official Catholic perspective, at least, Catholics and Protestants were now brothers, not enemies.

In some tension with the new ecumenical emphasis, the council reaffirmed the church's missionary role in *Ad Gentes*. Since the church was missionary "by her very nature" and since mission was its "greatest and holiest task," it was always and everywhere dedicated to the conversion of all human beings by preaching the gospel and planting itself among different peoples and groups. This work was far from over. As in *Lumen Gentium*, the laity would play a central role, this time not only as "a leaven working on the temporal order from within, to dispose it always in accordance with Christ" but also in groups organized specifically "to announce Christ to their non-Christian fellow-citizens by word and example." For a region that had long considered itself a Catholic society with little need for evangelization or missionary activity, *Ad Gentes* was a surprising challenge.

Catholics responded to Vatican II in three basic ways. First, and most influential in the decade after the council, came the idea that the importance of Vatican II lay as much in the expectation of profound change that it had created as in its specific decrees and calls for reform. Holders of this view, including Latin American bishops Helder Camara and Sergio Méndez Arceo, recognized the importance of the sixteen Vatican II documents but focused more on the sense of possibility and transformation that the council had opened up. At the same time, a traditionalist response held that the council had veered into heresy or near heresy in its pronouncements on religious freedom, the use of the vernacular in the Mass, and treating Protestants as separated brethren. Few went as far as Brazilian Bishop Antônio de Castro Mayer, who was excommunicated in 1988 for participating in the ordination of four bishops from the traditionalist Society of Saint Pius X against the express command of the Vatican, but he had sympathizers across Latin America, including more than two dozen priests of the Brazilian diocese of Campos. (The Catholic Church welcomed the traditionalists of Campos back into the church in 2002 as the special "Apostolic Administration of St. Jean Marie Vianney," a sort of traditionalist diocese within a diocese.) Finally, and most influential in the period from 1978 to the present, was the idea that the true "spirit of Vatican II" could be found in the documents themselves. Pope John Paul II, the most influential holder of this last interpretation, organized dozens of study groups to examine the council documents when he was archbishop of Krakow, wrote a book that called the council documents a primary source of renewal for the church, and then devoted his papacy (1978–2005) to implementing his interpretation of those documents.[27] Bishops appointed by John Paul often shared this orientation, leading to a generational tension between younger bishops who pointed to the texts of the council and older bishops who thought more of its spirit. Because of John Paul's long papacy, his interpretation of the council became increasingly influential in Latin America and around the world.

## *Five Areas of Rebirth*

The tens of thousands of new foreign missionaries that the Vatican sought never materialized, but Catholicism in Latin America managed to survive and even to thrive over the next half century, and by 2009 the region had almost 500 million Catholics—over 40 percent of the world's Catholics.[28] Protestantism too managed to thrive. In fact, a rebirth of Latin American Christianity—Catholic and Protestant—occurred in the midst of major and ongoing challenges such as urbanization, industrialization, and the rise of Marxist thought. New challenges from modernity ultimately brought forth new life.

This book argues that Christianity in Latin America was reborn in five ways reminiscent of the vital church of the early colonial period: (1) as a movement of witnesses and evangelists, (2) as a prophetic movement committed to the poor and the oppressed, (3) as a Pentecostal movement oriented toward spiritual and emotional religious experience, (4) as a lay movement, and (5) as a universal religion. Each of these areas is treated in two chapters that examine the issue in general terms and then in more specific examples.

Unlike Africa and Asia, which experienced Christian growth in traditionally non-Christian societies, Latin America has been Christian for five centuries and therefore could best be described as experiencing a rebirth and a transformation of a preexisting Christianity. As the center of gravity of Christianity shifts to the south, Latin America might well become a theological and philosophical leader for both the global South and the developed world. Indeed, such has been the case already in the rapid propagation of liberation theology around the globe. Christianity in Latin America has been transformed in the years since 1950 into a more vital movement that has returned to the dynamism of the early colonial period. Protestantism has not merely made the religious field more diverse and more competitive; it also has served as a catalyst for the revitalization of Catholicism and has forced Catholicism to become more catholic. Latin American Christianity is now expanding its influence by sending missionaries to the developed world (especially to the United States, Spain, and Portugal) and to Africa and Asia. As Christianity shifts more and more to the global South, Latin America may come to seem more and more like the center of World Christianity. The election in 2013 of the first Latin American pope, Argentina's Jorge Bergoglio, is both evidence of the region's religious revitalization and a harbinger of increasing influence in the future.

# Witnesses and Evangelists: The Rise of Protestantism

"THIS IS A Catholic home. We do not accept propaganda from Protestants or any other sects."[1] Signs with these or similar words greeted visitors to many homes in Mexico in the 1980s and 1990s. Although they clearly reflected inter-religious tensions, these signs also highlighted the profound impact of Protestant evangelism: visits from Protestant missionaries were common enough that Catholic families thought it worth their time, effort, and money to find a warning sign, to buy it, and to mount it on their homes. The signs also meant that such families, although aware of people who had become Protestants, had decided not to convert but rather to reaffirm their Catholic identity.

This dynamic was not limited to Mexico. In Bolivia, for example, in a neighborhood where almost everyone had converted to Protestantism, the last remaining Catholic was so accustomed to Protestant "witnessing" that when two American professors approached his home, he rushed to the door and shouted, "I'm Catholic. You're never going to convert me."[2] For him and for other Catholics throughout the region during the second half of the twentieth century, Protestants' door-to-door evangelism and other forms of outreach posed a real challenge. Some of them adopted the new faith; others became stauncher Catholics. Whatever the outcome, *they had to decide.* No longer would Latin Americans be presumed Catholic. In such an environment, Catholics eventually realized they too must adopt a missionary mindset.

It was Protestants who revitalized the missionary nature of the faith in Latin America, in large part because evangelism and missionary activity were central to their identity. Because Catholicism was pervasive in Latin

America, the main way that Protestantism spread was through active and intentional sharing of its message, initially by missionaries and then by converts. In the same vein, Protestants, as converts and the children of converts, understood that they were members of a minority faith, that it had started through missionary work, and that it could grow only through continued evangelism. Because they had endured the costs of conversion, including social stigmatization and violent persecution, Protestants were especially committed to their faith.

Protestantism in Latin America had expanded in the nineteenth century largely through the missionary activity of what are now referred to as the "historic" denominations, the Baptists, Methodists, Presbyterians, and other mainline groups largely from the United States, and through Bible distribution by the British and Foreign Bible Society and the American Bible Society. At the beginning of the twentieth century they were joined by the "faith" missions, such as the Central American Mission and the Latin America Mission, new fundamentalist organizations that had emerged from the fundamentalist-modernist split in American Protestantism in the early decades of the century. As for the techniques of evangelism, both the mainline Protestants and the fundamentalists started with preaching and then developed other methods, such as schools, literature, and radio programs. The 1950s and 1960s were transitional decades, as foreign missionaries ceased to be the main drivers of evangelism, and local believers, especially Pentecostals, became the main agents of expansion. In other words, although foreigners, mostly from the United States, established the beachheads of Protestantism, Latin American Protestants themselves fueled the dramatic growth that made their religion ubiquitous in the region, mostly through "witnessing" to their friends and relatives.[3]

This was facilitated by the anti-colonial attitudes of the 1960s. Latin American believers wanted more control of their churches, and mission boards generally acceded to their requests. The Presbyterian Church, for example, recalled all their American missionaries from Mexico and ended most forms of financial support in 1972.[4] Anti-colonial feelings were stirred by the active role of the Central Intelligence Agency (CIA) in Latin American politics, which cast suspicion on all Americans working in the region.[5] Even more, though, the explosion of witnessing, evangelism, and church planting came from denominations and movements that had broken off from American organizations or that never had been part of them in the first place. In other words, it was not so much the descendants of the mainline denominations and the faith missions who evangelized the continent as it was their bastard children and the heirs of the Pentecostal revival. Pentecostal spirituality and practice is discussed in more detail later, but suffice it to say that there was something profoundly attractive to newly industrialized and urbanized Latin Americans in its forms of worship and healing, even as its greatest weakness, an ingrained disposition toward division and redivision through "church splits," was a surprisingly effective method of growth.

Catholics, on the other hand, had a difficult time making sense of the new religious environment and their role in it. In the 1950s and 1960s Catholic Action and Jesuit scholars assembled reams of sociological data that began to alert the hierarchy and concerned members of the laity to the superficial nature of Catholic belief and practice in the region, but the vast majority of Catholics took little notice. Occasionally they heard warnings from their bishops about the dangers of the "sects," usually phrased in such a way as to make them sound like cultish groups of foreigners. Such warnings did little to prepare them for visitations from "missionaries" from their own neighborhoods, especially if those neighbors were respected members of the community or if they had demonstrated positive lifestyle changes after conversion.

While Protestants had a clear message and could assume that almost any Catholic was fair game for evangelism, Catholics struggled to identify who, exactly, they were supposed to be evangelizing and what they were supposed to be saying. For instance, in Ecuador the Catholic Church successfully championed agrarian reform laws that ended the traditional rural land tenure system and thus liberated peasants from an oppressive social system. Nevertheless, the institutional church played a minimal role in peasant life in some rural areas, leaving easy pickings for Protestant groups who took advantage of the new rural freedom for which the Catholic Church had fought.[6] Even when urban Catholics did imagine that remote indigenous communities might need missionary attention, they had a harder time seeing their own neighborhoods as areas for mission. The region's bishops, in their general conferences of 1979 (Puebla), 1992 (Santo Domingo), and 2007 (Aparecida), adopted explicitly missionary themes and tried to awaken the missionary vocation of the whole Latin American church, but most Catholics struggled to see themselves as missionaries and their cities and towns as mission fields. Meanwhile, some Latin American elites encouraged the growth of Protestantism as a wedge against Catholicism. Protestant conversions were not matters of choosing one "denomination" from a menu of religious options; they were more like social dynamite, especially in rural areas.

## Protestant Growth in Mexico

In 1936 Mexico's nationalist president, Lázaro Cárdenas, visited an indigenous pueblo in the state of Morelos where an American missionary
named Cameron Townsend had been experimenting with various projects to improve village life, including vegetable gardens, a basketball court,
and irrigation systems. Cárdenas was so impressed with Townsend's practical efforts that he asked him to bring in as many helpers as he could to
Mexico and even agreed to pay their salaries. The president also supported
Townsend's larger project of creating written versions of the country's indigenous languages and then translating the New Testament into those
languages. Cárdenas's successors continued the Mexican state's support
of Townsend's organization, which became known as the Summer Institute of Linguistics (SIL), and which worked closely with the government's
indigenous agencies. In 1951 the SIL signed an agreement to work for the
Mexican Department of Education to help the nation's Indians through
a program of linguistics and "all that signifies the betterment of those
indigenous groups," which meant that it functioned as a de facto arm of
the state until the agreement was terminated in 1979.[7]

Why would a revolutionary nationalist like Cárdenas, who fought in the
Mexican Revolution and expropriated American oil companies in 1938,
extend the red carpet to American fundamentalists bent on converting
Mexico's Indians? Why would a regime whose legitimacy depended on its
revolutionary pedigree and particularly on its assertion of Mexican independence vis-à-vis the United States not only continue Cárdenas's policies
but institutionalize them at the highest levels? The answer can be found
in the tense relationship between Mexican elites and Catholicism. Since
the nineteenth century, liberal leaders had seen the Catholic Church as
the institution most directly opposed to liberal reforms and folk Catholicism as a superstition incompatible with the kind of modern nationalism
that they espoused. The Mexican Revolution (1910–20) only intensified
such feelings, as radicals prevailed in writing an anti-clerical constitution
that privatized religion by prohibiting religious schools, outdoor religious
observances, and the public wearing of distinctive religious attire. The
constitution even went so far as to confiscate all real estate from churches
and to deny religious bodies the status of legal entities.

President Plutarco Elias Calles's attempt to put these prohibitions into
effect provoked the bloody Cristero Rebellion (1927–29), in which Catholic rebels fought the revolutionary state to a draw. The conflict was halted,

but was not truly resolved, by an agreement in which the anti-religious policies stayed on the books but were not strictly enforced. Although lacking Calles's visceral hatred for Catholicism, Cárdenas too wanted to roll back the public role of the faith. Cárdenas saw the SIL as a potential ally in this quest. Although not a Protestant himself, Cárdenas appreciated the passion and moral seriousness that he saw in Townsend and other Protestants. More important, he saw in their goal of converting Indians a twofold boon for the nationalist project: first, conversion to Protestantism detached indigenous Mexicans from the control of the Catholic hierarchy and made them more appreciative of the Mexican state; second, Protestantism itself seemed to him less superstitious than Catholicism and more open to the scientific mindset that he wanted all Mexicans to adopt. Thus, Cárdenas and his secular, nationalist successors in the 1950s and 1960s continued the attack on Catholicism that the Constitution and President Calles had started, but they did so in a subtler manner that downplayed direct confrontation and emphasized instead the substitution of Protestantism and nationalism.

By 1962 the SIL was working among eighty-one different indigenous groups throughout Mexico. Of course, some of these groups barely tolerated the American linguists and resisted conversion. Others saw dozens or hundreds of conversions; some, such as the Mezquital Otomi and the Mazahua had a thousand converts; and a few, such as the Chols and Tzeltals, two Mayan groups from the southern state of Chiapas, had over 5,000.[8] In other words, by the time of Vatican II, the strange partnership of Mexican nationalists and American fundamentalists was starting to bear fruit. This fruit would multiply dramatically in later years.

Meanwhile, in a manner generally unconnected to American missionaries or Mexican politicians, Protestantism also was expanding at the grassroots level as simple believers with little education and no official church positions shared their faith with friends, family members, and neighbors. Often, migrants to a Mexican city or to the United States encountered Protestants (frequently for the first time), became attracted to the religion, and eventually adopted it. On their return home, they shared the faith throughout their social networks, occasioning profound crises in rural communities.

To understand why the conversion of just one resident of a rural village could result in dissension, violence, and even murder, it is necessary to understand the nature of rural life in mid-twentieth-century Mexico. Many villages, especially indigenous ones, featured a hierarchy in which men, over the course of a lifetime, worked their way up a series of year-long civil and religious posts known as cargos. Although the lower level cargos, such as cleaning the local church or being a sort of gofer for the town officials, were relatively easy to fulfill, higher level posts demanded large amounts of time and money. The most important religious cargo, sponsoring the fiesta (often lasting several days) for the town's patron saint, could be so costly that men had to take out loans or even to sell off land to pay for it. The trade-off for those who fulfilled all the cargos and who sponsored the important fiestas was the status of elder, the highest in the community.

Hand in hand with the cargo system went a kind of folk Catholicism in which alcohol played a major role. The saints' festivals that dominated the yearly calendar usually featured large amounts of alcohol, paid for by the sponsor and available freely to the adults of the community. All residents were expected to participate in the festivities—that is, to imbibe copiously. Although such communities were never as closed to outsiders as some anthropologists once thought—after all, the alcohol had to come from somewhere—they often did exhibit a marked suspicion of outsiders, who were seen as potential exploiters and threats to unity. The rural village, therefore, could function to some degree as its own little cosmos, a world in which religion, politics, and culture were so closely intertwined that they could not easily be separated.

The presence of even a few Protestants in a village posed a grave challenge to such a system. First, Protestants in Mexico generally did not drink and therefore refused to participate in or to support financially the villages' most important festivities. Second, they rejected the cult of saints as a form of idolatry. Third, their new religion had come from outside and thus seemed like a betrayal and an alien imposition. Fourth, any public sort of Protestant worship introduced an open religious division in the community that could easily spread to other aspects of life. Added together, these various facets of Protestant belief and practice undermined the civil-religious hierarchy and ruptured the little cosmos of the village. No longer was it a village with a unified worldview and a comprehensive political-social-cultural system; it had become a collection of individuals, some practicing folk Catholicism, others practicing Protestantism. In a sense, then, Protestants introduced modernity, liberalism, and secularization to rural villages. Intending only to spread their religious message, they undermined the foundations of one world and laid the foundations of a new one.[9]

## Violent Reactions

It is not surprising that some villages responded angrily, but it is remarkable how violent such reactions could be and how widespread they were. I found records of 164 violent acts (most Catholic versus Protestant but a few of the opposite) for the years 1945 to 1955 in the Mexican national archives and more than 200 in the state archives of Oaxaca for the years 1948 to 1965.[10] In 1948, David Ruesga, founder of the Church of God denomination and leader of an organization that protected Protestant rights, was sending the Interior Ministry weekly reports of attacks on Protestants; he estimated that an attack on a Protestant occurred on average once a day.[11] The records from the national archives and the Oaxaca state archives go on and on; in small town after small town, Protestants were attacked. In many cases they were injured or even killed, their church buildings were destroyed, and they were chased out of town and threatened with death if they returned.

Three examples from the state of Hidalgo, north of Mexico City, give a sense of the dynamic. In one instance, a Protestant pastor named Tiburcio Maya from the Rancho Pedregoso neighborhood of the municipio of Huichapan complained to state authorities that a group of thirteen men under the leadership of a local politician had broken up his church service, firing rifles and pistols at his congregants as they fled. A few months later, as the Protestants were leaving their church, six of the same men again attacked, shooting and wounding a man and his daughter. The next day, the same group wounded one Protestant with machetes and beat two others with a chair. A local official investigated the claims, found that a girl named Pascuala Cruz Resendiz had been shot eleven times and that a man named Tomás Resendiz had received life-imperiling wounds from a sharp implement. Several individuals were arrested. Some of the detainees indicated that Pompeyo Rufino had recruited a group of twenty-five to attack and kill the Protestants. The official concluded his report by suggesting: "The directors of the League of Agrarian Communities of the State should be commissioned to go to this town or to the Pedregoso neighborhood to give the campesinos there a class on religious liberty so that they stop persecuting the Protestants."[12]

In another instance a retired general phoned the state attorney general to report that a group of Catholics led by Ponciano Pérez had attacked a small Protestant church in Mixquiahuala three times before tossing a smoldering bomb into the church, disrupting the service. The local police chief reported complaints that Catholics had seized and burned the Bibles of several Protestants. The state attorney general traveled to the town to interview the various parties and concluded that the "intellectual author" of the attacks was the local parish priest, Luis Sánchez Flores.[13]

The most dramatic events occurred in the muncipio of Tepeji del Rio, Hidalgo. The small group of Protestants in Tepeji had long experienced problems with both the local authorities and with Catholics.[14] In 1948, municipal authorities, apparently at the urging of the local priest, began harassing a group of Protestants led by Justiniano López Salcedo. On one occasion the police broke into López's home and put him in jail. They claimed it was to protect him from a lynch mob that was planning to kill him. Twenty-four Protestants protested to the governor that they were "not in agreement with this kind of protection" and that it was not fair that López had to pay a 50 peso fine to get out of jail when he had done nothing wrong.[15]

The simmering tensions boiled over again in 1952 when Protestants attempted to open an official church building (which became a federal matter because the Constitution of 1917 made all churches federal property). The municipal president protested that since Tepeji already had two Catholic churches and since the vast majority of its residents were Catholics, there was no need for a Protestant church. "Only an insignificant group of these people are evangelicals, and when they showed up here so too did relatively serious difficulties," he claimed. If they were allowed to open a Protestant church, "these difficulties would happen again, with deadly consequences."[16]

In the spring of 1953 the situation became even more explosive. The Protestants, not having received a response from the federal or state governments about their application, began to build the church without official authorization. Starting in early June, the municipal president, the local priest, and leader of the union at La Josefina textile factory joined forces to close the church, to prevent Protestants from working in the factory, and ultimately to expel all Protestants from the town. On June 9, Félix Servín, the leader of the local chapter of Catholic Action, and Toribio Rangel, one of the Protestant workers at La Josefina, had a violent altercation, attracting the attention of the state government, which told both sides to calm down and to refrain from violence. One week later, 900 workers from La Josefina marched out of their factory with the intention of removing a sign advertising the new Protestant church. Hundreds of local residents joined the workers in the streets. The crowd demolished the Protestant church and the army sent a platoon of soldiers from the state capital to restore order.[17]

Meanwhile, the workers of La Josefina decided that they would not return to work as long as Protestant workers remained in the plant. And the Catholic townspeople decided that they would not rest until they had expelled all Protestants and their family members from the town, employing, in the words of the state official who examined the case, "direct action" against them if necessary.[18] In the end, federal and state authorities sent in more soldiers to protect Protestant lives and to preserve "tranquility and order," but not to protect individual civil liberties. Yet Protestants applauded these actions as if President Adolfo Ruíz Cortines was a Protestant Constantine because his actions, as limited as they were, represented a positive change in the federal government's policy toward non-Catholics. Protestant writer Gonzalo Baez-Camargo, for example, rejoiced: "Once the government intervention came, it was quick and to the point. Seldom has official action to maintain the law and to insure their constitutional rights to Protestants been more prompt and determined."[19]

## Indigenous Conversions in Chiapas

The introduction of Protestantism, therefore, provoked a crisis for rural Mexico and for folk Catholicism. Community division and violence were signs of the grave challenge that Protestantism posed to the traditional way of life; religious competition and a free marketplace of ideas simply were not social phenomena that the leaders of these communities could accept without a struggle. Still, by the 1990s, most villages and towns had come to some sort of equilibrium in which Protestants were tolerated or even accepted, although some villages remain battlegrounds to the present day.

The history of Chiapas, a heavily indigenous state in southern Mexico, highlights three stages of this religious evolution, resulting eventually in a vibrant religious marketplace. After beginning work among the Tzeltal Maya in the highland area of the state in 1938, the SIL struggled for many years to make much of an impact in the municipality of Oxchuc. Suspicion of outsiders, deep commitment to their saints and customs, and tight political control by village elders all contributed to an atmosphere in which the presence of linguists Marianna Slocum and Florence Gerdel was barely tolerated, with the medical work of Gerdel, a nurse, serving as a decisive factor in their favor. In the summer of 1950, however, the nearby village of Corralito invited the two translators to relocate.[20] The combination of evangelism that was "non-coercive, patient, and entirely in the Tzeltal language" with "impressive medical results" proved to be the perfect recipe for reaching the local residents.[21] By the time Slocum and Gerdel finished the Tzeltal New Testament in 1956 there had been hundreds of Protestant conversions, and converts were heading to other Tzeltal villages to share the faith. Corralito converts also built Gerdel a large medical clinic, where she continued her medical ministry and used Tzeltal language medical textbooks that she had written to train three dozen practical nurses. When Slocum and Gerdel were transferred by the SIL to Colombia in 1965, they left behind seventy-two Tzeltal Protestant churches, at least 6,000 converts, and fourteen medical clinics staffed by those they had trained. In 1985 they returned to find 300 churches and 44,000 converts.[22]

Of course, such rapid religious change did not happen without conflict. Shamans from Oxchuc had opposed Slocum and Gerdel from the start, and only pressure from the state government allowed them to remain. Local elders sensed as well that religious conversion would undermine the civil-political hierarchy on which their power was based. Even in the more hospitable Corralito, enemies of Protestantism burned the first Protestant church to the ground. Also, in the early 1950s, the large numbers of converts in Corralito began attracting attention outside of the highlands. Catholic Action, a lay movement of catechesis and evangelization, began warning Tzeltals about the dangers of "La Marianna" and her "false and adulterated" Bible. However, as Catholic Action's lay evangelists spread through the area, they were actually introducing a faith as different from traditional Tzeltal religion as Protestantism. Ironically, then, Protestantism not only opened up a rigid political-religious system but also spurred orthodox Catholic evangelists into competition with traditional indigenous religion.[23]

Another Mayan group, the Tzotzils, proved even more resistant to Protestantism. Ken and Elaine Jacobs of the SIL never got permission to live in the Tzotzil town of San Juan Chamula, so they lived in the market city of San Cristóbal de Las Casas and tried to find Tzotzils there who would help them learn the language and translate the New Testament. In 1964, after a decade of work, they had only two converts, Miguel Gómez Hernández and Domingo Hernández, but over the next year those two men converted thirty-three friends and relatives in San Juan Chamula. By 1976 there were about 1,000 Protestants and by 1983 that number had quadrupled.[24]

The rapid growth of Protestantism among the Tzotzils was all the more remarkable because it took place in the face of intense persecution. In August 1976, municipal authorities in San Juan Chamula expelled 600 Protestants from the village. For the rest of the decade these tribal elders waged a campaign that resulted in house burnings, beatings, and expulsions, culminating in 1981 in the torture and murder of Miguel Gómez Hernández, not only the first Tzotzil convert but also the most effective Tzotzil evangelist. By the 1990s, local authorities had driven as many as 35,000 Protestants from San Juan Chamula and thousands of "expulsados" were living in the shantytowns around San Cristóbal, unable to return to San Juan Chamula but still clinging to their Tzotzil language and culture in a difficult urban environment. Catholic Bishop Samuel Ruiz recruited Sister Josefina de la Torre, of the Community of Mary, to help the desperate refugees. She eventually developed several agricultural, educational, and humanitarian projects, including building hundreds of homes in partnership with Habitat for Humanity. Bishop Ruiz sympathized with the Protestants because, among other reasons, the priest he had sent to Chamula also had been expelled.[25]

Another Tzotzil municipality, San Pedro Chenalhó, had a similar experience. Presbyterians and other Protestants began evangelizing the town in the 1950s, leading to conflict and, in 1957, the murder of a preacher by religious traditionalists. In the 1970s and 1980s there were acts of violence and some expulsions, but several Protestant churches (of different denominations) continued to grow. Meanwhile, Bishop Ruiz sent liberationist catechists into the town and they won many followers with their denunciations of economic injustice and political domination. At the same time, and partially as a result of the growing religious pluralism, religious dissidents began supporting political parties other than the long dominant Partido Revolucionario Institucional, while progressive Catholics formed a nonviolent organization called Las Abejas (The Bees) to fight for human rights. Subcomandante Marcos's Zapatista uprising of 1994 enjoyed considerable support in Chenalhó, but Las Abejas stayed committed to nonviolence. Consequently, the massacre in 1997 of forty-five Las Abejas members by right-wing paramilitaries, who tended to lump all leftists together, was particularly tragic.[26]

It is one thing to look at Mexico's 2010 national census and to note that 10 percent of its population of 112 million was Protestant (or some other non-Catholic religion such as Mormonism), but it was quite another to understand the process by which Mexico reached that point. Starting in 1950, when less than 2 percent of the population were non-Catholics (about 460,000 out of 26 million), the nation saw a remarkable change in its religious composition.[27] As seen in the previous pages, Protestant conversion was not some inconsequential choice, like deciding what to have for dinner or what television show to watch; it was a life-changing—and in some cases life-ending—decision for those who made it, exposing them to social isolation, expulsion from their communities, and extreme forms of violence. That so many continued to embrace the faith indicated the persistence of Protestant witness, the attractions of biblical and Pentecostal religion, the ongoing weakness of Catholic catechesis, and the virtual absence of Catholic evangelization during the first half of the twentieth century. At the same time, these ongoing conversions both responded to a growing religious marketplace and helped to create it. More recent developments, detailed in the next chapter, indicate that the Catholic Church has awakened from its slumber and that Protestants will not have such easy pickings in the future.

## Guatemala

Mexico's southern neighbor is today the most Protestant of all the Latin American nations. In 1920, after four decades of missionary work, Guatemala had only 2,000 Protestants, but steady growth in succeeding decades paved the way for impressive Protestant growth in the 1960s and 1970s, and then astounding growth in the 1980s. By 1985, with about one third of the population Protestant, some believers were asserting that Guatemala would become the region's first majority Protestant nation.[28] In 2009 a Catholic aid agency released data indicating that this milestone had been reached. Even if the national census of 2004 was more accurate in saying that Protestants composed 40 percent of the population, it was still clear that Guatemala had experienced a rapid and dramatic religious transformation in the second half of the twentieth century.[29]

The period from 1944 to 1954 was a pivotal one for Guatemalan politics and for Protestantism. After decades of dictatorial rule by Miguel Estrada Cabrera and Jorge Ubico, progressive military officers deposed Ubico and allowed a free election that resulted in the presidency of Juan José Arévalo, a believer in "spiritual socialism" and an advocate of nationalism, universal education, and labor unions. Just as the SIL's linguistics work had appealed to Mexico's President Cárdenas in similar circumstances, Protestant missionaries had certain talents that were valuable to Arévalo. Their rural schools, for instance, were the only ones in the nation that used indigenous languages for instruction and were therefore a key resource in the new president's plans for national literacy. In the same way, missionaries and their converts proved ready allies in Arévalo's campaigns to educate workers. For the president, the Protestants were free labor; for the Protestants, literacy work was a natural way of gaining access to the working class. In fact, the association of Protestants with the Arévalo regime was so strong that for a time conservative Catholics associated progressive politics with Protestantism. Jacobo Arbenz, who was elected president in 1951, had a more negative view of Protestantism, but during his presidency Presbyterians and converts of the Central American Mission worked closely with peasant unions on the agrarian reform program, and missionaries generally voiced no opposition to such cooperation.[30]

Church-state relations changed when Carlos Castillo Armas deposed Arbenz in 1954. Seeking strong allies, the conservative Castillo Armas threw his support behind the Catholic Church and effectively severed the government's ties to Protestants. After all, the Protestant community was still quite small and Catholics had numbers and an institutional structure that could shore up his political base. In the countryside, this withdrawal of support from Protestants and the government's new alliance with Catholicism had violent repercussions, as previously favored Protestants felt the brunt of simmering resentment in many communities, much as in Mexico.[31]

Paradoxically, another source of community division and religious pluralism in the countryside was the arrival of institutional and doctrinal Catholicism in the form of Catholic Action, Maryknoll missionaries, and European religious orders, who were responding to the growing Catholic awareness of the vulnerability of the countryside to Protestant missionaries. These groups presented rural communities with a religion that was almost as disruptive of traditional indigenous religion as Protestantism— it too condemned intoxication and presented ideas and practices clearly at odds with traditional indigenous religion—but was more difficult to reject. Since the doctrinal Catholicism of, say, a Maryknoll priest, had the backing of the institutional church it was difficult for local authorities to refuse it outright or to threaten the priest with expulsion. Evangelized from two sides, communities often responded violently against the weaker Protestants, but Catholic missionaries and catechists were presenting a message almost as challenging as the Protestant gospel.[32]

The department (region) of El Petén, where both Protestant evange-lists and Spanish missionary priests presented new religious messages in rural villages, was a microcosm of the increasingly complex and competi-tive religious dynamic in the countryside. In the 1930s and 1940s, Naza-renes (of the Protestant Church of the Nazarene) encountered varying levels of violence and acceptance in different villages, depending on the local political, economic, and cultural conditions. On one hand, the Maya community of San José found its traditional "ritual of three skulls" and a practice called "dinner-to-the-milpa" so much more comprehensible, compelling, and practical than the message preached by the Nazarenes that not one person converted. They similarly tolerated the presence of a missionary priest but threatened to run him out of town if he tried to remove their precious skulls from the church. On the other hand, in the nearby village of San Andrés, many residents became Nazarenes, many others accepted the doctrinal Catholicism of the missionary priests, and still others joined two Pentecostal churches that arrived in 1959—even as a large portion of town maintained their traditional folk Catholicism. In the region as a whole, the Spanish priests' attempts to end alcoholism and indigenous religious practices led to resentment and resistance by local communities and eventually to the priests' withdrawal from most villages by the early 1960s.[33]

In the late 1960s and the 1970s a succession of military governments faced both a growing leftist guerrilla uprising that was becoming a full-fledged civil war and, in 1976, a devastating earthquake that killed thou-sands and left as much as 25 percent of the nation homeless. In 1982, Efrain Rios Montt, a general and Pentecostal convert, seized the presi-dency and began a brutal but ultimately successful campaign against the leftist guerrillas in which military and security forces probably killed 200,000 people. In the mid-1980s, with Rios Montt gone and the civil war at a low ebb (it ended officially in 1996), the nation continued to suffer from crime, violence, and corruption. Despite, and to a degree because of, these traumatic experiences, the 1970s and 1980s proved to be a period of explosive Protestant growth.

After years of slow but steady growth under missionary leadership, in the 1970s Guatemalan Protestants asserted control, either taking over denominations or starting their own. Just as in Mexico, local leadership proved more successful at evangelism than missionaries had ever been and, when the earthquake struck, quite skilled at responding to an emer-gency in a way that both met practical needs and brought new members into their churches. Meanwhile, as the countryside plunged into a spiral of violence and as the cities witnessed soaring levels of crime and corruption, Protestantism provided refuge, community, and meaning for many who had been devastated. As surprising it might seem, Protestantism seemed to integrate itself very tightly with Guatemalan culture, especially indigenous culture.[34]

For instance, Protestants of the Mam ethnic group (speakers of a Mayan language who lived in the western highlands) quickly developed their own distinctive theology and religious practices that distinguished them from Mams who still practiced folk Catholicism as well as from ladino (mestizo) Protestants. Using the Mam New Testament, the Protestants emphasized three concepts: Tyol Dios (God's Word), Kman Dios (God the Father), and Kajaw Crist (Christ Our Lord). They developed a distinctive Christology that focused on Kajaw Crist's power over evil spirits and illness and ability to offer colbil (rescue/salvation) to believers in both the present world and in the afterlife. Mam Protestants rejected the traditional practice of burying work implements and cigarettes with the dead, and took a more hopeful approach toward death, distinguishing them from the traditionalists. Surprisingly, Mam Protestants never displayed crosses in their churches because of the symbol's prominence in traditional Mam religion. Thus, Mams maintained their ethnic identity, even as they developed a distinctive set of Protestant beliefs and practices that differed from both traditional religion and from mestizo Protestantism.[35]

What is most important here is not so much the depth and complexity of their adaptation of Protestantism, as interesting as it was, but rather the simpler point that evangelism often worked, that new messages could be accepted and internalized by populations previously committed to different beliefs and practices. Protestant evangelism varied considerably, including practices as different as one-on-one sharing, decades-long Bible translation projects, and nationwide campaigns, but the simple fact that it was done and that it often resulted in conversions changed the religious composition of Guatemala and served as a powerful challenge to Catholics.

A second key point is that the greatest Protestant growth occurred during the bloody years of the early 1980s when much of rural Guatemala was being devastated by the army. As complicit as Rios Montt was in this very devastation, his moral pronouncements on his weekly radio show and his plans to renew national morality went a long way toward legitimizing Protestantism as a plausible religious option at a time when many Guatemalans were desperate. The evident religious influence of the morally problematic Rios Montt highlighted the importance of evangelism. His message would have been much more coherent, and perhaps more successful, if he had coupled it with respect for human rights, but even in its incoherent and contradictory form it had a remarkable impact on his nation.

## Protestant Unity and Division

From their earliest days in Latin America, Protestant laypeople excelled at being active and committed, to a degree that put most lay Catholics to shame. As converts in an overwhelmingly Catholic culture, Protestants knew that they bore the responsibility for evangelism, training, and service—if they did not spread and teach their faith, it would simply die out. Protestants, however, struggled mightily with the basic Christian concept of unity. They were always divided among themselves, sometimes simply ignoring each other but sometimes enmeshed in rivalry and antipathy. Churches and denominations tended to splinter as liberals and conservatives, Pentecostals and fundamentalists went their separate ways, with nothing like the hierarchy or the official doctrines of Catholicism to hold them together.[36] After tentative steps toward unity in the 1960s there was some improvement in the 1980s, partially through the Billy Graham and Luis Palau evangelism campaigns that brought churches together in various cities, partially through the Pentecostal worship styles that spread from denomination to denomination, and partially through concerted local efforts to bring Protestant pastors and churches together.

In the 1960s, the World Council of Churches began encouraging the creation of an umbrella organization to represent Latin American Protestants. After exploratory meetings in 1977 and in 1978, in 1982 representatives of the "historic" Protestant churches, such as the Anglicans, Methodists, and Presbyterians, formed the Consejo Latinoamericano de Iglesias (CLAI, Latin American Council of Churches) "to promote unity, solidarity and cooperation among Latin American Christians." Even inside CLAI itself, however, unity was made difficult by the great diversity of beliefs, exemplified by Nancy Cardoso, plenary speaker at the 1995 general assembly, who said, "There is not only one God, there is not only one Lord, Jesus Christ, and there is not only one people of God."[37] Evangelist Luis Palau and other Protestants who were suspicious of the ecumenical movement founded a more conservative organization, the

Confraternidad Evangélica Latinoamericana (CONELA, Latin American Evangelical Fraternity), in 1982 as an alternative to CLAI. A third organization, the Fraternidad Teológica Latinoamericana (FTL, Latin American Theological Fraternity), founded in 1970, tried to appeal broadly to Protestant theologians and succeeded in bringing a wide spectrum of believers together at its Conferencia Latinoamericana De Evangelización (CLADE, Latin American Evangelization Conference) meetings.[38] CLADE III, held in Quito in 1992, served as a reconciliation of sorts between CLAI and CONELA, as the presidents of the two groups insisted on their respect for each other and agreed to preach in each other's churches, while members of the two organizations affirmed their support for both evangelization and social work.[39] Despite some successes, FTL and CONELA often viewed each other with suspicion, with the former accusing the latter of being fundamentalists who welcomed North American paternalism, and the latter seeing the former as liberation theologians inside the Protestant camp.[40] Because these attempts to unite Protestants struggled, spontaneous local movements for Protestant unity rose up to fulfill that goal.

In Buenos Aires, for example, in addition to the groups formed for Billy Graham and Luis Palau crusades, Pentecostal evangelist Carlos Annacondia played a major role in bringing pastors together. In 1982 Norberto Sarraco (Pentecostal), Carlos Mraida (Baptist), and Pablo Deiros (Baptist) formed the Buenos Aires Council of Pastors, which, by 2010, grew to include 180 pastors from 150 of the city's approximately 350 Protestant churches. At first the pastors simply tried to get to know one another, but by 1999 they were developing ambitious goals. In that year the more liberal members of the council, who had stood up against the dictatorship of the 1980s, publicly forgave the more conservative members for their lack of commitment to justice. In the late 2000s, churches of different denominations began helping each other financially—for example, several churches donated funds to save a Pentecostal church from losing its building to foreclosure. The pastors began working together to reach Buenos Aires, dividing up "spiritual responsibility" for every one of the city's thousands of blocks, and cooperating on a media campaign that would splash messages from the *Didache*, a first-century pastoral manual, across the city in newspapers, television commercials, and billboards at regular intervals for five years. They also shared responsibility for sending a team of Baptist missionaries to Africa. Perhaps most notably they began talking about being "one church in Buenos Aires," modeling themselves consciously after the early Christians. "When the New Testament speaks of the church in a city such as Ephesus, it is always singular, never plural," said Mraida.[41]

Despite the formation of the FTL, CLAI, and CONELA, and despite the remarkable coming together of groups like the Buenos Aires pastors, division remained a great weakness of Latin American Protestants. Their impact was probably less than their numbers might suggest because, despite considerable growth over the past sixty years, their failure to get along with each other made it more difficult to present a clear message to their Catholic compatriots.

## Conclusion

The history of Protestantism in Mexico and Guatemala and the struggle for Protestant unity suggest some larger themes about the dynamic of religious change in Latin America. First, Protestantism was generally introduced locally by foreign missionaries, such as those from the SIL, but soon the active role passed to local converts. With both the Tzeltals and the Tzotzils, for example, once the SIL linguists had established their bases of operation they were largely stationary, while it was the indigenous Protestants who took the message on the road. The Jacobs case was particularly noteworthy, for they seem to have had only two direct converts. It was these two men and then *their* converts who performed virtually all of the Tzotzil missionary work. Indeed, Chols, Mams, and other Chiapas indigenous groups joined the Tzeltals and Tzotzils in converting to Protestantism in large numbers, starting with mestizo or foreign missionaries, but almost always seeing the largest growth when indigenous believers took the reins. These native missionaries were so successful that by 1980 only 76 percent of Chiapas identified as Catholic, and that number dropped to 67 percent in 1990, making it the most Protestant state in Mexico.[42] Some Catholic leaders still have not grasped the fact that the most dynamic Protestant growth in the region was led by Latin Americans, not foreigners, and that Protestantism has become thoroughly indigenized.

Second, the period of rapid expansion often coincided with various levels of conflict, extending all the way to bloodshed and murder. Historian Karl-Wilhelm Westmeier goes so far as to say, "in order to grasp the nature of Latin America's Protestantism, it is necessary to study it from the perspective of conflict."[43] Foreign missionaries were taunted and pressured to leave but were seldom attacked physically, probably because they enjoyed the protection of the state and of foreign governments. The first converts, however, had no such immunity and often were killed or otherwise violently attacked. These efforts to repress Protestantism were counterproductive because they emphasized the villainy of local authorities and produced Protestant martyrs whose willingness to die for their faith spoke powerfully to their communities. Even the glimmerings of ecumenism, such as Bishop Ruiz's outreach to the Chamulan expulsados, was the result of conflict. Protestants and institutional Catholics (both progressives and conservatives) came to see each other not as friends or allies, but as fellow victims of traditionalist persecution.

Lest one think that it was only Mexico and Guatemala where such conflicts occurred, it is important to emphasize that while this is a topic on which little research has been done, it is probably fair to say that almost every history of Protestantism in any given Latin American nation lists acts of violence against missionaries and early converts.[44] The widespread attacks on evangelicals in Colombia, often instigated by priests, during the period known as La Violencia (1948 to 1958) have not received the attention they deserve, but they are better known than similar violence that occurred in most Latin American nations.[45] Memory of this sort of persecution continues to be an integral part of Protestant identity, a part that Catholics do not understand and that therefore serves as one of the hidden barriers to ecumenism in the region.

Third, this spread of both Protestantism and religious conflict helped to create a religious marketplace and was "a catalyst for change" in the Catholic Church.[46] When, despite persecution, Protestantism survived and even thrived, village elders lost control of their people's religion, and this change created opportunities that even those initial Protestants had not dreamed of. Once a Protestant group had established itself in an area, it would not be long before another arrived. The new denominations would challenge whatever church had first made inroads in an area and could even surpass it, especially when late-coming Pentecostals eclipsed Presbyterians and Baptists. This grudging acceptance of religious pluralism then raised new challenges for Catholics. If religion was genuinely up for grabs, how could they stem the tide of conversions to Protestantism without resorting to violence? What was the role of Catholicism in a pluralist society? Meanwhile, the door forced open by Protestants admitted new versions of Catholicism, including both liberation theology and more conservative movements, and also allowed the entrance of political pluralism, further destabilizing the countryside.[47]

Fourth, the growth of Protestantism in Latin America was often associated with state support, as was true also during the European Reformation, but not, as is often supposed, only by conservative governments. For example, Lázaro Cárdenas, the most progressive of Mexico's modern presidents, and Juan José Arévalo, Guatemala's first freely elected president and an advocate of "spiritual socialism," viewed Protestants as allies in the struggle against conservative forces. Although neither was himself a Protestant, both found Protestant beliefs more congenial than what they perceived as Catholic superstition and obscurantism. When conservative governments did support Protestants, as happened later in Chile and Guatemala, it was often because they wanted allies in the struggle against the newly prophetic Catholic Church of the 1970s or because they wanted the sheen of moral legitimization that religion projected but that the Catholic Church no longer would extend.

Protestants generally proved open—one might even say vulnerable—to political allegiances because of their minority status and their experience of violent persecution. Poor, outnumbered, and associated with foreigners, they were often desperate for the legitimacy and protection that these regimes offered. This is not to deny the traditional Catholic alliance with the state, which exists in a constitutional form to the present day in Argentina, Peru, and Costa Rica, and in an unofficial form in other nations and parts of nations, but it should complicate the common stereotype of Catholics as allies of the state and Protestants as its enemies.[48] In some situations—including some situations in which Protestantism experienced dramatic growth—it was closely allied with the state.

Finally, Protestants recognized their internal divisions as problematic and made various attempts to unite themselves in regional bodies like CLAI and CONELA and on a local level, as in Buenos Aires. The partial success of these endeavors should not obscure, however, the largely divided nature of Latin American Protestantism. The movement's great strengths—its lay character, its dynamism, its low barriers to leadership, its flexibility and adaptability—also served as its great weaknesses. Disenchanted leaders could easily break away from existing churches and denominations to start new ones.

## 2

# *Witnesses and Evangelists: Large-Scale Evangelism and the Catholic Response*

INDIVIDUAL LOCAL ACTORS were the main engines driving Protestantism, but it is worth examining large-scale evangelism because it presents another window into the growth and influence of Protestantism. In addition to being more visible and better documented, these programmatic and event-oriented approaches to evangelization were significant because they were public. No longer a tiny minority and no longer shrinking from attracting attention to themselves, Protestants were asserting a role in the public square and thereby contesting more directly the dominance of Catholicism in the region. Among the most important practitioners of large-scale evangelism were the Latin America Mission, Billy Graham, and Luis Palau (Carlos Annacondia and other Argentine Pentecostals, also important, are treated in Chapter 5). The tradition of large-scale evangelism continues to the present day and is now mostly the province of homegrown Latin American evangelists.

## *The Latin America Mission*

Founded in 1921 by Harry Strachan of Scotland, the Latin America Mission (LAM) initially focused on energizing and empowering dispirited Protestants, who tended to have small churches—both physically and in numbers of believers—and to live with constant anxiety about the precarious state of their religious freedom. In terms of evangelism, they feared doing anything more than share their faith quietly with their friends.

Strachan decided to bring in the best evangelical speakers he could find to give addresses in public places, thus evangelizing non-Protestants while emboldening local Protestants.[1] In 1948 LAM took an even more public approach when it pioneered radio evangelism in the region with TIFC, "the Lighthouse of the Caribbean," in San José, Costa Rica. The mission also started radio stations in El Salvador, Nicaragua, Panama, and Mexico and then helped to create the Pan American Christian Network of Protestant radio stations (today known as Difusiones InterAmericanas).[2]

Harry Strachan's son, Kenneth Strachan, took over the leadership of the mission and soon adopted an even more ambitious approach to evangelism. After organizing Billy Graham crusades on several Caribbean islands in 1958, he felt a sense of disappointment: had any lives really been changed or had the "converts" simply had fleeting emotional experiences? His disquiet led to months of study and eventually to a program called Evangelism in Depth. Three related convictions drove this new approach. First, Strachan argued that "every Christian, regardless of his position, is faced with a commission that does not permit him to hide inside sheltering walls but thrusts him out into the world." In other words, every Protestant had to support Jesus's "Great Commission" to "make disciples of all nations." Second, Strachan theorized, "The growth of any movement is in direct proportion to its success in mobilizing its total membership in the constant propagation of its beliefs." Third, he emphasized that Christian unity was a necessary corollary to the massive mobilization of believers, not simply as a practical matter, but as a command based on Christ's prayer "that they all may be one" (John 17). "For how can a multiplicity of distinct groups, living and working in isolation or even in competition with each other," he asked, "testify effectively to a skeptical world that Christ is Lord and Savior?"[3]

Evangelism in Depth, which operated between 1959 and 1971, attempted to mobilize all Protestants in a given country so that every non-Protestant could hear or read the gospel message in a period of one year. It included "organized prayer, training for lay Christians, preparation for counselors, follow-up of converts, widespread publicity, door-to-door visitation, local and regional evangelistic meetings, regional and national parades, radio and television programs, and widespread Bible and tract distribution."[4] To Dayton Roberts, vice president of the LAM, Evangelism in Depth was an overwhelming success: "Christians were united and mobilized in twelve Latin American nations. Evangelistic witness became the church's first concern. Thousands of Christians began praying together.

Pastors were revitalized. Financial resources were discovered and stewardship developed. New leadership was recruited and trained. Many thousands were born again. Backsliders returned to the fold. Missionary vision multiplied. The unbelieving world was made aware of the evangelical dynamic in its midst."[5]

Critics disputed the results and pointed to problems such as excessive bureaucracy, limited follow-up, and lack of permanent reorientation toward evangelism.[6] LAM leaders said that they disagreed, but they did not run another Evangelism in Depth campaign in Latin America after 1971. Despite the massive preparation, coordination, and mobilization in each campaign, the real motor of Protestant expansion, LAM had to admit, was more spontaneous. For instance, David Howard, later president of LAM, started his missionary career in Costa Rica but made only one convert in four years—and that young man one day simply renounced Protestantism. Later, in the 1960s in northern Colombia, Howard saw thousands of conversions, but these were the work of Victor Landero, a Colombian who was "the greatest personal evangelist" Howard had ever encountered. In a similar manner, the arrival in northern Colombia of Pentecostal phenomena, which Howard eventually recognized as "a wonderful blessing for new believers" and a "sovereign work of the Spirit," was totally unplanned by LAM and opposed by many veteran missionaries.[7]

Finally, in 1971, LAM responded to rising tensions between foreign missionaries and national leaders by thoroughly reorganizing itself. In the new organization, known as the Community of Latin American Evangelical Ministries, the former American-based missionary parent organization became known merely as the "Latin America Mission USA," one of many independent entities in an alliance of organizations, the majority of which were based in Latin America and run by Latin Americans. LAM relinquished its leadership role, focused on fundraising, and sent its missionaries to work for Latin American churches. Now the missionaries were the "employees" and the locals were the "employers."[8] Thus, LAM's story encapsulated the larger history of Protestant expansion. Just as the "historic" denominations were faltering in the early twentieth century, independent missions like LAM breathed a breath of fresh air into the Latin American religious environment with their bold public witness and their introduction of religious broadcasting; yet even as LAM's most ambitious plans for nationwide mobilization were being implemented in the 1960s, they were being overtaken and made almost irrelevant by unplanned and spontaneous indigenous revival. Even the Evangelism in Depth program was based on Latin American agency: LAM introduced the concept and provided high-level organization, but the premise of the project was that average Latin American Protestants would do the real work of evangelism.

## Billy Graham

Billy Graham offers another example of the evolution of Protestant outreach in Latin America. The evangelist did several of his trademark stadium "crusades" in the period from 1960 to 1995, visiting Brazil three times, Mexico and Puerto Rico twice, and most other countries in the region at least once.[9] His first Latin American crusade, which took place in Brazil in 1960, reached a total of 590,000 people in its various venues, including 160,000 who filled Rio de Janeiro's Maracana stadium for its largest event. Despite warnings from Catholics, Graham received a great deal of generally favorable attention in the press and attracted crowds that were about 50 percent Catholic. In the end, the Billy Graham Evangelistic Association (BGEA) recorded over 30,000 decisions for Christ over the crusade's five days.[10]

Not all of Graham's Latin American crusades were so successful. For instance, his 1962 visits to Venezuela, Colombia, and Ecuador featured thirteen events but reached only 150,000 people and saw only 4,567 conversions, largely because Catholic bishops and religious orders took a more active role in warning Catholics to stay away. Carlos Maria de la Torre, Cardinal Archbishop of Quito, prohibited Catholic attendance in his archdiocese; Jesuits mocked Graham in Venezuela; and in Barranquilla, Colombia, Catholic pressure led to a last-minute decision to deny Graham the use of a city stadium.[11] In general, though, Graham's crusades only increased in popularity, as religious freedom expanded and Protestantism slowly became more socially acceptable. In Argentina, for example, Graham's first events, in 1962, took place in a 5,000-seat venue, but by 1992 he was packing more than 80,000 people into River Plate Stadium in Buenos Aires. The Argentina crusade of 1991 also marked a transition of sorts, as the seventy-three-year-old evangelist was cutting back on public engagements and the BGEA was developing new approaches to mass evangelism. In conjunction with Graham's traditional stadium events, BGEA trained 18,000 Protestants in "discipleship" and evangelism and also sent his messages via satellite and videotape to 852 other sites in Latin America. Volunteers invited people to the events and then followed up with new converts. This massive effort, which included translation into Portuguese and four indigenous languages, testimonies by famous converts from the worlds of sports and entertainment, and special music videos for each location, actually had a higher response rate than the stadium events.[12]

Eventually, after Graham had his last Latin American stadium crusade in Puerto Rico in 1995, the BGEA developed a new program called "My Hope Evangelism Through Television" in which the BGEA mounted massive national campaigns reminiscent of LAM's Evangelism in Depth. First, BGEA trained hundreds of local pastors throughout the target country in the methods of My Hope. Then, the pastors taught their own congregants. Finally, the congregants invited friends and neighbors into their homes, showed recorded or televised gospel messages, told their own conversion stories, and urged their guests to make decisions for Christ. Starting in 2002 in Costa Rica, Honduras, Nicaragua, and El Salvador, with the BGEA claiming 196,900 conversions, the program spread to Panama, Paraguay, and Venezuela in 2003; Bolivia, Colombia, and Ecuador in 2004; Argentina, Chile, Guatemala, and Peru in 2005; Mexico in 2006; Uruguay in 2007; and Brazil in 2008. In Mexico alone, the BGEA asserted, more than 20,000 churches trained their people to host over 200,000 home events for an estimated audience of 2.4 million, with 479,000 people indicating their new commitments to Christ.[13]

The Brazilian effort of 2008 highlighted the massive scale of the My Hope campaigns. BGEA opened a Minha Esparança Brasil national office in August 2007, trained a national coordinator for every participating denomination (plus hundreds of others), and then bought air time on the Bandeirantes national television network so that the evangelistic programs could be seen across the nation. Meanwhile, the coordinators convinced 53,000 pastors to sign up for the program; these pastors then trained 840,000 people in their churches to implement it. On three successive nights in November those hundreds of thousands of Protestants invited their friends and neighbors into their homes, first to hear soccer star Kaká's conversion story and a message from Billy Graham, then messages from Franklin Graham (son of Billy), and singer Paulo Baruk, and, on the third night, a movie about a man who considers leaving his sick wife for another woman but through God's grace decides to remain faithful. Over 300,000 decisions for Christ were reported across the nation.[14]

Thus, in a process similar to what happened with LAM, Billy Graham became progressively less important to his own ministry. First the crusades revolved around him and his stadium events. Then his organization began organizing thousands of volunteers to run remote events, which ended up being more evangelistically successful than the larger stadium events. Finally, the My Hope initiative limited Graham's personal involvement to taping a message that served as a small part of a vast program. In Minha Esparança Brasil it was the coordinators, pastors, and lay Brazilians who did the real work of training, inviting, hosting, and following up. Billy Graham served as a unifying force and the BGEA acted as a catalyst, but overwhelmingly the Brazilian Protestants themselves were the evangelists.

## *Luis Palau*

Perhaps even more indicative of the transition in Latin American evangelism was the story of Luis Palau of Argentina. Baptized Catholic, Palau made a decision for Christ at a Protestant summer camp as a twelve-year-old in 1947.[15] Five years later a Billy Graham radio broadcast sparked his desire to become an evangelist. After studying at the Multnomah School of the Bible in Oregon, Palau worked for Graham as an intern in 1962 and then translated for several Graham crusades in Latin America over the next few years. As president of an evangelism organization called Overseas Crusades and then through his own Luis Palau Evangelistic Association (later the Luis Palau Association, LPA), Palau led more than 100 crusades in the 1970s and 1980s, mostly in Latin America, but also in Europe, Africa, Asia, and Australia.[16] Among his many successes were doubling the number of Protestants in Paraguay from 5,000 to 10,000 in the course of his 1976 crusade and assembling an audience of 700,000 in Guatemala in 1982, the "largest Christian gathering" in Latin American history up to that point.[17]

Although influenced by Graham and the BGEA, Palau developed a style more attuned to Latin American culture and more reflective of the typical Latin American Protestant reading of cultural issues. For instance, Palau realized early in his career that even though the upper class would not come to stadium events, they still might be interested in his message. "Wherever there's a measure of sophistication, where people feel 'I'm above being emotionally rattled in a rally,'" Palau noticed, "they will come to luncheons."[18] All his crusades, therefore, also featured meals in hotels and conference centers where he could share his message with segments of the population that Graham rarely reached. At the "Banquet of Hope," for example, in his 1977 campaign in Colombia, 2,500 civic and political leaders including President Alfonso López heard his plea to turn to God.[19]

Moreover, Palau did not shy away from controversial Latin American social issues. "In Latin America," he claimed, "most men, when they get into their 30s, have had three women, and most have children with them." He argued that Protestantism could solve a wide array of social problems, such as the poverty, prostitution, and despair that stemmed from sexual irresponsibility. "When a man gets converted, he wants to see his children educated," he argued. "He wants to see his wife elevated."[20] On another occasion he said, "Poverty in South America is not because of a lack of resources, and it's not mainly from oppression, although that is there. It's because people sleep around, gamble, and drink, wasting the few resources they have."[21] Graham never made such confrontational remarks and would not have gotten away with them if he had, but Palau, as a native Argentine, could present such words in the spirit of self-criticism.

Similarly, Palau showed more awareness than Graham of the theological currents in Latin America and more willingness to confront them directly. He contrasted one of Protestantism's emerging rivals in the struggle for the hearts of the poor, liberation theology, which he said was "not a theology" and "does not liberate" because "it starts from man and works outward," unlike true Christianity, which "starts from God's standpoint."[22] He also made veiled attacks on mainstream Catholicism, saying that Latin America was "oriented to a dead Christ," a reference to the prominence of the crucified Christ in Catholicism. "Our emphasis," he said, "is that he is alive. He can touch your life now, revolutionize your home, make you a different person."[23]

In the 1990s Palau led fifteen crusades in the United States, but there and in Latin America he noticed that the style that he and Billy Graham had used for decades was not working as well as it had in the past.[24] "We began to realize," he said, "that the classic campaign model—uniformed choir, the suits on the platform, the old hymns—wasn't the way to go for us." Palau and three of his sons then developed a new model called "festival evangelism" that started with a "Season of Service" by volunteers doing service projects in city neighborhoods and ended with enormous festivals featuring free food, contemporary music, and short evangelistic messages.[25] Starting in 1999, the Luis Palau Association sponsored many large festivals in Latin America, focusing on Argentina, Mexico, and Central America:

1999: Villahermosa, Mexico; Formosa and Corrientes, Argentina; Viña del Mar, Chile.
2000: Monterrey, Mexico; Rosario, Argentina.

2001: Managua, Nicaragua; Cordoba, Argentina.
2003: Buenos Aires, Argentina.
2004: Mar de Plata, Argentina; Lima, Peru.
2005: Mendoza, Argentina.
2006: San José, Costa Rica.
2007: Monterrey, Mexico.
2008: Buenos Aires, Argentina; Huatulco, Mexico; Oaxaca, Mexico.
2009: Guatemala City, Guatemala.

These campaigns became truly massive. For instance, the "Luis Palau Festival Buenos Aires" attracted 800,000 people to downtown Buenos Aires over two nights in 2008 and, according to the Luis Palau Association, witnessed more than 16,000 "documented decisions for Christ." Meanwhile, daily radio shows in English and Spanish on more than 3,000 stations in forty-eight nations extended Palau's ministry and made him more and more of a household name in both Latin America and the United States. By 2011 the LPA was boasting that through festivals, radio, and television, Palau had shared the gospel with more than 1 billion people, resulting in more than 1 million conversions.[26]

The Luis Palau Festival Monterrey, held in Mexico's leading industrial city in 2007, showcased the ways in which Palau's new strategy could inspire extensive Protestant cooperation and massive local attendance. His event in Buenos Aires the following year was larger, but Buenos Aires was home to almost 3 million people, with another 9 million living in a ring of suburbs, while Monterrey and its suburbs had only about 4 million residents. Therefore, the 400,000 people who attended the events in Monterrey represented about 10 percent of the local population, an even more impressive number than the approximately 5 percent of the Buenos Aires region who attended its festival.[27]

After recruiting a team of 18,000 volunteers from 980 churches in Monterrey, the LPA organized an array of events and services designed to attract the widest possible spectrum of people. The centerpiece of the festival was two nights of concert-type events at the Parque Fundidora, where the LPA built an enormous stage several stories high for the approximately 200,000 people who attended each night, crowds that the LPA described as the largest in Monterrey's history. Music in various styles, from traditional Mexican mariachi to heavy metal, warmed up the crowd each night before Palau took the stage. "This is the mystery of the cross," he preached. "If I give him my heart tonight, God is going to forgive me absolutely." For those who did not travel to the park, the music and preaching were broadcast on radio, television, and the internet, and summaries and articles were featured in the city's newspapers. In the end, the LPA recorded 16,000 decisions for Christ.[28]

How did such a large crowd get assembled? Most were invited by those 18,000 volunteers, signaling that, as with BGEA's work in Brazil, local agency played an essential role in the eventual success of the campaign. A massive advertising campaign, including nine trucks with twenty-foot-long signs that circulated throughout the city, also contributed. A meeting with the governor of Nuevo León, Natividad González Parás (including joint prayer), a breakfast with other politicians, and a meal with 700 businessmen simultaneously gained goodwill from the powerful and generated more media attention. In the same way, a luncheon with 1,100 "ladies of high society" that featured Puerto Rican television personality and singer Jailene Cintrón and Venezuelan singer José Luis Rodríguez heightened the public's awareness of the upcoming festival. Lest anyone imagine that Palau only cared about the rich and famous, he also presented his message at three different prisons and provided the inmates with food and toiletries. Meanwhile, at the Cintermex convention center, next door to the Parque Fundidora, 200 different organizations, including book publishers, music labels, and charitable organizations, provided 5,000 square meters of exhibits and the First Ibero-American Leadership Conference brought together 1,900 evangelical leaders from twenty-two countries to hear presentations from Protestant leaders such as Dante Gebel, the Argentine pastor of Hispanic ministries at California's Crystal Cathedral megachurch, and Harold Cabelleros, founder of Guatemala's El Shaddai denomination and leader of the Visión con Valores political party. Medical services and a children's festival also attracted crowds to Parque Fundidora. Two hundred eighty family doctors and twenty-nine physicians specializing in everything from allergies to surgery offered free care to thousands of people, while 155 dentists worked on their teeth. Nearby, 65,000 children played games, received free snacks, and then watched a two-hour evangelistic musical show.[29]

Added together, the events of the Palau festival in Monterrey created a sort of parallel universe in which leading government, business, and entertainment figures visibly identified with the Protestant message, in which Protestantism was the religion of the multitudes, and in which Protestantism, not Catholicism, was the dominant faith in Latin America. This diligently constructed oasis of Protestantism was central to LPA's project in two senses. First, it presented itself as all that Latin America hoped to be—modern, technologically advanced, generous, open, peaceful, centered on the family—while being thoroughly Protestant. Thus, the festival could present conversion to Protestantism as uncontroversial and at the same time as a bridge to the "goods" presented at the festival. History, tradition, family, theology—all the common barriers to Protestantism—were submerged by a tidal wave of popular culture, gifts, and services, freeing the potential convert to make a decision that otherwise might have been unthinkable. Second, the festival was forward-looking. The world of the Festival Luis Palau offered not only a vision of a hoped-for Protestant Latin American future but also a glimpse of a heaven designed by and for Latin American Protestants. Thirty years earlier, a Uruguayan Methodist bishop had criticized Billy Graham for coming all the way to Latin America but not "taking seriously the context and people in their context."[30] Such a charge was much harder to level against Palau.

The attention I have paid to Evangelism in Depth, Billy Graham, and Luis Palau could leave the impression that these highly organized campaigns were the most important or most representative form of evangelism. It should be emphasized again that personal evangelism through social networks and door-to-door evangelism on the local level played a significantly larger role in the growth of Latin American Protestantism than these public evangelistic crusades.[31] The point is that these campaigns were *spectacles,* that is, public events that were hard to avoid and that impressed on the Latin American psyche a picture of bold, public, unapologetic Protestant outreach. Far beyond the thousands who made those "documented decisions for Christ" were the millions of people who attended these events without making a decision or who were invited to attend but declined or who encountered the crusade in the media. These "unconverted" Latin Americans, the vast majority of them Catholic, could not help but learn lessons about evangelism and about Protestantism: these Protestants had a clear message, thought it applied to everybody, and put large amounts of time and money into spreading it. Each crusade consequently functioned as a loud warning to Catholics that they needed to get their act together to avoid continued losses to Protestantism. At the same time each crusade provided a model of evangelism that Catholics had to take seriously and at least to consider emulating. As mentioned earlier, Luis Palau was just the tip of the iceberg. By the 1990s many Latin American Pentecostal evangelists were drawing large crowds throughout Latin America and around the world.

# *The New Evangelization*

In 1975 Pope Paul VI released a document, *Evangelii Nuntiandi*, that had special resonance for Latin America. There were allusions to liberation theology and base ecclesial communities, but they were not the central point of the document. Rather, Paul emphasized that "evangelizing is in fact the grace and vocation proper to the church, her deepest identity," and that the church "exists in order to evangelize."[32]

More than reining in radical liberationists or spurring conservative clerics into a more holistic gospel, Paul wanted to promote "the clear and unequivocal proclamation of the Lord Jesus," by example and by word, especially preaching and catechesis, using traditional methods and the modern media. Catholics should not neglect person-to-person evangelism, he admonished. "In the long run," he asked, "is there any other way of handing on the Gospel than by transmitting to another person one's personal experience of faith?" Unbelievers and children needed to hear the message for the first time, but they should not be the only ones to hear the gospel. "As a result of the frequent situations of dechristianization in our day," he explained, "it [the gospel] also proves equally necessary to innumerable people who have been baptized but who live outside the Christian life, for simple people who have certain faith but an imperfect knowledge of the foundations of the faith, for intellectuals who feel the need to know Jesus Christ in a light different from the instruction they received as children, and for many others." The Catholic Church also must evangelize Protestants, for "she would be gravely lacking in her duty if she did not give witness before them of the fullness of revelation whose deposit she guards."[33]

*Evangelii Nuntiandi* served as a clear message from the pope that the church was not going to take its losses to Protestantism and secularism lying down. Catholics had a sacred obligation to re-evangelize nominal Catholics and to win back Protestants. It was the bishops who most internalized this message, who saw firsthand the superficiality of much Catholic practice and the massive defections to Protestantism. CELAM's 1979 meeting in Puebla has attracted scholarly attention mostly because of its emphasis on "the preferential option for the poor," but more than anything it was a response to *Evangelii Nuntiandi* that focused on "Evangelization in Latin America's Present and Future."[34] Vatican II and CELAM's previous meetings had made clear, said the bishops, that evangelization was the church's "fundamental mission." Admitting the church's "inadequate proclamation of the Gospel," the bishops called all Latin American Catholics to a renewed commitment to evangelization as their "primordial vocation." First the church had to reenergize those already within the fold, "to fashion Christians who are mature in their faith and nourish them with adequate catechesis and a revitalized liturgy." Then the church should go out to those in most need: indigenous groups, African Americans, migrants, students, and laborers. Cities and "those most exposed to the influence of sects and ideologies that do not respect their identity and that provoke confusion and divisiveness" (a reference to Pentecostals and other Protestants) demanded special attention.[35]

Despite the many positive aspects of popular religiosity, the bishops identified many significant problems, ongoing ones such as "superstition, magic, fatalism, idolatrous worship of power, fetishism, and . . . syncretistic reinterpretation," and new ones such as secularism, consumerism, non-Catholic religious movements, and urban poverty. The people therefore "must be constantly evangelized over again" by a pastoral approach in which their religion was "purified, completed, and made dynamic by the Gospel." While this message was inextricably tied to justice and human development, but it was essential to remember that the point of the preferential option for the poor was "to proclaim Christ the Savior."[36]

After the deaths of both Paul VI and his successor John Paul I in 1978, the new pope, John Paul II, continued to focus on Latin America, a region that now comprised almost half of the world's Catholics. He responded quite favorably to the conclusions of CELAM's Puebla conference of 1979, which he considered "more important" than those of CELAM's Medellín conference of 1968, but he felt the need to clarify the meaning of the preferential option for the poor. "The following stand out," he said, "among the elements of a pastorate bearing the seal of a predilection for the poor: interest in solid and accessible preaching; in catechesis embracing the whole of the Christian message; in liturgy respecting feeling for the sacred and avoiding dangers of political instrumentalization; in a family pastorate defending the poor man against unjust campaigns that offend his dignity; and interest in education, bringing it to less favored sectors; a concern for popular religion, in which the very soul of peoples is expressed." He then mentioned various social concerns and matters of justice, but the point was clear: the preferential option did include social action, but it started with traditional religious issues such as preaching, catechesis, and liturgy. It was invalid if it omitted the most important teachings and practices of the church.[37]

In 1983 John Paul renewed his call for the evangelization of the poor. Expressing concern at the defections caused by other "religious groups," he exhorted the Latin American bishops to make a commitment to a program of outreach that would be "new in its fervor, in its methods, and in its expression." This "new evangelization," as it came to be known, should focus on the recruitment and training of priests, the formation of a corps of lay evangelists and catechists, and the recovery of the true message of Puebla, "without distorted interpretations, without false reductionism, and without overemphasizing one part at the expense of others." In other words, he wanted a preferential option for the poor that, as the bishops at Puebla and he himself had emphasized, was oriented toward the proclamation of the gospel.[38]

The bishops' next general conference met in Santo Domingo in 1992 to mark the 500th anniversary of Christianity in the Americas and to take up the call for a "new evangelization." John Paul opened the conference with a rousing speech that celebrated the missionary heroes of the region's first era of evangelization and then spelled out what the new evangelization should look like. Because "rapacious wolves" were conducting "active campaigns of sectarian proselytism," the pope warned, large numbers of Catholics were in danger of losing their faith. The bishops needed to preach the true gospel—and to avoid being led astray by dissenting theologians—by focusing on catechesis, Bible study, and new methods of evangelization that would translate timeless truths into contemporary language. Particularly important was the creation of local church communities with strong biblical teaching, excellent liturgy, real support for families, active social programs, and the fostering of a "culture of life." In vital parishes, "the sects and the cults cannot implant themselves or grow" while a revitalized culture could protect and nurture faith. In the same way, popular religiosity, if properly evangelized and reoriented, could become "an antidote against the sects."[39] The most recent CELAM general conference, in Aparecida, Brazil, in 2007 struck similar themes.[40]

Base ecclesial communities, which spread throughout Latin America in the 1960s and 1970s, with a particularly large presence in Brazil, provided one method of Catholic evangelization. In these small groups, lay Catholics, sometimes with support from a priest or religious sister, met to study the Bible and to apply it to their surroundings. Another approach was taken by movements such as the Neocatechumenal Way and Opus Dei, which catechized urban Catholics and provided models of Catholic living in the challenging religious marketplace of the late twentieth century. These groups fulfilled the mandate of the new evangelization by reaching and training nominal Catholics so that they would not be tempted by Protestantism or secularism and so that they could rebuild a thoroughly Catholic culture. (These movements are treated in more detail later.) Activities that might have seemed purely pastoral or cultural to Protestants functioned for Catholics as significant forms of evangelization. In the same way, Luis Palau's painstakingly constructed Protestant oases made clear that it was not just Catholics who understood the ways in which culture could aid or hinder evangelization.

The views of CELAM and the papacy toward evangelization should not be taken to represent those of all Catholics. It was one thing for a pope to give a speech or for CELAM to issue a document; it was quite another for those words to filter down to Catholics on the street or in the fields. In fact, it is quite likely that most Catholics had very little familiarity with the hierarchy's repeated calls for evangelization. The Catholic Church usually moves slowly, often thinking in terms of decades and centuries, and it surely did so in the case of evangelization. The signs in Mexico saying "This is a Catholic home" and the man in Bolivia yelling that he would never convert were more representative responses to Protestant evangelism than were the statements of popes and bishops. Still, the continued attention to evangelization at the CELAM general conferences and from Paul VI and John Paul II indicates the seriousness with which the hierarchy was responding to Protestant advances. That an ecumenist like John Paul II, who stressed the priority of working for unity with all Christians, could refer to his religious rivals as "rapacious wolves" signaled how strongly he believed that the Catholic Church faced a grave crisis of evangelization.[41]

Some Catholics did take up the challenge, building strong grassroots evangelization movements, often in the very places where Protestants were making the most headway. Two of the most impressive responses to the Protestant challenge sprang out of the Catholic Charismatic movement in Mexico.

Father Alfonso Navarro of the Missionaries of the Holy Spirit developed a program called Sistema Integral de Evangelización (SINE, usually translated in English as Systemic Integral New Evangelization) that trained and mobilized lay Catholics for evangelization by focusing on the kerigma, or basic Christian message, and catechesis. Starting in 1975, Navarro introduced his catechetical program to most of the centers of the Charismatic Renewal around Mexico, thus harnessing its energy for evangelization in a way not seen in most other countries. In 1981 Navarro pioneered the concept of the "missionary parish" at a church in Mexico City, with the idea of mobilizing all the believers there into an "evangelizing community." Eventually SINE spread beyond the Charismatic Renewal movement to over 1,000 parishes and Catholic organizations, mostly in Mexico but also in twenty-four other countries. SINE trained parishes to become "intensively missionary, implementing the integral mission of the Church in an organized and systematic manner." The organization boasted that parishes that adopted its plans saw a "total halt to the advance of Protestants and other sects, and a firm commitment of Catholics to their own church, the fruit of numerous apostolically committed lay people."[42]

The second influential Mexican figure in Catholic evangelization, José "Pepe" Prado, a layman active in the Charismatic Renewal since 1971, created a similar program of training and action. In 1980, starting with an evangelism class for forty-three lay Catholics in Chilpancingo, Guerrero, Prado slowly developed his methods. At first he envisioned his mission as training the leaders of small groups and Charismatic communities, but he eventually focused on evangelization and the building of the church. The mature program taught the basics of the Christian life, then evangelization, and finally how to train others in evangelization. By 2011 the schools were operating in 2,000 locations in sixty countries.[43] The Brazilian charismatic movement had a similar evangelistic dynamism that is examined in Chapter 10.

## *Conclusion*

The prophetic church, base ecclesial communities (comunidades eclesiales de base, or CEBs), new ecclesial movements, and the Charismatic Renewal all functioned to one degree or another as forms of Catholic evangelization. They captured the attention of secular society, brought new people into the church, and deepened the faith of other Catholics. They provided Catholic alternatives to Protestantism that appealed to rich, poor, and middle-class people across Latin America. Challenged by Protestant successes, Latin American Catholics did not fold up their tents and retreat; they began their own attempts at evangelization, training, and catechesis.

At times Protestantism seemed like an unstoppable juggernaut. Its lay character and its evangelistic successes convinced many that Latin America was indeed "turning Protestant." Across Latin America, simple Protestant believers led their friends and neighbors to radical commitments to the new religion. For instance, a Protestant convert described his life in a Honduran shantytown with no running water, no indoor plumbing, no electricity, muddy streets, and a partially built Protestant church building as follows: "We are rich in Christ. What is most important is to finish the church, make the walls—when it rains or it's cold we suffer. The only thing that is of value in life is to serve the Lord. We work when we can; He gives health."[44] In the face of such fervency, did Catholicism have any hope? Yes, it did, in large part because Protestant successes had exposed both weaknesses that could be exploited and strengths that could be imitated.

One of those weaknesses, Protestants were realizing, was that the religious marketplace could cut both ways, as new versions of Protestantism "stole sheep" from earlier ones. In the 1960s and 1970s the historic (mainline) denominations and the faith (fundamentalist) missions were complaining about Pentecostals. More recent still is "neo-Pentecostalism," represented by the Trinity Broadcasting Network (TBN), which a professor at a Protestant university in Costa Rica characterized as propagating "abstract, foreign theologies which guarantee little sensitivity towards Latin America's objective realities." Sounding like a Catholic bishop from a few decades earlier, this professor lamented that TBN's radio and television shows served as "veritable training camps that compete with denominational teachings" and that had created a new "post-denominational" Protestantism in which "competition between churches and pastors is more and more pronounced." As believers hopped from church to church in search of more entertaining worship experiences, they were ignoring discipleship and displaying "the dangerous tendency to dilute the person of Jesus Christ and his redemptive work by absorbing 'cheap grace' currents."[45] Some Protestant churches were selling vials of "spiritual oil" and promising specific blessings in return for financial contributions, exactly the kinds of abuses against which Luther and the other reformers had railed in the sixteenth century.[46] Not only was Protestantism internally divided, but it had also created a religious marketplace that magnified its own worst tendencies.

Protestantism had grown to the point that Hispanic Latin American Protestantism had come to seem "natural." With thousands of churches, millions of believers, round the clock radio and television shows, and its own bevy of star pastors and musicians, Protestants could forget (or never realize) that La Santa Biblia was a translation and that their cultural incarnation of Christianity was just one of many. Specifically, mestizo Protestants tended to deprecate indigenous languages and cultures, even those of their indigenous Protestant brothers and sisters, not understanding that the Spanish-language Bible and the vibrancy of Hispanic Protestantism were proof not of Hispanic superiority but rather of the translatability of the gospel. For converts and children of converts—in other words, those who in recent memory had received their religion from foreign missionaries—to insist on the primacy of their language and culture signaled a new stage in the development of Latin American Protestantism, a stage of maturity and confidence but also of myopia and failure of memory, and thus of vulnerability.[47]

Finally, as one Protestant writer admitted, "wherever priests and lay Catholics have started to imitate the pastoral and missionary methods of evangelicals, it seems that the evangelical churches do not grow at the same rate as in those places where the Catholic Church is absent or inactive."[48] This trend worried Protestants, since most of those Catholics who converted to Protestantism in previous generations were nominal Catholics, who would presumably be as amenable to a Catholic message as to a Protestant one. Even more worrisome, studies suggested that Protestants were not as observant or committed as previously thought, with most Chilean and Mexican Pentecostals skipping church in a given week and with almost 70 percent of those baptized as Protestants in Mexico no longer practicing a decade later. Since Protestants proved much better at conversion than at retention, Catholic evangelists could follow the example of a missionary priest in Guatemala who persuaded almost 2,000 lapsed Catholics in his diocese to return to the Catholic Church.[49] Similarly, where Catholic catechists were working, even in regions without priests, Catholicism proved surprisingly resilient.[50]

Consequently, although Protestant evangelism had made Latin America more Protestant over the past sixty years, it also, in a sense, made Latin America more Catholic. In isolated villages indigenous religion had functioned as a barrier to other religions, including both Protestantism and doctrinal Catholicism, because local elders viewed those religions as foreign and unattuned to local realities. But once Protestantism broke the local religious monopoly, indigenous people also became more receptive to doctrinal Catholicism. At the same time, when Protestant conversion became widespread in a given area, as happened in areas of Mexico and Guatemala, it attracted Catholic missionaries and catechists. These representatives of the institutional church introduced a version of Catholicism that—in an environment in which a purely local religion seemed more and more inadequate—demonstrated more resistance to Protestantism than traditional indigenous religion had. This "new" Catholicism provided doctrinal, theological, and philosophical bulwarks that had been developed over centuries and refined in ongoing ideological competition with Orthodoxy and Protestantism—something local indigenous religion could never hope to offer.

The rise of Protestantism thus served as a catalyst to Catholic revitalization. Roused from its slumber by the Protestant challenge, the Catholic Church not only returned to evangelization but also embraced new movements—including basic ecclesial communities, the Charismatic Renewal, and the new ecclesial movements—that reestablished vibrant Catholicism in different social sectors. Recent research by Rodney Stark and Buster Smith makes the connection between Protestant growth and Catholic resurgence explicit. They point to the results of Gallup polls in 2007 and 2008, which showed that eight of eighteen Latin American nations had Protestant populations of 20 percent or higher and that four of those eight—El Salvador, Nicaragua, Guatemala, and Honduras—had Protestant populations of 36 percent or higher. Yet the same polls showed "a truly remarkable level" of church attendance by Catholics across Latin America. In an area where in the 1950s only 10 to 20 percent of Catholics attended Mass weekly, more than 30 percent were attending weekly in every country except Uruguay, and more than 50 percent were doing so in twelve of eighteen countries. Most remarkably, three of the four most Protestant countries—Honduras, El Salvador, and Guatemala—demonstrated the highest weekly attendance by Catholics, with rates of 66 percent or higher. In other words, the polls suggested that the places that experienced the most Protestant successes also witnessed remarkable Catholic revivals.[51] "Is Latin America turning Protestant?" asked David Stoll in an influential 1990 book.[52] The answer two decades later was that it had become more Protestant, but that this very change had eventually made it more Catholic.

One barrier, however, that Catholics had to overcome in their new evangelization was the legacy of anti-Protestant violence. The "culture of life" and "civilization of love" that John Paul proclaimed could not go very far as long as memories of threats, church burnings, expulsions, and murders lingered. Of course, much of the violence came from indigenous traditionalists with minimal knowledge of doctrinal Catholicism, but some of it, as in Tepeji del Rio in Mexico and in Colombia, was encouraged by priests. If Catholics wanted to win over Protestants and other non-Catholics they needed to revisit the violence that their brave resistance to injustice, which we see in the next chapter, enabled them to forget.

# 3

## *Prophetic Christianity: Origins and Development*

IN 1982 CHILEAN General Fernando Paredes declared that the Catholic Church had been taken over by Marxists. The next year, the government of Augusto Pinochet repeatedly harassed Catholic churches across Chile and expelled three foreign priests who had been fighting for human rights and running a soup kitchen in Santiago. The nation's leading Catholic official, Cardinal Raúl Silva Henríquez, complained, "Police visit parishes, asking questions that sow doubts and fears among humble people. Sites for chapels are denied to Catholics and given to other denominations. At the bottom of this we see that the church's activism is misunderstood. It is thought that feeding those who have no jobs or organizing those who have no place to live is done for political reasons."[1] A year later three Chilean bishops made the break with the Pinochet regime official by refusing to celebrate the annual Te Deum Mass, in which the church traditionally had celebrated Independence Day with government officials sitting in the front row.[2]

In 1985, the Jesuit journal *Mensaje* published a number of editorials by its editor, Renato Hevia, blaming the violent atmosphere in Chile on the "repression, abuse of power, misery, and that irritating injustice that can no longer be borne passively" of the Pinochet regime. He denounced all forms of violence, but said "state violence is objectively more grave because authority by definition is called to repress crime with the arms of truth and justice." Hevia was charged with several violations of the country's new constitution, convicted, and sent to jail. Far from being intimidated, Hevia seemed to relish his imprisonment: "This experience has been for me a gift from God because it has made me feel injustice in my own flesh, drawing me a little closer to so many in Chile who suffer such injustice."[3]

The Chilean case highlighted a major change in the Catholic Church's role in Latin America. Where once it had been a bulwark of the traditional order, by the 1970s the church's position had changed so dramatically that it was often seen as an advocate of revolution. Protestants often seemed more acceptable to military regimes. Nevertheless, despite government antagonism and the threat of losing adherents to apolitical or pro-military Protestant groups, throughout the region bishops denounced governments, priests and sisters defended human rights, and lay Catholics organized for justice and peace. As a result, by the 1980s almost every Latin American nation had its list of new martyrs, men and women who had died—almost always at the hands of their own government—in the struggle for justice. Three major developments gave rise to this newly prophetic Catholicism: (1) the unjust dictatorships, human rights abuses, and revolutionary movements that characterized the region in the Cold War years; (2) the growth of Protestantism and its emergence, in some cases, as an apolitical religious option; and (3) the Second Vatican Council's profound influence. Latin America was experiencing a particularly difficult chapter in its history. The Cold War had split the world into camps, and the United States wanted to make sure that Latin America remained firmly within its sphere of influence. Still economically underdeveloped and with much of its land in the hands of a traditional oligarchy, the region would need some deep changes if it was to improve the lives of most of its people. Although Soviet-style communism had limited appeal, something along the lines of the Mexican Revolution, a mix of nationalism and state-led industrialization, had widespread attraction in other Latin America nations. By the 1960s talk of "revolution" filled the region, but its aims remained vague. While joining the Soviet bloc seemed unlikely, some sort of dramatic social transformation seemed almost inevitable.

The US approach to retaining its influence in Latin America had serious flaws. The United States supported governments (often dictatorships) that could suppress any revolutionary movements that might emerge, while simultaneously providing aid to encourage the economic growth that would make such movements less attractive. In addition to direct military aid, the United States also sent military advisors to some countries and began training Latin American officers in counterinsurgency tactics at the School of the Americas in the Panama Canal Zone. On the economic side, the United States began the Alliance for Progress, the Peace Corps, and the Agency for International Development, among other programs. Unfortunately, supporting dictators proved much easier than making economies grow in ways that truly helped the impoverished masses.

The Cuban Revolution of 1959 shocked American officials, especially when Fidel Castro openly used Marxist language and aligned Cuba with the Soviet Union in 1960. This revolution had particular relevance for Latin America because it showed that a nation thoroughly dominated by the United States not only could throw off the American yoke but could also transform its society rapidly through socialism. For the Latin American left, the Cuban Revolution was a beacon of hope. If Cuba could do it, they reasoned, so too could other nations. Ernesto "Che" Guevara, the Argentine physician who fought under Castro and then became a top official in the new revolutionary government, encouraged them in this idea, arguing that the Cuban situation was not exceptional and that the "objective conditions" necessary for revolution existed throughout the region.[4]

For the US State Department, the Cuban Revolution seemed like a nightmare. Policymakers had realized, of course, that Cuban dictator Fulgencio Batista was corrupt and violent but had supported him because they believed the "strength" that he supposedly projected would serve as a protection against communism. To lose Cuba to a Marxist intent on creating a socialist society ninety miles from Florida was bad enough; to see Castro and Guevara becoming the inspiration for Marxist revolution across the region was worse. The failure of the attempted Bay of Pigs invasion in 1961 caused even more consternation.

US Cold War policy in Latin America and the sometimes related emergence of radical guerrilla movements pushed most of Latin America into the hands of unsavory military dictators. By the late 1970s, Latin America seemed to be composed mostly of governments that oppressed their own people. In Argentina, General Jorge Videla led a government that waged an undeclared "dirty war" against its radical opponents, kidnapping thousands of suspected enemies and torturing and murdering as many as 20,000 of them. In Chile, General Augusto Pinochet, who had taken power from a democratically elected Marxist, Salvador Allende, used similar tactics against his opponents. In Brazil, a military government that ruled from 1964 to 1985 defeated an urban insurgency through the use of repression. In Uruguay, the Tupamaro urban guerrilla movement ushered in an era of harsh military governments and jails full of political prisoners. Peru's military government bucked the trend by adopting a left-ist reform program, but as soon as that regime allowed democratic elections, the Maoist guerrillas of Sendero Luminoso (Shining Path) began a campaign of sabotage and terror.

In Central America, the military had dominated Guatemala (despite some governments that were technically civilian) since a US-sponsored coup in 1954. In the scorched earth campaigns of the 1970s and 1980s, the army destroyed entire villages of those suspected to be working with Marxist guerrillas. In El Salvador, a 1979 military coup by reform-minded officers did nothing to halt the nation's descent into full-fledged civil war. An exception of sorts occurred when Nicaragua's Sandinistas managed to overthrow the US-backed Somoza dictatorship in 1979, but the US-supported Contras so weakened the government that the Sandinistas allowed democratic elections and relinquished power in 1992.

Costa Rica and Mexico escaped the period without military dictatorships. Costa Rica enjoyed uninterrupted democracy but experienced spillover in its border region from the Contra-Sandinista conflict in neighboring Nicaragua. Mexico proved that democracies could be quite repressive, as exemplified most clearly in the 1968 massacre of hundreds of student protestors at Tlatelolco square. Not incidentally, Mexico also experienced guerrilla activity in the central part of the country. Thus, from Mexico to Argentina, a repressive political climate called out for a response from the Catholic Church.

As military dictatorships and radical guerrilla movements spread throughout the region, Protestantism was not only continuing to grow but was also becoming a more public actor. Most nations in the region saw massive Protestant growth in the period from 1960 to 1985, with the number of Protestants in Brazil, for example, increasing from 4.4 to 15.95 percent and in Chile from 11.71 to 21.57 percent. The least Protestant nations, such as Colombia and Peru, saw the most dramatic growth, with their Protestant populations multiplying by five or six times during this period.[5] In the nineteenth century, Protestantism had seemed exotic, and indeed had been the domain of immigrants and political liberals, but this new wave of Protestant growth meant that Protestantism could present itself more and more as a religion of normal Latin Americans. The poor, the working class, and the middle class were turning to the new gospel in increasing numbers.

Meanwhile, Protestants were also gaining a higher profile, perhaps best symbolized by Pentecostal Efraín Ríos Montt, a general who ruled

Guatemala from 1982 to 1983 and who made Pentecostal Christianity a major aspect of his public persona. His El Verbo Church, which had connections to American evangelical celebrities such as Pat Robertson and Jerry Falwell, fed all the traditional fears of Protestantism as a vehicle for American cultural imperialism. Ríos Montt's weekly radio address to the nation, which featured the language of evangelical moral reform, and his army's policy of working closely with Protestants in the countryside made Protestantism not only socially acceptable, but a safer religious option than Catholicism, which increasingly was associated with resistance. Ríos Montt may have been the most visible figure in Latin American Protestantism, but that was not always good for the faith. Under Rios Montt, Guatemala's army committed unspeakable crimes, including massacres of indigenous communities. Was he hurting or helping the evangelical project in Latin America? It is difficult to say, but Rios Montt certainly represented a more assertive Protestantism that could challenge Catholic dominance.[6]

Across Latin America, Protestantism had achieved a degree of stability and social status. No longer the religion of immigrants and intellectuals, Protestantism seemed at home in the region. Catholics therefore faced a real dilemma. They had to respond in some way both to Protestant growth and to the murderous regimes ruling over them. Should Catholics match the apolitical stance of most Protestants? Or should they confront these murderous regimes?

Vatican II's *Gaudium et Spes* helped Catholics face this difficult situation. With persistent poverty and suffering amidst never-before-seen material abundance, with the Cold War threatening all life on earth, with scientific advances and industrialization thoroughly changing human lifestyles, the modern world had a complexity unlike any previous age, the document said. The answer to humanity's many questions could be found in Jesus Christ, who, as "the key, the focal point and the goal of man, as well as of all human history," shed light on "the mystery of man." Christ's unique and essential role did not imply a rejection of atheists and other non-Christians; instead, the document said that Catholics should pursue "sincere and prudent dialogue" with non-believers. Based on the "exalted dignity proper to the human person," Catholics should work with all those of good faith to build a human society "founded on truth, built in justice, and animated by love." Because of the "basic equality" of all people, Catholics should work to end all types of discrimination and "excessive economic and social differences."[7]

*Gaudium et Spes* also addressed economic development, an area of special interest to Latin America. All economic activity, it argued, must be based on the needs and the dignity of the human person. It thus rejected laissez-faire capitalism and collectivization alike, since they both made human beings into means rather than ends. Basic rights included work, a wage that provided the necessities of life, and the freedom to found and to join unions. Although they should start with dialogue and negotiation, workers could legitimately resort to strikes to protect their rights.[8]

The document affirmed the value of private property but made clear that such a right was not absolute. The traditional Catholic concept of "the common destination of earthly goods" put the right to the material goods that correspond to basic human needs ahead of the right to private property or the right to free trade. A section seemingly written specifically for Latin America applied this idea to "extensive rural estates which are only slightly cultivated or lie completely idle for the sake of profit, while the majority of the people either are without land or have only very small fields." In such circumstances "insufficiently cultivated estates should be distributed to those who can make these lands fruitful."[9]

## *Medellín and Puebla*

The official Catholic response to the military dictatorships, Protestant expansion, and Vatican II came at the general conferences of CELAM in 1968 and 1979. After the close of Vatican II, the Latin American bishops had about two years to prepare for CELAM's general conference in Medellín, Colombia. At various meetings and conferences they examined conditions in the region in light of the recent council and with a growing appreciation for data from the social sciences. Several factors influenced the preparations.

First, several members of the Brazilian bishops' conference—with Dom Helder Camara, Archbishop of Olinda and Recife leading the way— began to emphasize that justice and economic development needed to be at the heart of the upcoming Medellín meeting. Camara, for instance, used principles gleaned from *Gaudium et Spes* and data from the growing number of Catholic social science "think tanks" that were sprouting throughout the region to point to unjust economic and political structures that the church should condemn and transform. "The number one problem is not priestly vocations; it is underdevelopment," Camara warned CELAM. A person subjected to dehumanizing and debilitating poverty simply had no real choices. "Such a person," he made clear, "cannot choose to be anything, much less a priest." With most peasants either subjected to neo-feudal oppression or relegated to subsistence on minuscule and inadequate plots of land—even as rich landowners kept enormous tracts of land idle—the region needed exactly the sort of agrarian reform envisioned by *Gaudium et Spes*. The church, and in particular its bishops, must expose the scandal of rural exploitation and advocate the needed reforms. Camara also called for radical changes in international relations. "The problem," he argued, "is not aid, but justice." The contradiction between rich nations' hefty profits on their investments in Latin America and the abysmally low prices for the raw materials that the region exported was a "discrepancy that cries to heaven for vengeance." The bishops, he believed, should work to rectify this situation by supporting a Latin American common market and efforts to reform international trade.[10]

A second influence on the preparations for CELAM was occurring at the same time, as a network of theologians had begun to develop a theology that incorporated sociological and economic data, history, and Marxist analysis. They would have a major impact on CELAM. Starting at a meeting in 1964 in Petropolis, Brazil, this group, which included Gustavo Gutiérrez, Juan Luis Segundo, and Lucio Gera, took pains to look closely at Latin American reality, as painful as it was, before building their theological systems. Chief among their concerns was "dependency," an economic concept in vogue at the time that pointed to the plight of nations of the "periphery" whose economies relied on exporting cheap raw materials but who were forced to pay exorbitant prices for the finished goods produced by the industrialized nations of the "core." In this theory, the prosperity of the core caused the poverty of the periphery; in effect, the underdevelopment of Latin America resulted not from the region's failure to institute proper economic policies but from the development of Europe and North America. Gustavo Gutiérrez did not present his talk "Toward a Theology of Liberation" until a month before the Medellín conference, but the notion of "liberation" that he and others were using began to circulate in the intellectual currents of the church. Consequently, in the years before Medellín, Gutiérrez and a network of priests, theologians, and progressive bishops laid the theoretical groundwork for the concept of liberation that figured prominently in the Medellín documents.[11]

A third influence on CELAM arrived in 1967 when Pope Paul VI released *Populorum Progressio*, an encyclical on economic development that extended and made more specific some of the council's recommendations. Paul rejected colonialism and called for a new global economic order of justice and compassion. He argued that every person had "the right to glean what he needs from the earth" and that rights of private property and free trade, although legitimate and important, were subordinate to the principle reaffirmed in Vatican II that "created goods should flow fairly to all." He repeated the council's call for the expropriation of unused landed estates and condemned "unbridled liberalism" as dangerous and deficient because "economics is supposed to be in the service of man." Wealthy nations, he said, had a duty to aid developing nations directly and to make the terms of trade more just, even to renegotiate loans to make them easier for the poorer nations to repay. "Continuing avarice" on the part of the wealthier nations, he warned, "will arouse the judgment of God and the wrath of the poor."[12]

Paul had reaffirmed the social teaching of Vatican II and had rephrased it in a way particularly suited to the developing world in general and to Latin America in particular. His rejection of colonialism, his harsh language toward the rich, and his elevated vision of human affairs served as an invitation to boldness, especially for the progressive Latin American bishops. If the pope had already blazed the trail, they could surely follow him by applying the council's recommendations and his encyclical to their specific situations. He even gave some encouragement for the small number of bishops with ties to the far left; although the encyclical generally advocated peaceful approaches to development and condemned violent uprisings for creating "new injustices" and "new disasters," it contained one sentence that showed that Paul VI had not absolutely ruled out revolution. Situations of "manifest, longstanding tyranny" and severe infringements of human rights, he implied, could justify armed revolt.[13]

Thus, when the Latin American bishops convened in Medellín, from August 26 to September 6, 1968, many of them had spent the previous six years in an intense period of reflection, growing familiarity with one another, and increasing understanding of the socioeconomic reality of their region.[14] They had come together as a group in Rome and had imbibed the teaching of *Gaudium et Spes* and the heady sense of change and possibility that emanated from the council. For three years they had been meditating on the implications of the council for their region. It is hard to imagine a series of events more likely to mold them into the kind of body that produced the bold and transformative document that soon came from the conference.

The urgency that the bishops felt shone forth from Medellín. The poverty, violence, dependency, and oppression around them led them to re-dedicate themselves to "a true scriptural poverty" and to call the whole People of God to work for "a new order of justice" and for the region's "liberation at the cost of whatever sacrifice."[15] First, the bishops called the entire continent to conversion, the prerequisite for the structural change that was clearly needed. Then, rejecting both capitalism and Marxism as damaging to the dignity of the human person, they called for a return to the principles established in Catholic social teaching. Echoing the council and *Populorum Progressio*, they advocated radical commitment to justice and peace at every level of society. In the international arena, they condemned the ways in which more powerful nations exploited weaker ones and asked for a greater role for international organizations. On the national level, they called for agrarian reform through land redistribution and for programs of "concientization" that would form true social consciences in the different strata of society. On the local level, the bishops endorsed "small basic communities," in which groups of Catholics could meet together for study, service, and activism.[16]

After serious reflection, the bishops concluded that because they lived in a poor region, they had a special duty to identify with and to serve the poor. Money and personnel should be distributed in a manner that gave "preference to the poorest and most needy sectors" and that demonstrated "solidarity with the poor." Priests, religious, and laity should all seek not merely to aid the poor but "to share the lot of the poor." When the church lived in this way, she would give the world "a clear and unmistakable sign of the poverty of her Lord."[17]

Accordingly, in the midst of the Cold War, in the middle of a region dominated by military governments with little respect for human rights, the Catholic bishops came out squarely for justice, liberation, human rights, and identification with the most vulnerable members of society. The Medellín conference served as a watershed, not so much because of new concepts but because of the bishops' willingness to adopt them publicly and emphatically. In fact, from a historical perspective, the episcopacy's open identification with and defense of the poor could be considered the real ending of the colonial era, as the church finally ended its traditional support for the status quo. Despite decades of pressure from liberal governments, the Latin American church usually had managed to remain in some measure part of the establishment. Medellín officially rejected that role. Henceforth, the bishops said, the church would side with the poor.

The network of Latin American theologians led by Gustavo Gutiérrez responded enthusiastically to Medellín. These theologians had already
contributed significantly to the conference through their development of a
theology that took seriously Latin America's situation of dependence and
its need for liberation. In the years directly after the meeting, they fleshed
out their ideas into a full-fledged theology of liberation. After presenting influential lectures and articles in 1969 and 1970, in 1971 Gutiérrez
published his groundbreaking A Theology of Liberation, in which he took
sociological analysis and dependency theory for granted but said that they
required another crucial concept from the social sciences. "The theory
of dependence," he said, "will take the wrong path and lead to deception
if the analysis is not put within the framework of the worldwide class
struggle." He was calling not only for the church to use Marxist class
analysis to understand the realities of Latin American society but also for
the church to join that struggle on the side of the oppressed. "To deny the
fact of the class struggle," he argued, "is really to put oneself on the side of
the dominant sectors. Neutrality is impossible." For Gutiérrez, therefore,
Christ's work of salvation, in the sense of forgiveness of human sin, was
only part of the larger work of liberation, which encompassed support of
the oppressed and the creation of a just society.[18]

Other theologians, such as Leonardo Boff and Hugo Assman of Brazil
and Juan Luis Segundo of Uruguay, joined Gutiérrez in developing their
own book-length contributions to the field. Presbyterian José Miguez
Bonino of Argentina and Methodist Rubem Alves of Brazil began to elab-
orate Protestant versions of the new theology. In general, these thinkers,
Protestant and Catholic, shared a few key ideas: they rejected the concept
of economic development and replaced it with liberation; they insisted on
history and current reality as the starting point of theology; they embraced
dependency theory and class analysis; they saw traditional theology as
reductive, in the sense of limiting salvation to spiritual healing, when
true liberation encompassed the whole individual and the entire society.
Clearly, such an approach would transform theology itself, as one early
practitioner made clear: "Theology, then, is to be fully included under the
historical sciences and subordinated to the social sciences that analyze
the facts of collective human life." In fact, he continued, "theology will be
an 'evangelical' rereading of politics as a liberation praxis, and a 'political'
rereading of the gospel."[19]

In the 1970s and into the 1980s these liberation theologians seemed
to be leading the Latin American church into a new era. In 1985, Edward

Cleary, for example, saw the networks of intellectuals and activists as "the driving force of the Latin American Church" and argued that among these networks, "at the core is a group of intellectuals, most of them active in the elaboration of a theology of liberation." These theologians were in his mind the "inner force" of the church. They had elaborated not only a new theological methodology but also a new ideology and way of life that influenced everything from church documents to local communities.[20]

Many bishops, however, had doubts about liberation theology, about the increasingly progressive trajectory of CELAM, and about the radicalization of many Latin American priests. The emergence of liberation theology and of groups of priests dedicated to socialism in the years directly after Medellín suggested to many bishops that the principles elaborated at CELAM lent themselves to misinterpretation and radicalism. The election of conservative Colombian bishop Alfonso López Trujillo as secretary general of CELAM in 1972 signaled a retrenchment of sorts, as a majority of moderate and conservative bishops turned to the pugnacious López Trujillo as a sort of dam against further radicalization. López Trujillo did not reject the teachings of Medellín but rather interpreted them in a way that emphasized continuity and harmony with previous church teachings. He had written a thesis on "Marx's Conception of Man" and had no sympathy for the liberationists' dalliance with Marxism, and had been asked by Paul VI to investigate the new theology. As the secretary general and later president of CELAM, he dedicated himself to the defense of what he called "the formidable ecclesial accomplishment" of Medellín and of Paul VI's teachings in *Populorum Progressio* and 1975's *Evangelii Nuntiandi*, which, to him, meant protecting the legacy of the meeting and the papal documents from liberationist distortions.[21]

Even as conservatives and traditionalists were complaining that the church was becoming too political, and liberationists were asserting that their perspective was the key to the church's future, in 1975, on the tenth anniversary of the closing of Vatican II, Paul VI surprised both groups by affirming the direction taken by the Latin American bishops at Medellín while simultaneously closing off some of the more radical interpretations of the documents. In his apostolic exhortation *Evangelii Nuntiandi*, Paul argued that the gospel could not be reduced to a mere spiritual message. Since evangelization involved the church's attempt to convert "both the personal and collective consciences of people, the activities in which they engage, and the lives and concrete milieu which are theirs," it necessarily spoke to issues and areas of life far beyond the confines of the church and religious practice. "Evangelization," he made clear, "involves an explicit message . . . about the rights and duties of every human being, about family life without which personal growth and development is hardly possible, about life in society, about international life, peace, justice and development." The church therefore had a duty to work for the liberation of those mired in "famine, chronic disease, illiteracy, poverty, injustices in international relations and especially in commercial exchanges, situations of economic and cultural neo-colonialism." Far from being a distraction from evangelization, the church's work in these areas flowed directly from the gospel message. Mission and justice were integrally related.[22] Traditionalists who rejected the social mission of the church were rejecting basic Catholic doctrine.

At the same time, Paul cautioned liberationists to avoid any sort of reduction of Christianity to a political project. Advocates of liberation, he said, were tempted to limit the church's mission to "a simply temporal project," but if this were to happen, the church would lose its "fundamental meaning." There was, and had to be, a "specifically religious finality" to the gospel message that could never be eliminated or watered down. "The Church links human liberation and salvation in Jesus Christ," he said, but they are not the same thing.[23] Advocates of liberation denied that they advocated such reductionism, but it was clear that Paul had laid down real limits for the new theology. With the pope having firmly supported the church's commitment to justice and liberation, there was no real possibility that the church could ignore or erase Medellín, for the pope had tied Medellín's principles to Vatican II and to the social doctrine of the church more generally and he had affirmed, developed, and clarified those principles in quite recent writings. He also had signaled to the liberationists, though, that they were in danger of departing from the teaching of the church if they overemphasized politics and downplayed the religious aspects of the faith.

Despite the pope's clarifications, it was evident that there would be a struggle over the meaning, legacy, and implementation of Medellín, over the direction of CELAM, and over the influence of liberation theology— with López Trujillo and his supporters on one side and the liberationists and their allies on the other—at the third general meeting of CELAM in Puebla, originally scheduled for October 1978. López Trujillo and his allies argued that they did not reject Vatican II, Medellín, or Paul VI's recent social teaching, but in fact were defending those documents from distortions. In their own minds they were integrating the principles of

Medellín with the doctrinal foundations of the church. On the other side Gutiérrez and his allies felt that they were defending the true legacy of Vatican II and Medellín.[24]

The deaths of Paul VI and his successor John Paul I just a month later delayed the Puebla conference until January 1979. Meanwhile, both conservatives and progressives were jockeying for position, sensing the meeting's potential to define the legacy of Medellín and to set the trajectory for the application of its principles in the coming decades. López Trujillo and his conservative and moderate allies in CELAM made sure that bishops rather than theologians would control the conference. In Puebla only the invited bishops and other official participants could enter the Palafox Seminary where the meeting took place and where all the participants ate and slept. Almost all theologians and social scientists had to stay outside, even if their own bishops had invited them. Progressives and their moderate allies scrambled to buttress their own possibilities for influence; many progressive bishops decided to bring their liberationist advisors to Puebla even though they had to reside and work outside of the official meeting.

Both sides courted French theologian Yves Congar, an architect of Vatican II who had written a generally supportive but somewhat critical book about liberation theology. The liberationists prevailed upon him and seventy other French theologians to sign an open letter urging the Latin American bishops not to give up the principles and spirit of Medellín. López Trujillo, hearing that the letter was soon to be released, traveled to France to convince Congar to remove his name. Despite a vigorous discussion in which López Trujillo told the aged theologian that the liberationists were manipulating him and that the Latin American bishops had no plans to repudiate Medellín's principles, Congar refused to back down and the letter was released.[25]

Longer and more nuanced than the Medellín document, the Puebla "Final Document" did bear the stamp of bishops, as opposed to theologians. The new document introduced the term "preferential option for the poor"—which is often associated with Medellín but did not appear in that document—even as it placed that option squarely in the context of evangelization. The bishops concluded that evangelization was the "fundamental" mission of the church, and in fact that the church "lives to evangelize." In this way, the bishops embraced Medellín's basic principles and consciously affirmed its "vision of reality" but also identified unacceptable extremes. As John Paul II had encouraged CELAM to do, the bishops developed and clarified Medellín's conclusions in light of

Vatican II and Paul VI's *Populorum Progressio* and *Evangelii Nuntiandi*. In a manner evocative of *Evangelii Nuntiandi*, which it quoted extensively and repeatedly, the document spoke of "Christ the Liberator" and throughout advocated the "liberation" of the poor and oppressed. At the same time, as Paul VI had done, it cautioned against violence, class struggle, partisan political activity by priests, and "applying social analyses with strong political connotations to pastoral work."[26]

What did the "preferential option for the poor" actually mean as outlined in the Puebla document? First, it meant priority for the poor *in evangelization*, because the poor were "the first ones to whom Jesus' mission is directed." The message in evangelization had to include forgiveness of sin and communion with God. Second, since evangelization included "the duty to proclaim the Christian vision of the human person to all peoples," in Latin America the church could not preach a purely spiritual gospel but also must emphasize the "inviolable nobility" of even the most seemingly insignificant and marginalized persons. Third, the preferential option meant denouncing all violations of human dignity, including repression, kidnapping, arrest without due process, large gaps between rich and poor, widespread poverty, and direct exploitation of the poor by the rich. Similarly, it meant denouncing "liberal capitalism," "Marxist collectivism," and the ideology of the repressive "National Security State," all of which led to "institutionalized injustice." Fourth, it meant active work on behalf of human dignity and continual encouragement of the various sectors of the population, from students to soldiers, to construct a just and humane society that respected the "universal destiny" of the goods created by God and produced by human beings. They affirmed John Paul II's statement that there was "a social mortgage on all private property," meaning that private property, although good and generally conducive to human flourishing, had limits. Governments could legitimately expropriate unused agricultural land, as Medellín and popes Paul VI and John Paul II had affirmed. Finally, the option for the poor did not exclude the rich or any other category of person. In fact, the bishops also called for a "preferential option for young people" and even called dialogue with politicians a "priority."[27]

Puebla thus clarified and preserved the social teaching of Medellín in a way that did not entirely please liberationists or conservatives, but did not horrify them either. In the end, the importance of Puebla was measured not so much by which ecclesiastical party scored more points, but by the reaffirmation and elucidation of Medellín's orientation toward the poor and toward justice. At a meeting many feared would be dominated by López Trujillo and a conservative cabal, the Latin American bishops came out squarely for "the preferential option for the poor" and for justice, and not just in one or two peripheral lines. The poor and the justice due them appeared on almost every one of the document's 172 pages. Regardless of the plans of any group before or during the meeting, what the bishops actually produced made clear that "the promotion of justice is an integral and indispensable part" of the evangelization and the mission of the church. There was no turning back.[28]

## *Conclusion*

While I have focused here on the Catholic bishops, Protestants were also developing a new social conscience. For instance, the Protestant Iglesia y Sociedad en América Latina (ISAL, Church and Society in Latin America), founded in 1961 in Peru, called for Protestants to commit themselves to social justice, even if it meant deemphasizing evangelism.[29] Most prominently, at the International Congress on World Evangelization in Lausanne, Switzerland, in 1974, two Latin American evangelicals played leading roles in pushing the 2,500 delegates to take a stand in favor of social justice. At the time, many evangelicals did not see social issues as an integral part of mission—many believed, in fact, that such action could distract Christians from proclamation and conversion, which they saw as essential. Rene Padilla of Ecuador responded to such concerns by attacking the "truncated Gospel" of American Christianity. He challenged his fellow delegates not to fall into the trap of portraying the evangelization of the world as a technological problem that American efficiency and the "systematization of method" could solve. Instead, he argued for a recovery of the whole gospel, a gospel that included ethics, politics, and economics and that had little to do with statistics.[30]

Similarly, Peruvian Samuel Escobar pointed to Jesus's seminal statement that he had come "to preach deliverance to the captives and recovery of sight to the blind" and to evangelical leaders such as John Wesley and William Wilberforce who had worked against slavery. He asked whether evangelicals of his day stood with the oppressors or the oppressed and called for a new kind of missionary who both evangelized and worked for social justice.[31] In the end, Padilla and Escobar's position carried the day and the "Lausanne Declaration," a seminal document in the history of the world evangelical movement, included a strong endorsement of social justice, based on God's identity as both creator and judge: "We therefore should share his concern for justice and reconciliation throughout human society and for the liberation of men and women from every kind of oppression." The delegates expressed sorrow for having seen evangelism and social concern as mutually exclusive and instead proclaimed it a "necessary" part of the Christian faith. The gospel compelled evangelicals "to denounce evil and injustice wherever they exist."[32]

These statements had special significance in the context of Protestants' usual political situation in Latin America. Foreign missionaries to Latin America, who could lose their visas if they caused political problems, had deemphasized the political implications of their faith. Their converts not only inherited this apolitical faith, but also, as small religious minorities in overwhelmingly Catholic countries, had their own reasons for keeping their heads down. To speak out, as ISAL, Padilla, and Escobar were doing, in a way that linked the gospel with social justice put them at risk. That some of the region's more thoughtful evangelical leaders had done so indicated the seriousness of the injustices confronting the region and perhaps, although none of them admitted as much, the influence of Catholics.

The oppression was so extreme and so widespread that Christians were forced to ponder the connections between their faith and issues of justice and peace. The Protestants showed that this reassessment of the relation between gospel and justice could happen in a faith based mostly on the Bible. The Catholics demonstrated that the depth of the hierarchy's attention would lead to popular acceptance of the new justice agenda. Individual Protestants and some Protestant bodies came to virtually identical conclusions, but, with no pan-Protestant distribution mechanism or authority structure, these ideas did not produce the same impact that the Catholic statements did.[33] Some Protestants always participated in the struggle, but Catholic bishops and Catholic organizations led the fight. Nowhere was that more true than in Chile and Brazil.

# 4

# *Prophetic Christianity in Brazil and Chile*

IN 1989, PEOPLE in the United States learned of the deaths in El Salvador of four American churchwomen who were raped and murdered by a death squad working for the government. But the women's work and gruesome murders represented just one small chapter of the larger story of the growth of prophetic Christianity in Latin America.[1] The development of the church's teaching on justice and the public proclamation of the church's preferential option for the poor, as exemplified in the CELAM conferences at Medellín and Puebla, would have meant little as mere statements of principle. The obvious injustice in most Latin American nations during the 1970s and 1980s made clear that Christians had to take action. In following the line of prophetic resistance laid out for them in the CELAM documents, bishops knew that they were taking serious risks, but they felt that to be neutral or passive would betray the people's trust. During this period not only bishops but also religious sisters, priests, lay Catholics, and Protestants of various sorts denounced injustices and stood up for the poor and oppressed, often risking their lives in the process. We focus here on Brazil and Chile, but similar things were happening throughout the region.[2]

## *Brazil*

Even before Vatican II and Medellín, the church in Brazil was developing its own option for the poor, in large part due to a bishop, an intellectual, and several lay movements. The bishop, Helder Camara (1909–99), had served as national chaplain of Catholic Action, the influential lay movement, in the 1940s. Although previously part of a conservative group with fascist tendencies, Camara had a gradual conversion to the interests of the poor—a result of his pastoral work and conditions in his home region, Brazil's most destitute. Influenced by Catholic Action's national meetings, once he became a bishop Camara worked hard to build a national bishops' organization. The Conferência Nacional dos Bispos do Brasil (National Conference of Brazilian Bishops, CNBB) was founded in 1952, in no small part because of support from his friend Giovanni Montini, then undersecretary of state for the Vatican and later Pope Paul VI. Camara served as general secretary from the beginning until 1964. Because of his progressive orientation, the CNBB assumed its founder's commitment to the poor and the landless.[3]

Camara highlighted the ways in which Vatican II, *Populorum Progressio*, and Medellín mutually reinforced each other. Perhaps no Latin American more greatly influenced Vatican II—he helped plan the council and organized the Latin American bishops there—yet Camara was at the same time decisively influenced *by* the council. His statement that "The post-Vatican II Christian is a man without fear" because "he is beginning to take command of history," applied to no one more than himself. Camara lived out the principles of Vatican II by defending the poor and landless, which clearly influenced Paul VI's *Populorum Progressio* of 1967, which in turn pleased Camara so much that he described himself as "a bishop who exults with *Populorum Progressio*." Energized by the ringing papal endorsement of what he held most dear, Camara played a major role in preparing and guiding the meeting of the Latin American bishops at Medellín.[4] To have a figure of international renown whose ideas were receiving such startling endorsement from CELAM and the Vatican could not help but confirm to the Brazilian church the priority of justice and concern for the poor.

The second key figure, Paulo Freire (1921–97), also born in the impoverished northeast, developed a distinctive pedagogy that combined elements of Marxism and Christianity and focused on adult literacy. Freire, who saw society as consisting of "oppressors" and "the oppressed," argued that the oppressed not only should learn to read but also to understand their oppression. Then they could put their newfound literacy to work. For instance, in Freire's scheme, the word "land" would have special resonance for landless and exploited rural workers and would thus be one of the first words taught in an adult literacy course. These same rural workers, once literate, would then use their new ability in the fight for land.

After working with illiterate adults in Pernambuco during the 1940s and 1950s, Freire came to national attention in 1962 when he taught 300 sugar cane workers to read in forty-five days. The federal government had agreed to implement his program on a national basis, but the military coup of 1964 put an end to such programs.

The first lay movement to influence the Brazilian church's move toward social justice, the Basic Education Movement (MEB), also originated in the northeast. Like Freire's programs, MEB emphasized literacy education for adults and the development of their social awareness. In the MEB's case, lay Catholic activists used "radio schools" in remote rural areas to educate adults. José Távora, bishop of the northeast diocese of Aracaju, worked out an agreement with President Jânio Quadros in which the federal government paid for the program, which lay Catholics taught and administered, starting in 1961. The program quickly turned politically radical and thus faced both budget cuts and efforts by the bishops to tone down its rhetoric, but it nevertheless had a profound impact on the rural northeast by educating and empowering the landless and helping them to develop organizations that played active roles for decades.[5]

Other lay movements, usually associated with Catholic Action—Catholic Youth Workers, Catholic Workers Association, Catholic Agrarian Youth, Catholic Rural Support, and Catholic University Youth—flourished in the 1950s and 1960s, especially in the northeast. These movements developed leaders among the laity and often led their members into political activism on issues of workers' rights, social justice, and agrarian reform. Although their importance faded during the 1970s, their militancy and commitment inspired a generation of Catholics to take social issues seriously. Although priests, bishops, and religious sisters often played the most prominent roles in later years, in many ways the laity served as the vanguard in raising the banner of social justice in Brazil.

In short, by the time Vatican II called for a society "founded on truth, built in justice, and animated by love" in 1965, Brazil already had three key elements in place.[6] It had an episcopal structure, created and staffed by progressive bishops such as Helder Camara, that could adapt and institutionalize the council's teachings; it had a homegrown educational and social ideology developed by Paulo Freire that both confirmed the council's teaching and gave an example of how to implement it; and it had large numbers of poor Catholics and lay Catholics who had participated in social, economic, and political activism. The council, therefore, was not the beginning of the Brazilian church's commitment to the poor or its work for justice. Rather, the words of the council reinforced and confirmed the approach that had already developed and the work that had already begun. Still, the council, followed by Medellín and Puebla, made clear that the stance of the Brazilian church corresponded to the vision of the universal church.[7] This affirmation and endorsement from Rome and from the Latin American bishops proved invaluable because from 1964 to 1985 Brazil faced a new and deadly challenge: an increasingly ruthless military dictatorship.

## Bishops, Priests, and CEBs (Comunidades Eclesiales de Base)

In 1964 the Brazilian military seized power from reformist president João Goulart. Although initially welcomed by some bishops as an alternative to a socialist takeover, most of them soon realized that the military government had little concern for human rights or the country's poorest citizens. After the promulgation of Institutional Act V in 1968 few doubted the oppressive nature of the new regime. The act allowed the government to censor all varieties of media, to suspend habeas corpus, to detain persons deemed dangerous to the state, and to forbid political meetings of any sort. In short, it gave the state almost unlimited powers and destroyed most vestiges of democracy. Meanwhile, the government began using "death squads" to kidnap, torture, and murder its perceived enemies.

The church, already losing support from the upper class for its work with the poor and landless, found itself lumped in with the radicals, socialists, and Marxists that the military government saw as its chief adversaries. Activism that had seemed controversial in the early 1960s became, by the late 1960s, subversive—at least in the military's eyes. More and more, the government came to see priests, bishops, religious, and lay activists as the adversaries of the government—and in many cases those priests, bishops, religious, and activists saw themselves in the same way.

A year after the coup, the Brazilian bishops adopted a unified pastoral plan that attempted to adapt the church in Brazil "as rapidly and as completely as possible to the image of the Church of Vatican II." Perhaps most significantly, a new emphasis on the role and voice of the laity included a clear endorsement of CEBs (base ecclesial communities, or comunidades eclesiales de base), small groups of believers in impoverished areas who met to study the Bible and to fight for neighborhood improvements and social justice. The Brazilian church could no longer think of itself as a simple hierarchy in which clergy were synonymous with the church.

Because of the poverty of most of the laity, this turn toward the laity was simultaneously a turn toward the poor.[8]

In some cases priests and religious sisters became more prophetic than their bishops. For instance, in 1968, 300 priests wrote a letter to their bishops in which they called for a new attitude of solidarity with the masses and of independence from the wealthy and powerful. "The basic need," they said, "is not only to face courageously the rules that govern capitalist production, but to help the church attain complete freedom from economic powers." Rather than being the voice of the state, a priest had to take on "the role of prophet" and "to live as the common people do, to have simpler houses and churches."[9] Some priests went so far as to insist that "Unjust laws should not be obeyed; to obey them is to submit to sin." Not surprisingly, they soon found themselves in jail.[10]

In 1969, as priests and bishops stepped up their criticism, the military regime murdered one of Helder Camara's close associates, social activist Father Henrique Pereira Neto, and left his corpse hanging from a tree at the university where he taught sociology. Camara did not take the hint. Soon after the murder he led thousands of students in a funeral procession at the end of which he called for their commitment to the "struggle for the material and spiritual liberation of our people."[11]

Even conservative bishops confronted the military government. Cardinal Archbishop of Sao Paulo Agnelo Rossi, for example, turned down the National Order of Merit from the president to show his solidarity with priests whom the regime had jailed unjustly. His successor, the politically moderate Paulo Evaristo Arns, also broke with tradition by failing to appear with military leaders. He devoted significant attention to visiting prisons, at first simply to see his own imprisoned priests and activists, but eventually as a way to put the public spotlight on what the military wanted to keep hidden. Arns also invited twenty-four priests and the bishop of the victim's home diocese to participate in the funeral mass for Alexandre Vanucchi Leme, a student activist killed in police custody. With 5,000 students in attendance at the Sao Paulo cathedral, Arns read the judgment scene from the Gospel of Matthew—"All the nations will be gathered before him, and he will separate people one from another as a shepherd separates the sheep from the goats"—a clear condemnation of the regime's injustice and a grave warning about the eternal destiny of its officials. Afterward he told the press that his archdiocese was experiencing "a situation of emergency in relation to wages, health, and public security."[12]

This infuriated the dictatorship. Already Arns had stirred their ire by using the diocesan newspaper, O São Paulo, to cast doubt on the legitimacy of the 1964 military takeover and using the archdiocesan radio station to question government policies. The dictatorship responded by closing down the radio station and heavily censoring O São Paulo. Each week a federal police officer arrived at the newspaper office and marked the articles and portions of articles deemed unacceptable, often focusing on the weekly editorials written by the archbishop. Arns argued that the government was only damaging its own reputation: "I never tire of repeating that, in the long run, rumors damage the image and the good works of a government more than the most implacable free circulation of the truth."[13] For over a decade, Arns received visits from twenty-five to fifty people a week seeking help in finding "disappeared" family members. He felt that he could not drop the battle for justice. "No one on earth can describe," he said, "the hurt of those who saw their dear ones disappear behind prison bars without being able even to guess what had happened to them."[14]

Ivo Lorsheiter, bishop of Santa Maria and secretary general of the CNBB from 1971 to 1979, also stood up to the military government. Although he was initially perceived as a moderate, clashes with the government radicalized him, especially his arrest in the middle of a talk he was giving at a Catholic university. He later praised the 50,000 base ecclesial communities that spread rapidly across Brazil in the 1960s and 1970s. "Every man who is accustomed to live according to his faith and to practice it is also capable of taking part in political discussions, and citizens who are aware of their responsibilities will be committed also in the social domain," he believed. His words, very much in tune with those of Vatican II and Medellín, seemed to the military like a threat to turn every CEB into a cell of counter-government activism.[15]

As the bishops fought the battle in the press and offered protection of a sort, members of 50,000 CEBs fought on the ground. The most effective of these groups acted as both spiritual communities and activist groups, with Bible study and liturgy inspiring and reinforcing commitment to concrete actions for their locales. For example, a CEB in Sao Paulo prayed the following:

That we may have the right to freedom of assembly and association, let us pray to the Lord.

That there may be free and independent unions, let us pray to the Lord.

For a basic living wage, let us pray to the Lord.

For an eight hour day, which our friends asked for as long ago as May 1886, let us pray to the Lord.[16]

This grounding of concrete demands in the context of God's will and the thorough integration of justice and religion made the CEBs a political force, precisely because they were not purely political.

When members of CEBs studied the Bible they often came up with fairly radical theology, such as the following:

I believe in the reality of the Bible, in which God is on the side of the people, the oppressed, the little ones, who suffer injustly. So, in this aspect of the Gospel, I believe that it is wrong for a rancher to have eleven thousand, or much more, hectares of land, without producing anything, while several thousand laborers suffer, dying of hunger, for the lack of a piece of land to plant, to harvest their bread. So based on the Gospel, I believed and continued to believe that this was the only way we had to take possession of the land, to set foot on this ground, to gather our own bread.

—Madeleine Adriance, "Base Communities and Rural Mobilization in Northeast Brazil," *Sociology of Religion* 55, no. 2 (1994): 173–4.

Often, study led CEBs to concrete actions, as in the following testimony from a CEB member in the Amazon region:

By means of the organization of the communities we learned the struggle for rights. The communities were studying together, that we also had the right to be people. And it was thus through that journey that we learned to unite, to organize, to struggle for our rights.

Those involved in land struggles often risked their lives, as landlords and would-be landlords employed armies of thugs who threatened and sometimes kidnapped or murdered leaders of CEBs.[17]

## The Northeast and Amazonia

Because of the poverty of their region, bishops of the Northeast and the Amazon regions tended to take the lead in agrarian issues. For example, in 1970 a regional episcopal group argued that the government's economic policies had serious flaws:

> The installation of agribusiness firms in the south of Pará, a result
> of fiscal incentives, is causing problems that affect a large segment of
> the poor population of our rural areas and forests. . . . The develop
> ment of the Amazon cannot become a reality if it is not directly ori
> ented toward the people. We believe this can be attained only through
> an authentic reform of the structures and rural policies.[18]

Through repeated statements like this, the bishops made the just development of the Amazon a national issue.

Perhaps the boldest words and actions from the Northeast came from
Pedro Casaldáliga, a Catalan priest who came to Brazil in 1967 and in
1971 became the prelate of Sao Felix do Araguaia, in the Amazon region.
After observing the extreme injustice, Casaldáliga worked both to protect
the land of those being robbed by corrupt officials and to develop programs for the landless. In his first pastoral letter (which ran to 120 pages),
he denounced the climate of violence and fear in his region, including
the recent destruction of an entire town that had left its 500 residents
homeless.[19] Casaldáliga demonstrated his bravery in 1976 when he and
Joao Bosco Penido Bournier, a Jesuit priest, intervened to try to stop the
torture and rape of two female activists by police in a small town. Officers
threatened both men and then shot Bournier in the head; he died the next
day. Instead of staying silent, Casaldáliga publicized the incident and continued his push for justice. "The regime's official policy for the Amazon,"
he argued, "is based on enormous fiscal incentives that benefit only the
large ranches owned by wealthy and national and international interests,
opening up huge highways to serve those same interests. Cattle are supposed to replace men, and if things continue as they are, I may end up as
a bishop of cows and oxen because there won't be any people left."[20]

In 1973 the bishops of the Amazon region and of the Northeast released two documents that one scholar has called "probably the most
radical statements every issued by a group of bishops anywhere in the
world."[21] The bishops explicitly excoriated the regime for its numerous
abuses of human rights, aware, of course, that in doing so they were exposing themselves to the danger of those same abuses:

> The legislature has no authority; urban and rural unions are force
> fully depoliticized; the leaders are persecuted; censorship has

gotten worse; workers, peasants, and intellectuals are persecuted; priests and activists in the Christian Churches suffer persecution. The regime has used various forms of imprisonment, torture, mutilations, and assassinations.

—Scott Mainwaring, *The Catholic Church*, 103.

Not content simply to denounce the manifold human rights abuses and injustices in their regions, they proposed radical solutions. "What is really needed," argued the bishops, "is to change the structure of rural production. . . . [W]e must overcome private ownership of land and have socialized use of the land." They even went so far as to condemn capitalism as "the great evil, the rotten root, the tree that produces those fruits we all know: poverty, hunger, sickness, death of the majority."[22]

Catholic bishops also organized the Pastoral Land Commission (CPT) in 1975 to coordinate responses to agrarian issues. After joining forces with some Lutherans, the commission began providing legal aid and agricultural education, as well as publicizing human rights violations. Using television and radio, the CPT informed rural people of their rights and gave them information about how to organize. Even more important, the CNBB, representing all the bishops of Brazil, denounced the regime's abuses on a regular basis. Under the leadership of men like Helder Camara and Aloisio Lorsheider, the bishops' conference steadily broadcast its judgments to the nation and the world. As the one group of elites that would not stay silent, it played an incalculable role in keeping hope alive in the nation's darkest hours.

## Documenting Abuses

Even before the dictatorship ended, in 1985, Catholics and Protestants began an important aspect of their human rights campaign: documentation of abuses.[23] In 1979, the generals in charge of the country began to loosen some restrictions. In the judicial realm, this meant that lawyers could access the files of many persons whom the military had detained over the previous fifteen years, files that lawyers soon realized recorded the damning details of the military's treatment of detainees. Cardinal Arns and Presbyterian Jaime Wright, with $350,000 from the World Council of Churches (the worldwide federation of Protestant churches), worked out a plan to have sympathetic lawyers make photocopies of relevant files and then to send them to Arns for safekeeping. They compiled hundreds of thousands of pages of files detailing the military's extensive use of torture against its enemies. In 1985, Arns released the book *Brasil: Nunca Mais*, a summary of the documents that covered topics such as "Modes and Instruments of Torture," "Torture of Children and Women," "How Suspects Were Detained," and "The Consequences of Torture." He also produced a twelve-volume, 7,000-page version for universities and human rights organizations. "The project was not motivated by revenge," the introduction to the book made clear. "What is intended is a work that will have an impact by revealing to the conscience of the nation, through the light shed by these denunciations, the dark reality of the political repression that grew unchecked after 1964. We thus observe the Gospel precept that counsels us to know the truth as a precondition for liberation ('You will know the truth, and the truth will make you free,' John 8:32)."[24]

This practical form of ecumenism focused not on theological dialogue but on uniting for a common cause. During the periods of military dictatorship, not just in Brazil but around the region, Catholics and Protestants could put aside their differences to work for justice and peace. This ecumenism of the trenches proved far more common and successful than any formal theological dialogue.

By the time the military dictatorship ended, the Catholic Church in Brazil had transformed itself into a prophetic defender of human rights. Although in coming years the church did not play as public a role, this was largely because the new democratically elected governments committed fewer rights abuses. Still, the bishops put human rights and social justice at the center of their plans for the nation.[25]

## *Chile*

In 1968 a group of young Chilean priests and nuns called for a radical reform of their church: "We want to be a church of the people. We want the church to live among the poor. . . . We say Yes to a servant church, Yes to a church which, by its faith in Jesus Christ and in man, dares to side with the poor."[26] Paradoxically, the very success of Chile's Christian Democratic Party, which enjoyed extensive support from Catholics, delayed the fulfillment of their dream. The Christian Democratic government (1964–70), which aimed to help the landless and other needy Chileans, tended to siphon socially minded Catholics away from the church. As in Brazil, it was a military dictatorship that catalyzed the church's prophetic role. Salvador Allende's democratically elected socialist government experienced increasing opposition during its rule, from 1970 to 1973. When a group of four generals led a coup in 1973, many bishops and other Catholic leaders expressed cautious optimism about the prospects for the country. Some, of course, staunchly opposed any form of socialism, but many moderates simply longed for an end to the extremely divisive and chaotic political situation that Allende did not seem able to rectify. Within weeks, however, the true nature of the new regime became apparent. Augusto Pinochet, the general who emerged as the driving force behind the dictatorship, eventually did improve the national economy—though not necessarily the economic situation of the poor—but he did it at the expense of freedom and human rights. He eliminated opposition parties—imprisoning, torturing, and murdering thousands of political rivals and exiling many thousands more. For instance, security forces detained and beat political prisoner Alfredo Bruno to such an extent that his muscles adopted "a permanent state of spasm." Guards routinely raped female prisoners.[27]

Religious groups, especially the Catholic Church, were the only organizations capable of standing up to the dictatorship in. In the early years, Santiago's Cardinal Raúl Silva Henríquez and two Protestants, Lutheran Bishop Helmut Frenz and Charles Taylor of the World Council of Churches, assumed leadership roles. On September 24, 1973, Silva had gone to the National Stadium, where the government was holding thousands of political prisoners incommunicado. Shocked by their sheer numbers and touched by their repeated pleas to let their families know where they were, Silva proved receptive when Frenz and Taylor asked him to work with them to safeguard human rights. In October 1973, just one month after the coup, these men founded the ecumenical Comité de Cooperación para la Paz en Chile (COPACHI, Committee of Cooperation for Peace in Chile). The committee initially included the Catholic, Orthodox, Methodist, Baptist, and Lutheran churches as well as Jewish groups, and received almost $1 million in financial support from the World Council of Churches. In its early months of existence the committee focused on workers who had lost their jobs for political or other arbitrary reasons as well as on those who had been arrested. The committee, which had over 200 employees by 1975, proved surprisingly successful at saving jobs, securing unemployment benefits, and defending prisoners in military tribunals. Although less successful, the committee's submission of 2,342 writs of habeas corpus for persons who had disappeared, which resulted in a dismal total of three prisoners produced by the courts, nevertheless publicized the grave injustice of government kidnappings. Similarly, a report on torture that the committee produced in 1974 played a major role in convincing the Catholic bishops as a body to speak out against the abuses of the regime.[28]

As in the Brazilian case, the cooperation of Catholics and Protestants (and in Chile's case, Jews) created a sort of practical ecumenism that brought believers from different faith communities together to work on a common project. Unfortunately for the committee, its very ecumenical nature represented an opening for the dictatorship. The regime's security agents identified weaknesses and used them to break apart the coalition. Helmut Frenz attracted special attention, as his active opposition to the government contrasted with most Lutherans' acceptance of Pinochet as an improvement over Allende. Newspapers and other media outlets trumpeted Frenz's supposed communist beliefs and claimed that he was stealing money from his church, resulting in a split among Chile's Lutherans in 1975 and the creation of a new Lutheran denomination that immediately expressed its support for the regime. Similar tactics whittled down the committee until, in late 1975, only the Catholic, Methodist, and Jewish leaders remained.[29]

Threats, claims that Cardinal Silva was embezzling funds, and actual violence against priests and nuns—three priests were murdered, forty-five arrested, and fifty deported in 1973 alone—eventually convinced Silva to shut down the committee in November 1975. But he almost immediately established the Vicariate of Solidarity, a program of his archdiocese that the government could not easily pressure. The placement of the Vicariate offices next door to the cathedral symbolized the new agency's identity as part of the archdiocese and made clear that any attack on it would be a direct attack on the church itself. The Vicariate continued the committee's work of investigating disappearances and offering legal services but also expanded into twenty regional offices that provided job training, health services, and free meals for children made destitute by the regime's policies. Although the government attempted the same sort of propaganda attacks that had broken the ecumenical committee, the nation's bishops proved almost unanimously supportive of the Vicariate. From the popular perspective, the argument that the Vicariate represented corruption or foreign domination had no traction. In 1980, for instance, the Vicariate operated seventy-four health clinics that served 22,000 people in low-income areas, 160 soup kitchens that fed thousands every day, and dozens of local craft projects designed to put the unemployed back to work. The Vicariate also published an influential magazine called *Solidaridad*, one of the only periodicals not controlled by the government. Its direct connection to the Catholic Church allowed it to function even as Pinochet was shutting down almost all other opposition media outlets.[30]

Cardinal Silva deftly used international attention to protect himself and others working for justice and human rights, even going so far as hosting an international conference on human rights in 1978. He also created a bank for his archdiocese to keep international donations and the disbursement of funds out of the prying eyes of the government, which had the legal right to review the files of commercial banks.[31]

In addition to the ecumenical committee and the Vicariate, other Christian agencies contributed to the fight for justice. After the ecumenical committee disbanded in 1975, Protestants formed three major organizations—Evangelical Christian Aid, Diakonia, and the Social Action Federation of Christian Churches—that provided social services such as soup kitchens, medical care, literacy courses, and agricultural cooperatives. These programs avoided the more dangerous advocacy and defense work of the committee, but they met definite needs in a country in which the working class was suffering from high unemployment and a drastic reduction in purchasing power.[32]

Even as Christian opposition to the Pinochet regime exposed priests, religious sisters, and lay activists to reprisals from security forces, the Catholic Church experienced a marked increase in active leaders at all levels. In 1972, the year before the coup, the archdiocese of Santiago had had no new seminarians; in 1976 it had fifty and in 1977 it had thirty more. By 1975 the church had already trained 10,000 new lay catechists, who in turned trained another 100,000 lay Catholics in home religious education methods. Most exciting for a church that had long strained to engage working-class Catholics, many of the new leaders came from poorer urban neighborhoods.[33] It seemed that the church's stance for justice and human rights won the allegiance and respect of its people.

## A New Bishop Continues the Resistance

When Juan Francisco Fresno replaced Cardinal Silva as archbishop of Santiago in 1983, the military breathed a sigh of relief, for Fresno had a conservative reputation and on occasion had had positive words for the regime. However, Fresno made sure to make the Vicariate of Solidarity one of his first stops in his early days as archbishop, signaling that he was not going to change his successor's policy of defending human rights.[34]

In 1984 Fresno used his first Te Deum service (the independence day Mass) to call, in the presence of the top government officials, for a return to peace, obviously implying that the government was responsible for the violence in the country. The church under Fresno also proved ready to fight for political rights. For instance, when the government arrested priests, religious sisters, and other activists for protesting against torture in 1984, Fresno and his colleagues worked behind the scenes to gain their release.[35] When the regime jailed Renato Hevia, editor of the Jesuit journal *Mensaje*, for an article critical of state violence, Fresno visited him in jail.[36] In the end, Fresno played a major role in bringing the Pinochet regime to an end by calling together the many different opposition parties and helping them to write and sign an agreement for a transition to democracy.[37]

For Pinochet, the Catholic Church's resistance presented a serious problem. Because he insisted that his regime represented Christian civilization in its ongoing battle against Marxist atheism and materialism, he craved the legitimization that only Chile's dominant church could grant. At first, he believed that the Catholic bishops would welcome him, but when they became critical after only a few months, he turned to Protestants, many of whom jumped at the chance to build ties with the regime. In December 1974, for example, thirty-two pastors signed a statement calling the coup "God's response" to a dangerous situation and referred to Pinochet as the "blessed soldier" who had fulfilled God's purposes. Soon afterward, the Methodist Pentecostal Church welcomed Pinochet to the opening of its new "cathedral" in Santiago. In 1975, a Pentecostal group went so far as to have a Protestant version of the traditional Catholic Te Deum service on Chile's independence day, implying that Protestants endorsed the regime, and vice versa. The regime in return allowed Protestants a free hand to spread the faith among soldiers and sailors, which served at once as a way for the government to build an alternative base of legitimacy and as a way of signaling to Catholics what the confrontational approach would cost. If Catholics continued to withhold their support, Protestants would become the institutional allies of the regime.[38] Of course, as indicated earlier, many Protestants sided with the Catholic Church; they tended, however, to come from the older "historic" Protestant denominations, with the newer and much more rapidly growing Pentecostals tending to stay neutral or to support the regime outright.

When a democratically elected government replaced the Pinochet regime in 1990, almost overnight the Chilean bishops assumed a quieter and less confrontational posture. The bishops' leadership in opposition to the abuses of the military government had sometimes obscured the reality that the vast majority of bishops had never adopted liberation theology, much less Marxism—they had no plans to democratize the church or otherwise to transform it in any essential way. They had responded publicly and decisively to violence and human rights violations—including the imprisonment, torture, and murder of their own priests, nuns, and lay activists—but they had not substantially modified their theology or ecclesiology. The discovery of the bishops' basic conservatism scandalized some but came as a relief to others.[39]

## *Conclusion*

On March 24, 1980, an assassin murdered Oscar Romero in San Salvador. The army and its paramilitary allies killed many people that year in El Salvador as they battled different Marxist guerrilla groups and other rivals of the regime, but Romero's murder stood out. First, he was the archbishop of the country's capital city and El Salvador's most prominent churchman. Second, he was shot at the altar while celebrating the Eucharist. His murderer could have given no clearer message that the church, in the person of the nation's highest-ranking cleric, no longer enjoyed the trust of the nation's oligarchs. Romero, who had a theologically conservative background that included receiving spiritual direction from an Opus Dei priest, had surprised almost everyone after he became archbishop in 1977 by standing up for human rights and by directly criticizing the army.[40] As his country experienced rising levels of bloodshed, Romero spoke out more and more. Just a few weeks before his murder, he denounced the indiscriminate killing by security forces as part of "a general program of annihilation of those of the left, who by themselves would not commit violence or further it were it not for the social injustice that they want to do away with." A suitcase full of dynamite left a week later at a funeral Mass Romero was celebrating failed to deter him from his chosen course. He soon made a special appeal to the enlisted men of the army and the Guardia Nacional: "Brothers: you are part of your own people. You kill your own campesino brothers and sisters. And before an order to kill that a man may give, God's law must prevail that says 'Thou shalt not kill.' No soldier is obliged to obey an order against the law of God." A day later he fell at the altar.[41]

Eighteen years after Romero's death, on April 26, 1998, three Guatemalan army officers beat Bishop Juan Gerardi to death with a slab of concrete. His murder came just two days after the Archdiocesan Human Rights Center, led by Gerardi, had released a detailed report on human rights violations during the brutal Guatemalan civil war of the 1980s. Gerardi had served as bishop of El Quiché in the early 1980s and denounced the army's murder of non-combatants. He had been exiled, and had then returned to the country as an auxiliary bishop for Guatemala City. There he worked as one of the directors of the National Commission for Reconciliation, which involved various church and social groups in the quest for peace. After peace was finally achieved, Gerardi played a major role in the Recovery of Historical Memory project, which documented in its 1,400 pages thousands of cases of murder, torture, and other human rights abuses, almost all committed by the army and its allies.[42]

The murders of bishops Romero and Gerardi demonstrated the great cost of principled opposition to injustice and the lengths to which some regimes would go in retaliating against that opposition. Both bishops, despite threats, continued standing up to the military and denouncing abuses. They represented thousands of less prominent believers who did the same thing. In one of Latin America's darkest hours, the years of military dictatorships from the 1960s to the 1980s, Christians, especially Catholics, emerged as fighters for justice and human rights. And they continued fighting after the dictatorships had faded away. Taking the words of Vatican II, Medellín, and Puebla to heart, they denounced torture, disappearances, murders, and other gross injustices, often at the cost of their lives. The Catholic Church changed so much that Murray Kempton, a Pulitzer Prize–winning journalist, admitted, "Even unbelievers like myself have to conclude that the Catholic Church has become the steadiest, and in many places, the only defender of human rights the wide world can show."[43]

The region's Catholic bishops taught the faithful that piety was not enough, that the gospel demanded a commitment to justice. They were not alone. At the grassroots level, millions of poor and working class Catholics, often members of CEBs, fought local battles for land, infrastructure, wages, and other matters of justice; and they did so as part of their faith.

These mostly Catholic struggles served as powerful examples for Protestants. For example, Mayan Presbyterians, caught in the crossfire of Guatemala's civil war, rebelled against the apolitical religion they had received from North American missionaries and came out strongly for human rights and against government oppression. In a similar vein, the pastor of a large neo-Pentecostal church in Guatemala City admitted that "the shame of the Pentecostal Church" in contrast to Catholics, "is its neglect of the poor, the sick, and the imprisoned."[44] Orlando Costas, former LAM missionary, condemned Protestant support for Pinochet as evidence of "an uncritical and naïve attitude toward the current government, together with an ahistorical and privatistic missiology, and, at most, a betrayal of the prophetic mission of the church."[45] Clearly the Catholic example had caught the attention of many Protestants.

In a similar vein, the struggle for justice served as one of the region's few achievements in the area of ecumenism. Although mistrust always remained, some Protestants and Catholics could agree on basic issues of justice. Outsiders, particularly North Americans, have difficulty appreciating the depth of the antipathy between Protestants and Catholics in Latin America; it is therefore also difficult for some to understand how significant Catholic-Protestant cooperation was. The fall of the military governments eliminated that common ground, making ecumenism of the trenches much less common.

Some observers feared that the Catholic commitment to the poor and to justice also would fade away as John Paul II loaded the Latin American episcopacy with conservatives, but such was not the case. The CELAM general meeting at Aparecida, Brazil, in 2007 reemphasized the importance of the option for the poor, with the phrase appearing fifteen times in the meeting's official document, and signaled that the church's decision to align itself with the poor was not up for debate.[46]

A period of military dictatorships, human rights abuses, and growing competition between Protestants and Catholics does not sound like the recipe for the revival of Christianity in Latin America, but it did present the perfect environment in which to answer an important question: were Christians serious? Did they really believe what they said they believed? Hundreds of thousands, perhaps millions, of Christians showed that they were serious, that they would risk their lives to fight for justice. We will see in the chapters ahead many other ways in which Latin American Christians revitalized their faith—through, for instance, charismatic practices and new forms of community. But the courage, witness, and martyrdom they displayed in the face of dictatorship should be seen as foundational for all that follows. As John Paul II pointed out, "Martyrdom, accepted as an affirmation of the inviolability of the moral order, bears splendid witness both to the holiness of God's law and to the inviolability of the personal dignity of man."[47] When Christians were willing to shed their own blood in defense of others, they made clear that their religion had substance. Neither mere emotional piety nor some antiquated cultural relic, this living faith made real moral demands. Even those who rejected Christian theological claims could not dismiss the suffering and death of Christians. At the most basic level, suffering and martyrdom made Christianity credible.

# 5

# *The Heartland of Pentecostalism*

IN JANUARY 1985 a barber named Pablo Bottari, along with his wife and two children, attended an outdoor rally held by evangelist Carlos Annacondia in San Justo, Argentina. Bottari, an elder in a conservative Free Brethren church, was surprised by the shouting and clapping during the period of praise and worship and by the "food stands and general informality of it all." He was even more taken aback when Annacondia preached a short sermon and then cried out, "And now listen to me, Satan! I come against you in the powerful name of Jesus Christ of Nazareth! I rebuke you, I bind you and I order you to get out of this place! Out!" After several minutes of such rebuking, Annacondia began his ministry of healing and deliverance. Bottari's astonishment increased when he saw people, including his wife, "falling to the ground when they were prayed for" and others who manifested "convulsions, spasms, yelling, crying, fainting, vomiting and occasional violence" as they were delivered from demons.[1]

When his wife emerged from her spiritual swoon she expressed thanks for what she described as a deep personal encounter with God. Despite discomfort with much of what was happening around him, Bottari decided that he too had felt the presence of God. Both the "spiritual authority and power" of Annacondia and the testimonies of those who said that their teeth had been healed, including some who said they had received miraculous bridges, crowns, and fillings, impressed him. A few weeks later, evangelist Edgardo Silvoso spontaneously anointed and prayed for Bottari in the middle of a church service because, he said, God had instructed him that Bottari would soon have a "renowned public ministry." Later in 1985 Bottari did indeed start a public ministry, first as part of Carlos Annacondia's prayer team and then in the evangelist's deliverance tent, where, during crusades, he ministered to people who manifested demonic symptoms. By 1986 Bottari was the leader of Annacondia's deliverance ministry. In the next twelve years, he estimates, he personally freed 20,000 people from their demons and oversaw the deliverance of 500,000 other people. In 1996 Bottari took a pastoral counseling position at Buenos Aires's Central Baptist Church and developed a deliverance ministry focused on pastors and church leaders.[2]

Many Catholic and secular Latin Americans scoffed at the kinds of experiences described by Bottari, but, even as they scoffed, the same sorts of things were happening in *Catholic* settings. For example, in Bottari's hometown of Buenos Aires during the 1990s, Catholics were singing contemporary praise songs, engaging in "spiritual warfare," speaking in tongues, giving prophecies, interpreting prophecies, and experiencing supernatural physical and spiritual healing—the so-called Catholic Charismatic Renewal (CCR).[3] Despite the disdain, born of ignorance, with which the intelligentsia treated them, the Pentecostal movement and the Catholic Charismatic Renewal were not weak colonial versions of more robust North American phenomena. Rather, Charismatic Catholicism and Pentecostal Protestantism utterly transformed Latin America between 1970 and 2000. Pentecostals and Catholic Charismatics were not the fringe—although many observers continue to see them that way—but rather the main attraction. These two heavyweights were fighting for the title of most influential religious movement in Latin America.[4]

In 2006, a study by the Pew Foundation estimated that Pentecostals or Charismatics (with both groups counted together as "Renewalists") made up 49 percent of Brazil's urban population, including almost 80 percent of all Protestants and half of all Catholics. The same study found that in Chile about three quarters of all Protestants and one quarter of all Catholics were Renewalists, amounting to 30 percent of the nation's population. In Guatemala the majority of Catholics and vast majority of Protestants— about 60 percent of the population—were Renewalists.[5] Although some scholars have disputed these numbers, even if they overcount Renewalists by as much as 30 or 40 percent they still represent a religious sea change. In most Latin American countries, since 1960 the most successful religious movements have emphasized the power of the Holy Spirit. We begin with the Pentecostals before turning our attention to the Catholic Charismatic Renewal in the next chapter.

## A Global Movement

Although there were similar revivals in Wales (1904), India (1905), and Korea (1907), the modern Pentecostal movement often traces its roots to Azusa Street in Los Angeles in 1906. A humble black preacher from the Wesleyan "Holiness" tradition named William Seymour, who had studied the possibility of experiencing a new "baptism in the Holy Spirit," led a series of small meetings in private homes in which people began falling to the floor and speaking in tongues. When crowds of those eager to see and to experience these strange phenomena became overwhelming, Seymour rented a dilapidated church building at 312 Azusa Street. The loud and lively services scandalized local elites and many church leaders but attracted a stream of visitors, first from Los Angeles and then from the nation and the world, over the course of three years. At Seymour's "Apostolic Faith Mission" these visitors found intense prayer and worship and various ecstatic phenomena, such as speaking in tongues, spiritual healing, deliverance from demonic forces, shaking under the influence of the Holy Spirit, and being "slain in the Spirit," which involved falling to the ground in a sort of trance. Seymour and others interpreted these manifestations as experiences similar or closely related to the account in the book of Acts, in which the disciples "were all filled with the Holy Ghost, and began to speak with other tongues, as the Spirit gave them utterance." They also saw the manifestations as fulfillment of a prophecy in the book of Joel of a "latter rain," or a new and more abundant outpouring of the Holy Spirit. In the key passage, God had promised, "I will pour out my spirit upon all flesh; and your sons and your daughters shall prophesy, your old men shall dream dreams, your young men shall see visions: And also upon the servants and upon the handmaids in those days will I pour out my spirit." Members of the Holiness movement who had been seeking this new Pentecost had predisposed themselves to see Azusa Street as the answer to their prayers.[6]

Often, an encounter with the Holy Spirit at Azusa Street led first to speaking in tongues and then to a devotion to Christian life and mission. A Chicago pastor named William Durham described it this way: "It seemed to me that my body had suddenly become porous," he said, "and that a current of electricity was being turned on me from all sides." After lying on the floor for two hours, Durham believed that he had received a great spiritual gift from God. The next night, after Durham's body shook for three hours, he began to speak in tongues, which he perceived as evidence of baptism in the Holy Spirit. "Then I had such power on me and in me as I never had before," he said. "And last but not least I had a depth of love and sweetness in my soul that I had never even dreamed of before, and a holy calm possessed me, and a holy joy and peace, that is deep and sweet beyond anything I ever experienced before, even in the sanctified life."[7] Another visitor, Arthur Shepherd, said that after a period of shaking and another of being in a trance he could sense new life entering his body. "Soon," he said, "my jaws and my tongue began to work independently of my volition and the words came out in a clear language." He felt that he had received new power for mission and service.[8]

In 1906 and 1907, the revival spread throughout Los Angeles and neighboring communities, and then to other cities such as Memphis, Cleveland, Indianapolis, and Dunn, North Carolina, as the curious came to Azusa Street and then brought its phenomena back to their homes. These new apostles proved prone to schism, with division often taking place along racial lines. In the end, Azusa spawned at least twenty-six different Pentecostal denominations, including the Assemblies of God, the Church of God in Christ, and the Church of God (Cleveland, Tennessee).[9]

Almost as quickly, the revival jumped to other countries. Sometimes it was carried by semi-official missionaries of the Apostolic Faith Mission, such as Frank Bartleman, who spread the message in Palestine, Europe, and Asia, and A. G. and Lillian Garr, who carried the new anointing to India, Japan, and China. The revival also came to new areas through already established missionaries who visited Azusa Street and then returned to the mission field.[10] Finally, and probably most important, the new Pentecostalism spread through lay Protestants, travelers and migrants, who shared it in the course of their journeys.

In the late 1950s and early 1960s the revival entered non-Pentecostal churches in what was soon called the "Charismatic Renewal." Members of mainline Protestant churches who had attended the Azusa revival and other Pentecostal events had often experienced speaking in tongues and related phenomena, but their denominations did not welcome the new form of spirituality. But soon the environment began to change. In 1960 Dennis Bennett, an Episcopal priest in Van Nuys, California, lost his job for speaking in tongues. His explanation that tongues represented "a freeing of the personality in expressing one's self more profoundly, particularly toward God" won over about a third of his congregation, but the rest were scandalized enough to demand his resignation. In his next position in Seattle, however, a friendly bishop gave him the freedom to

pursue the Pentecostal gifts, which eventually transformed a once struggling church into a thriving congregation of more than 2,000 people.
Over the next decade, the Charismatic Renewal spread quickly across
denominations so that by the 1970s almost every church and denomination had its pocket of "Charismatics." They acted more sedately than
their Pentecostal cousins and had different theological interpretations of
Pentecostal phenomena, but Lutherans and Methodists and even Catholic nuns were speaking in tongues, praying for healing, and receiving
dreams and visions.[11]

Pentecostalism and the Charismatic Renewal grew spectacularly in
the century after the Azusa Street revival, particularly in Latin America, Asia, and Africa. In many countries around the world, Pentecostals
today constitute a majority of Protestants. In most nations Pentecostal
churches are the fastest growing and most dynamic churches. In fact,
it is clear that, at least from a numerical perspective, Catholicism, with
1.1 billion adherents, and Pentecostalism (including Charismatics) with
600 million, make up the two major sectors of contemporary World
Christianity.[12] The speed of the Pentecostal and Charismatic ascent is
truly remarkable.

## *Protestant Pentecost in Latin America*

Latin America has a special place in the global explosion of Pentecostalism because of its geographical, political, demographic, economic, and
cultural connections to the traditional birthplace of the movement (both
Los Angeles and the United States more generally), because of the un-
matched success of Pentecostal and Charismatic movements within its
borders, and because of its role in spreading the new spirituality to Africa,
Europe, and the United States. Starting with the first person healed at
Azusa Street in 1906, who was Mexican, Latinos became enthusiastic
exponents of the new Pentecost and carried it around the United States
and to Mexico, Puerto Rico, and other Latin American lands.[13] Starting
in Chile in 1909, Pentecostalism spread to South America, finding particularly enthusiastic receptions in Brazil and Argentina but affecting
every Latin American nation to some degree.[14] At first, foreign missionaries played an important role, but local believers took over the work
at an early stage. To a greater extent than in mainline and fundamentalist missions, the new churches quickly became self-supporting and
self-propagating.

For example, the Chilean Pentecostal movement started with Willis Hoover (1856–1936), a Methodist physician and missionary from Illinois who became the rector of the Colegio Inglés in Iquique, northern Chile, in 1889 and pastor of a church in Valparaiso in 1903. Hoover's successful but controversial methods, including street preaching and close contact with the poor, kept him in constant conflict with mission authorities in the United States and with more traditional missionaries in the field. In 1909, in the midst of escalating tensions with the mission board, Hoover received a pamphlet on a Pentecostal revival taking place in India. After following the directions in the pamphlet, he began speaking in tongues and soon shared this gift with members of his church. The Pentecostal experience spread throughout his denomination and into other evangelical churches, mostly in poor urban areas. After the mission board compelled Hoover to resign and local church authorities expelled many advocates of spiritual gifts, Hoover and Chilean pastors started the Iglesia Metodista Pentecostal (Pentecostal Methodist Church) to free themselves from foreign control. In the coming years, the denomination prospered, growing to 520,000 members by 2000, even as it suffered a major church split in 1933 that produced the Iglesia Evangélica Pentecostal (Pentecostal Evangelical Church), another important Pentecostal body. Despite splintering into many churches, the movement as a whole grew among the marginalized sectors of society and, with the exception of Hoover, with little foreign involvement.[15]

Brazil had a similar experience. In 1910 Swedish immigrants Gunnar Vingren and Daniel Berg received the baptism in the Holy Spirit at the Chicago church of William Durham and believed that God was calling them to mission. Without any official standing or financial backing the two men arrived in Pará, Brazil, and took whatever work they could find. But their lack of financial support actually worked to the benefit of their mission, as their poverty prevented the growth of an economic divide between them and their converts. Tensions arose only in the 1920s when more missionaries arrived. After 1930, when the nationals and missionaries took responsibility for different territories, the nationals saw greater growth.[16]

Bolivia, on the other hand, provided a counterexample. This country attracted many Pentecostal missionaries, particularly a large Swedish community that boasted "hundreds of missionaries, millions of Swedish kroners to spend on social programs, a complete Swedish school for missionary children, its own radio communication system, its own airplane,

[and] a proper Swedish consulate." Despite some notable successes, including the work of Astrid Jansson among the Weenhayek (Mataco) people, the large concentration of missionaries seems to have worked against the success of the mission. Only when the missionary presence waned or when movements independent of missionary control developed did Pentecostalism thrive.[17]

The movement's approach to leadership development contributed to its rapid growth. In contrast to Catholic priests, who were required to hold the equivalent of a graduate degree before starting their ministries, and mainline and fundamentalist Protestant pastors, who often required significantly more education than those in the pews, Pentecostal pastors generally had the same educational background as their congregations. In Chile in the 1960s, for example, 56 percent of Pentecostal pastors had not even finished primary school and only 7 percent had finished secondary school, while *no* pastors in other Protestant churches had failed to finish primary school and 43 percent had university degrees.[18] This dearth of education among Pentecostals had certain disadvantages, but it had one overwhelming advantage—pastors came from the same environment as their congregations and had no intellectual and class issues that separated them from their flocks.

A second advantage of the Pentecostal approach to leadership was that it was inexpensive, accessible, and practical. As people without many financial resources—and virtually all Pentecostals until the 1980s were poor—most Pentecostals could not even consider secondary education, university training, or graduate theological education. Even staying in primary school, if one was available, posed significant financial obstacles, since a family might need children to work rather than keeping them in school. Instead of earning degrees, Pentecostal leaders proved themselves through a series of progressively more important challenges: "Soon after his conversion he starts as a preacher in the street, where he proves the depth of his convictions and the quality of his witness. He will then be given responsibility for a Sunday school class and will accede to the status of a preacher: he will then have the right to lead worship. If he gives satisfaction, his pastor may entrust to him the task of opening a new preaching place in his neighborhood. . . . If he succeeds in gathering a small group, the elders and the pastor will regard this as adequate proof of his vocation, because they are convinced that it is not man who converts, but the power of God within him; a vocation which does not bear fruit cannot be of God."[19]

The candidate's spiritual authority also received particular scrutiny. Throughout all of these steps, he needed to demonstrate the ability to heal, to cast out demons, and generally to display the supernatural gifts valued by Pentecostals.[20] Poor churches thus did not waste resources on those who liked studying theology but had no affinity for the demands of daily ministry. Similarly, candidates did not study esoteric theories with little practical application but rather learned and practiced exactly what Pentecostal churches required. A weakness, of course, was that few Pentecostal pastors had the theological resources to deal with complex doctrinal, philosophical, and moral issues and most had little understanding of Christian history and tradition.

A third strength was that instead of separating ministerial candidates during years of college and seminary, the Pentecostal method propelled them into sustained social contact with the people around them. Where priests and seminary-trained Protestant pastors could become alienated from their roots by years of immersion in academic study, those who climbed the Pentecostal leadership ladder became, if anything, more attuned to their people and their culture. Preaching on street corners, door-to-door evangelism, healing the sick (common in their neighborhoods), and attempting to start a church on a shoestring budget, all while supporting themselves by working at some other job, gave them a deep understanding and appreciation of the struggles and tribulations of the poor.

Thus, by the 1950s Pentecostalism had established itself in Latin America. Other Protestants still looked down on it as a fringe phenomenon, but it had thoroughly indigenized itself. The political, social, economic, and cultural atmosphere of the 1950s and 1960s in Latin America provided an ideal environment for the next stage of Pentecostal development, which included explosive growth, the formation of new national denominations, and the achievement of a certain prominence (sometimes notoriety) in national affairs. These achievements resulted from Pentecostalism's strongly indigenous character and its ability to expand without missionaries and at low cost, even as its critics tended to charge that it was funded and directed by foreigners.

## The Option of the Poor

Urbanization and industrialization tended to create "zones of misery," or rings of shantytowns around capitals and industrial centers. Lured by the promise of a better life, migrants settled in the only places they could afford—slums that lacked electricity, running water, sewers, schools, police stations, and, important for this story, Catholic churches. These areas, full of transplants from different regions of a country, had no common culture, no traditions, and often no real local government. To make matters worse for their poor and desperate residents, crime and disease ran rampant in these slums.

The institutional Catholic Church, unprepared for what amounted to the creation of entire new cities over the course of just a few years and suffering from both a priest shortage and a growing panic about the superficiality of the faith in places that *did* have priests, responded weakly. The hierarchy sent few priests to the shantytowns and built few churches and virtually no schools in these areas. In effect, most of these new urban areas had to fend for themselves as far as religion was concerned. From the migrants' perspective, this institutional neglect proved more damaging than might have been expected. Since rural folk Catholicism had a strong local element that revolved around local patron saints, specific sacred places, and festivals infused with local customs, it did not transfer well to the new urban environments where people came from different regions of a given country, where the sacred caves and springs were only a distant memory, and where people from other regions had no familiarity with the rituals and distinctive calendars of their neighbors. Consequently, even devout migrants faced a religious dilemma: how could they keep the faith in the new environment?

The global contest between the United States and the Soviet Union and the related phenomenon of decolonization added another complication. Latin America served as a battleground of the Cold War. Sometimes this took benign form, for instance, in President John F. Kennedy's attempt to win allies and to foster development through the Alliance for Progress. On the other hand, many actions of United States—such as the Central Intelligence Agency (CIA)-sponsored coup that deposed progressive Guatemalan president Jacobo Arbenz in 1954, the attempted invasion of Cuba at the Bay of Pigs in 1961, and the invasion and occupation of the Dominican Republic in 1965—reinforced and exacerbated Latin American suspicions of that neighbor to the north. Meanwhile, many African colonies of European nations gained their independence in the 1950s and 1960s, especially in the landmark year of 1960, when seventeen nations became independent.

Consequently, the 1950s and 1960s offered significant opportunities for Pentecostal expansion and for the creation of national denominations, both of which finally brought Pentecostals to the attention of politicians, social scientists, and the Catholic hierarchy. With Catholics and historic Protestants underserving the urban poor, Pentecostals had methods and "religious products" almost perfectly aligned with the needs of this immense "religious market."[21] At the same time, despite claiming to be apolitical, Pentecostals experienced the winds of nationalism, anti-Americanism, and decolonization in a way that, while rarely radicalizing them, still made them receptive to the idea of severing ties to missionaries and mission boards. The new denominations that they created completed the indigenization process and eventually made Latin America the true heartland of Pentecostalism.[22]

In Chile, after decades of growth, in the 1960s Pentecostals were attracting academic attention, most notably from scholars Emilio Willems and Christian Lalive d'Epinay, and starting to set their sights on public influence. Having grown from a handful of people in 1909 to more than 500,000 in 1960, they began to feel less like a peripheral group than one that could change society. For instance, in 1967 the leader of one denomination had a transformative experience at a conference in Berlin, but not in the traditional Pentecostal way. "I, who am nothing," he said, "found myself with the great men of this world. I, the least important, was with the great theologian X and with the great evangelist Y . . . and when I passed through London, a minister received me. . . . This is what God has done with us, with me who am the least of all." His congregation answered each line of his report with "Amens" and "Alleluias," perhaps seeing his elevation in the world as a sign of their own improving circumstances. Pentecostals also developed the financial wherewithal to erect large buildings, such as the "basilica" of the Iglesia Pentecostal de Chile in Curicó and the "cathedral" of the Iglesia Metodista Pentecostal, for which construction began in 1967.[23] When Pinochet came to power in 1973, some Pentecostals made the fateful decision to align themselves with the new regime. That Pinochet would consider Pentecostals worthy of his attention as a counterweight to the Catholic Church indicated the great numerical success that Pentecostals had achieved by the 1970s and their increased prominence as public actors.

Pentecostals also enjoyed marked successes in Brazil in the 1980s and 1990s. By the early 1990s five new Pentecostal churches were opening their doors every week in Rio de Janeiro alone.[24] In the poorest neighborhoods of Rio there were seven Protestant (almost always Pentecostal) churches for every Catholic church.[25] Their primary clientele, the urban poor, were struggling mightily. After visiting Brazil, American theologian

Richard Shaull found that most Pentecostals lived with "broken families, material deprivation, addiction to drugs and alcohol, and the culture of violence surrounding them" but that they could nevertheless experience "ecstasy and joy" because through their faith "the impossible becomes possible time and again."[26]

Across the region, healing and exorcism played important roles in the growth of Pentecostal churches. Because of their location in poor and even desperate neighborhoods, where the lack of sanitation services made disease more likely and where people's poverty put expensive medical treatment out of reach, Pentecostal churches put a special emphasis on divine healing, which often served as a decisive factor in attracting potential converts. In a similar vein, in an atmosphere in which people took the spirit world for granted and in which they explained suffering by reference to curses and demonic possession, Pentecostals provided the sought-after deliverance.

Believers also found emotional and spiritual encouragement for their difficult lives. The Pentecostal style of praise, prayer, and preaching seemed to meet believers' needs in a profound and powerful way:

> A typical Latin American Pentecostal service takes place in a large, poorly decorated meeting hall, with a full-blown band leading the singing, shouting, whistling, clapping, and dancing. As the service begins, the congregants become deeply immersed, their eyes closed, some crying, others singing at the top of their voice or "speaking in tongues," and still others lifting faces and hands toward heaven. The music goes on and on, building from soft strains to a fast, arresting rhythm that after nearly two hours reaches a deafening climax—and suddenly drops back again to quiet strains. With the entrance of the pastor, the whole congregation shouts and claps, while he begins to preach a simple message of salvation through Jesus: you must convert now, while there is still time; no more drinking, cheating, and lying; the Lord is coming soon. The music softly restarts while the pastor asks all who want to "accept the Lord" to come forward. As the leaders pray, the people start falling down—"slain in the Spirit," the outward expression of the Holy Spirit come into their lives.[27]

The music, which ranged from rock to local popular styles, almost always took a form that seemed natural and appropriate for the expression of deep personal emotions in a given sociocultural milieu. Even if not "slain in the Spirit," worshippers often entered a trance-like state that could last for thirty minutes or more. Whatever the exact nature of this occurrence, believers experienced it as a direct and almost physical encounter with the divine. "I feel it in the heart as odd, something strange . . . a kind of electricity inside," said one Chilean woman. "This is how I feel it when I'm in church, and there are instruments, and they dance, and all that. I feel an electricity which is mine, as if the whole body has needles."[28] Preaching did not so much explain or teach as challenge and encourage. The "altar call" near the end of a service invited personal response, highlighting the active participation of the congregation. They were worshippers—not spectators—who consciously responded to what they perceived as God's call in their lives.

Gifts such as speaking in tongues, prophecy, and healing served a dual purpose. First, they met individual needs in a powerful and decisive way. Tongues, for instance, gave new spiritual vitality to those who had become dry and tired, while prophetic "words" provided the type of personalized encouragement that made believers feel God's special concern. Healing, similarly, met an obvious crisis in a believer's life, in a way that had special relevance in the lives of the poor. Second, the more dramatic charismatic phenomena served as a major means of what one scholar has called the "re-enchantment of the world."[29] If modernity had stripped away layers of religious explanations of the world, Pentecostalism had the ability to re-infuse reality with the supernatural. Its practitioners did not reject science per se but rather seemed able to live supernaturally in urban environments. Rural migrants had brought their own supernatural folk Catholicism to the city but never had as much success as Pentecostals.

A new wave of Pentecostalism, often referred to as neo-Pentecostalism, emerged in the 1970s and became a major religious player in the 1980s. Although there was no black-and-white difference between the newer version and its predecessors, neo-Pentecostalism tended to differentiate itself in three ways: an emphasis on "health and wealth," an elevation of "spiritual warfare," and an appeal to the middle and upper classes. Pentecostals had long practiced physical healing and, to a lesser extent, understood themselves to be in a spiritual battle; this new wave added financial prosperity to the mix. It also built on the foundations that other Pentecostals had built among the poor to reach into upper social strata, where people often latched onto the financial aspects of the message.

The most prominent example of neo-Pentecostalism was Brazil's Igreja Universal do Reino do Deus (IURD, Universal Church of the

Kingdom of God), started by Edir Macedo in 1977. The IURD grew dramatically in the 1980s and became a political and cultural force in the 1990s. By the 2000s it had hundreds of foreign missionaries, including dozens in the United States. At the heart of the IURD's appeal was its bold reliance on spiritual warfare, not in some vague philosophical way, but in direct confrontation of the spirits, saints, and deities of other religions—Umbanda, Mucumba, Candomblé, and Catholicism. In a backhanded way this direct attack took seriously the concerns of the poor, who believed strongly in those spiritual forces, and offered them the sort of spiritual protection that they longed for but were not receiving elsewhere.[30]

Together, Pentecostals and neo-Pentecostals changed the religious landscape of Latin America dramatically. As Paul Freston argues, Pentecostalism and organized crime became the two institutions that "really functioned," in poor urban areas that were "virtually untouched by other sectors of civil society or indeed the state." In fact, Freston contends, Pentecostal pastors acted as one of the few forces against violence in those neighborhoods, "whether by dissuading young males from becoming criminals, converting prisoners, or providing 'protection' for potential victims of violence."[31]

## *Argentine Pentecost*

Although all Latin American nations experienced Pentecostal growth in the second half of the twentieth century, the most remarkable developments took place in Argentina. During the years after the fall of Juan Perón in 1955, conservatives and the military (who ruled the country from 1966 to 1973) tended to see the Catholic Church as a bulwark of Argentine nationalism, even as a group of priests, the Movement of Priests for the Third World, signaled the emergence of a Catholic left. When the military came to power again in 1976 and waged their infamous "Dirty War" against their leftist opponents, the Catholic left often fell victim to "disappearances" and violence. After the military's rule came to an end in 1983 the hierarchy faced a crisis on two fronts. First, it was criticized for its inaction during the years of human rights violations by the military—in stark contrast to the bishops of Chile and Brazil. And then the new administration of President Raul Alfonsín tried to separate church and state and to introduce various new laws that undermined Catholic teaching on marriage and family.[32]

Protestants in general and Pentecostals in particular fared poorly during most of the period from 1950 to 1983. With the notable exception of American evangelist Tommy Hicks's stadium-filling crusades in 1954 (in the midst of Perón's anti-clerical period), the conservative and military governments that led the nation during these years emphasized a sort of *argentinidad* in which Catholicism played an integral part. The military dictatorship of 1976 to 1983 went so far as to prohibit large Protestant events, especially evangelistic campaigns, and meetings of any number of Protestant pastors. The one Pentecostal evangelist who thrived during the dictatorship did so despite numerous arrests and threats.[33]

## Omar Cabrera

Omar Cabrera (b. 1936) was an anomaly in that he had had a successful ministry that emphasized healing, miracles, and deliverance before the mid-1980s. Cabrera believed that he had a divine vocation, "especially and uniquely oriented to those who were immersed in the ritualistic and sacramental religion of the state, Roman Catholicism." Focusing on non-practicing Catholics, Cabrera fashioned a persona for himself that minimized any discomfort they might feel at his meetings. He wore clerical attire, including a collar, presented himself as "Reverend Cabrera," and tried to avoid direct attacks on Catholicism. "My purpose," he said, "was not to convince people that they should abandon the Roman Catholic Church, but rather that they should enter into the kingdom of God through their faith in Jesus Christ." In fact, he said, "I have tried to avoid the impression I am asking anyone to change their religion."[34] He called Catholics not to "conversion," but to "the miracle of the new birth"; they did not have to call themselves evangelicals, but only to reject "idolatry" and "Mariolatry."[35]

Another integral part of Cabrera's message was prosperity. "When we meet Jesus Christ," he said, "we receive the power to change and replace poverty with abundance." If believers simply learned the "Marvelous Law of Abundance" their gifts to his ministry could open up new levels of blessing from God.[36] Such open courting of financial favor seemed heretical to the majority of the nation's small evangelical community, but to some of its struggling citizens it had great appeal.

In the late 1960s, in Entre Rios province, Cabrera, at that time the pastor of a small church, saw a Billy Graham film and marveled at the "thousands and thousands coming to the Lord." He began to pray for a similar sort of revival in Argentina. After committing himself more deeply to fasting and prayer, Cabrera put up a platform in an outdoor lot and preached there for 540 nights in a row, to crowds of as many as 15,000.[37] Not surprisingly, he eventually exhausted himself. After rest, study, and training in the United States, he returned to Argentina in 1971. From this point on his ministry prospered, despite frequent problems with the law and almost total rejection by other Pentecostals.

Cabrera's methods were quite distinctive for the time. When conducting a campaign in a new area, he first bought air time on a local radio station and broadcast a weekly show for about three years. Then, without needing to do much in the way of publicity, he announced that he was coming to town and crowds of 3,000 or more would assemble every night for a week or two. He returned for two days a month during each month of the next year, and slowly turned the reins over to homegrown pastors, although he and his wife Marfa technically remained the senior pastors of each new church.[38] He also came to believe that spiritual warfare played a crucial role in successful evangelism. After fasting and prayer, he would "engage the spiritual hosts of evil keeping peoples and cities in spiritual darkness," with the result that "areas formerly marked by apathy and indifference would suddenly open up" and many people would convert.[39] Finally, he put a great deal of emphasis on leadership development.

By 1985 Cabrera had built up a multi-site church of 145,000 people with 1,200 of them serving in leadership roles.[40] Not until Carlos Annacondia transformed Argentine evangelicalism, however, did Cabrera join the mainstream of Argentine Pentecostalism. Previously, his emphasis on healing, deliverance, and prosperity and his insistence on wearing clerical attire had put him on the fringe of the Pentecostal movement. Once Annacondia legitimized healing and deliverance, Cabrera's clericals posed much less of a barrier and Pentecostals and other evangelicals more readily accepted him.[41]

## Carlos Annacondia

Although Cabrera prospered under the years of military dictatorship, it took the return of democracy in 1983 and the ensuing expansion of religious liberty to provide the conditions for the larger Pentecostal movement to achieve serious growth. The propitious political situation and the national soul searching that accompanied Argentina's embarrassing defeat by the British in the Falklands/Malvinas war in 1982 made the mid-1980s ripe for some kind of spiritual awakening. The catalyst for revival came in the unlikely form of the owner of a nuts and bolts factory and the father of nine, Carlos Annacondia (b. 1944). Although many other leaders played important roles, Annacondia created a template for evangelism, healing, and deliverance that not only won converts and united Pentecostals but also forged "a new Argentine evangelical identity" that made Protestants a major social force for the first time in the nation's history.[42]

In 1981, two years after a life-changing decision for Christ and without any formal training, Annacondia began a ministry of open-air preaching and praying for the sick in poor neighborhoods in the province of Buenos Aires. In that same year, his wife, Maria Lujan, interpreted a prophecy in tongues from one of their sons as a message from God that meant "Soon, soon, soon, great revival in Argentina. Argentina will be mine."[43] Over the next four years Annacondia refined his methods until, in 1985, he had arrived at an approach that he used successfully for the next twenty-five years. Based on the "Great Commission" passage in the Gospel of Mark, he emphasized salvation, deliverance from demons, the anointing of the Holy Spirit, and healing, all in his own idiosyncratic fashion. Most distinctively, he practiced a type of "spiritual warfare" that he saw as essential to true evangelistic success:

> I learned to rebuke, strongly and directly, the high-ranking principalities of darkness; to address Satan and his demons with full authority in the name of Jesus; to bind them publicly; and to cast them out of the lives of the captives in my audience. . . . I find myself investing an incredible amount of energy in this strategic-level spiritual warfare.[44]

After this spiritual preparation, he typically saw many conversions, deliverances, and healings, especially miraculously filled teeth. The more practical elements of his methods included contemporary worship music, a large stage with powerful lights, deliverance and healing tents behind the stage, and a general atmosphere designed to approximate "the climate of a popular fiesta." Once established in a city, he preached for many nights in a row, sometimes for as long as two months without a break. In 1985 alone, he said, these methods allowed him to lead more than 130,000 people to Christ.[45]

Annacondia's approach to evangelism differed markedly from the practices of other Pentecostals and evangelicals in Argentina (except for

Cabrera). Heavily influenced by the North American missionaries who had founded their churches (and in some cases still led them) and cowed by anti-Protestant pressures from the political and religious right, most evangelicals practiced a religion at once resistant to change and divorced from popular culture. Meanwhile, denominational rivalries prevented any meaningful sort of cooperation. Annacondia, as a recent convert without a long denominational history and with no experience of being under missionary tutelage, had no patience for either the timidity or the rivalry that he came to see as characteristic Argentine Protestantism. In fact, he saw the lack of trust between churches as evidence of demonic activity.[46]

"When I started to attract attention," Annacondia said, "I made one rule regarding my participation in crusades: I always invited all of the churches in the area to join the campaign. If the pastors had a problem with that, I would not preach in that area until they could resolve their differences."[47] The success of the crusades, including 83,000 converted in the 1984 Mar del Plata campaign, pushed churches to consider participating. Even non-Pentecostal churches, overwhelmed by spiritual power evident at Annacondia's events, overcame their scruples to join the team. Like Pablo Bottari, these non-Pentecostal evangelicals simply could not argue with the healing, deliverance, and conversion that they saw. As they became more involved with the crusades, they began to imitate Pentecostal practices, even if they never adopted the label. Bottari, for instance, came from the conservative Free Brethren denomination and eventually took a position in a Baptist church that never called itself Pentecostal but that nevertheless wanted to have a full-blown deliverance ministry. Annacondia's campaigns filled churches with new believers who wanted to experience more of what had led them to convert.[48]

After focusing almost all of his efforts on the province of Buenos Aires, Annacondia began visiting cities outside the region in 1987. That same year, Korea's David Yonggi Cho, pastor of the world's largest church, visited Argentina. The 7,500 church leaders who heard him speak represented a new generation of outward-looking leaders who could put aside the deep denominational suspicions that had marked Argentine Protestantism in the past. In the following years, as Annacondia conducted crusades around Argentina and in El Salvador, Peru, Uruguay, the United States, Finland, Japan, and several other countries, other Pentecostal evangelists rose to fill the vacuum created by his absence.[49] Of these evangelists, Hector Giménez, Omar Cabrera, and Claudio Friedzon played the most important roles, but dozens, perhaps hundreds, of influential Pentecostal leaders emerged, all following the basic pattern set by Annacondia.

## The Normalization of Pentecostalism

The most controversial of these new leaders was Hector Giménez (b. 1957). A former drug addict and criminal with only a primary school education, Giménez converted to Pentecostalism in the late 1970s and in 1982 began his own ministry, Ondas de Amor y Paz (OAP, Waves of Love and Peace), in converted theaters in Buenos Aires. From the beginning, Giménez attracted both the popular classes and celebrities but scandalized the middle class and other Pentecostals. His flashy clothes, sports cars, and continual association with public figures such as the singer Johny Tedesco and the comedian Mario Sapag seemed clownish, if not suspicious, to more traditional Protestants. Wearing "white or pastel suits [and] shoes with big heels" and sporting long curly hair and gold chains, Giménez simply did not seem like a pastor to most Pentecostals. But his target audience—the down and out and the desperate—obviously found him appealing.[50] By 1989, his ministry was flourishing. His main church in the former Roca movie theater was holding services from 8:00 A.M. until midnight every day, for about 14,000 people each week. He had his own radio and television shows. And OAP had expanded to twenty-four locations, including Uruguay and Miami, and had started a training school with 1,000 students.[51]

Giménez's approach to ministry has been described as "the permanent crusade" and "bringing the revival into church"—in other words, as an institutionalization of the revival catalyzed by Annacondia. OAP succeeded in duplicating many attractive aspects of an Annacondia crusade in the confines of a local church. Matthew Morostica describes a pastor's revelation that a woman in the audience needed deliverance:

Everyone in the hall put their hands in the air, stamped their feet, and began to pray individually in tongues. Down in front the pastor decided which of the six or seven women that was claiming to be possessed was the one with the demon he had felt. Once she was discovered, the pastor began to pray very loudly into the microphone so that there was a total cacophony of voices underscored by the screams of the possessed woman and the heavy Christian

rock of the ever-present band on stage. Then, using phrases originated by Annacondia—"Out, out, out unholy spirit. Let her go! Let
her go!—the the pastor laid his hands on the woman and exhorted
the evil spirit to leave. The woman collapsed on the floor and was
carried out to receive further prayer, while the church erupted in
cheering and prayer that lasted ten more minutes. The pastors on
stage danced and clapped while everyone present praised the Lord
for delivering the woman.

—Marostica, "Pentecostals and Politics," 104–5.

With Giménez presiding over services similar to Annacondia's campaigns
for sixteen hours a day and only seeing his children "between meetings,"
it was not clear that this was in fact a reproducible model, but it definitely
brought in the crowds.[52]

Claudio Friedzón, an Assemblies of God pastor and seminary professor from Buenos Aires, actually maintained a daily schedule almost as
long as Giménez's, working fourteen hours a day, seven days a week on
his radio show, counseling, preaching, and teaching, with only five days of
vacation per year. In 1992, however, it did not seem that he would be the
one to extend the reach of the Argentine revival. He felt burdened, spiritually dry, and unproductive. After his mentor rebuked him for not taking
time to listen to the Holy Spirit, Freidzón traveled to evangelist Benny
Hinn's Orlando Christian Center in Florida. There Freidzón believed that
he received a special "anointing" when Hinn laid hands on him. After returning to Buenos Aires, Freidzón began to draw larger and larger crowds
to his Rey de Reyes church.[53] The main attraction was "the anointing,"
which consisted of "drunkenness in the Spirit, uncontrollable laughter,
and crying with joy." By November 1992 Freidzón was attracting 6,000
church leaders to outdoor events and 40,000 people to an auditorium
designed for 12,000. At the former event, "Freidzón spent the entire afternoon inviting pastors and other church leaders onto the platform, where
he would blow into a microphone, throw his suit jacket, lay his hands on
heads, or simply wave his arms in the direction of an individual or a group
of individuals," which caused people to collapse and laugh.[54]

This new anointing extended the "normalization" of Pentecostal
practices and beliefs that Annacondia had begun. Conservative Protestants, including pastors and other leaders, came to Freidzón's events and
then returned to their own churches with the anointing. "It is interesting to note," said Baptist pastor Pablo Deiros, "that this phenomenon,

of a distinctly Pentecostal-charismatic nature, is experienced differently with the framework of each denominational tradition and is adjusted to the theological perspective of each one, yet retains many common characteristics across the board."[55] Even more remarkably, the anointing made Argentina not only a draw for spiritual pilgrims from other nations but also a sort of launching pad for global revival. For instance, Canadian pastor John Arnott traveled to Argentina in 1993 specifically to experience the revival. "We were powerfully touched in meetings led by Claudio Freidzón," Arnott related. "After I stood up Claudio came over to me and said, 'Do you want the anointing?" When he responded in the affirmative, Freidzón slapped Arnott's hands and transmitted the anointing.[56] After returning to his Toronto Airport Vineyard church, Arnott invited another Vineyard pastor, Randy Clark, to speak in January 1994. The "Toronto Blessing" that began brought the Argentine-style anointing to hundreds of thousands of North Americans, often in the form of "holy laughter." Steve Hill, a missionary in Argentina who had received the anointing from Carlos Annacondia and other Argentine pastors, brought the anointing to Florida, where the Brownsville Assembly of God in Pensacola experienced its own revival for several years, starting in 1995.[57]

One of the more surprising achievements of the Pentecostal movement in Argentina occurred in the Olmos maximum security prison, where 1,450 of the 3,000 prisoners joined an on-site church between 1985 and 1996. Assemblies of God pastor Juan Zuccarelli, feeling called to reach the prisoners, had started working as a prison guard in 1983. Although the prison authorities told him that he could not preach, they did allow him to bring in a member of his church, José Luis Tessi, to preach to the inmates directly and over the prison's radio station. Prison authorities at first merely tolerated the Pentecostals in their midst, but as they came to see that converted prisoners caused fewer problems and had a low recidivism rate, they became more accommodating. When a local pastor, Antonio Arcadio García, was arrested for armed robbery and sent to Olmos, Zuccarelli and Tessi gave him the chance to redeem himself by becoming the pastor of a church that would operate entirely inside the prison. Eventually Christ the Only Hope Church incorporated the entire fourth and fifth floors of the prison and began its own Bible institute. Church members committed themselves to a strict moral code—no smoking, violence, television, or drugs—and to a rigorous schedule that included two Bible studies and one church service each day. Every night

132 believers spent the period from midnight to six in the morning praying for the other members of the church.[58]

In short, Argentina, a nation struggling with economic, military, and political crises throughout the period from 1960 to 2000, became a worldwide leader of the Pentecostal movement. Its financial difficulties and its human rights problems grabbed the headlines, but in one area, at least, it became a global leader.

## *Conclusion*

Pentecostal growth in Latin America tends to be a topic that stays quarantined in the ghetto of "quirky religious stories from the Third World." Academic and media specialists of course know about the "Pentecostalization" of Latin American Christianity, but even they can sell short the significance of the phenomenon. Religion, especially of the Latin American variety, simply does not fit into the common narratives of what is truly important—usually politics and economics—in the globalized world of the twenty-first century.

Consider, however, the European Reformation of the sixteenth century. Martin Luther's broadsides against the Catholic Church did not simply provide more religious options for Europeans. The strength and plausibility of his arguments and those of other Protestant reformers challenged the faith of Catholics around Europe, empowered German princes to assert more independence, detached large portions of Europe from the Catholic Church, and ultimately led to major church reforms. One does not have to believe in the religious sincerity of the reformers to see that the profound religious changes they introduced opened up new avenues of action for many political actors. All this was made possible by the fact that Protestantism had a life of its own, that it appealed to common people, and that it inspired many to risk their lives for its progress. If it had functioned merely as a theoretical possibility or a superfluous addition to people's lives, it would have had little social impact, but its profound appeal to millions of Europeans meant that it had real cultural, political, and economic effects. Global conflict between England and Spain, the early industrialization of England, the later rise of the evangelical movement—these are just a few of the results of the Protestantization of England alone.

Inhabitants of the global North should at least consider that the Pentecostal explosion in Latin America could have similar results. Why?

Because religion involves what is deepest and most important in people's lives. Without minimizing the significance of the latest debt crisis or political upheaval, is it not at least possible that the profound religious experiences recorded in this chapter are ultimately more influential? If religious change matters—and the Reformation demonstrates that it does—the Pentecostal transformation of Latin America is one of the major stories of our age, especially when combined with the similar transformation that took place inside Catholicism.

# 6

# *The Heartland of Charismatic Catholicism*

*As night falls, the largest Catholic church in downtown Sao Paulo is filled with raucous "hallelujahs" and the beat of drums and electric keyboards. Hundreds of worshipers, many in T-shirts, raise their hands and shout "Amen" as if at a Baptist revival. . . . Services are animated, marked by catchy music, faith healing, and speaking in tongues.*[1]

THE CATHOLIC CHARISMATIC Renewal (CCR) might be even more significant than the rise of Pentecostalism. But it is less visible. If few inhabitants of the global North are aware of the rapid growth of Pentecostal churches and the strong Pentecostal influence on other Latin American Protestants, even fewer have recognized the growth of the CCR. Yet in 2000 there were more Catholic Charismatics in Latin America, 75 million, than there were Pentecostals, at most 66 million.[2] In 2011 Edward Cleary described the CCR as "the most important religious movement in Latin America," but it still tended to attract less scholarly and journalistic attention than either Pentecostalism or liberation theology.[3]

The Charismatic Renewal came to the Catholic Church in 1967 when a group of students from Duquesne University in Pennsylvania began crying, laughing, and speaking in tongues during a retreat. The experience next arrived at the University of Notre Dame, which began hosting international CCR conferences that grew from eighty-five people in 1967 to 30,000 in 1974. As the movement spread across the United States and then the world, reaching 350,000 adherents by 1974, it also occasioned considerable confusion and criticism. A significant factor in the survival of the CCR was the encouragement it received from Belgian Cardinal Léon-Joseph Suenens (1904–96). The cardinal first encountered Charismatic American nuns at a conference in Philadelphia in 1972, and, after some investigation, was impressed. In 1973 he told the 23,000 participants at Notre Dame's annual conference, "I will tell you a secret which will help you to welcome the Holy Spirit: it has a name; it is union with Mary." His advocacy of the renewal at the highest levels of the Vatican, including to Pope Paul VI himself, and his intervention to keep the CCR distinctively and clearly Catholic both eased the movement's acceptance into the church and ensured that its members stayed within the confines of Catholicism.

Like Charismatic movements around the world, the Latin American CCR usually explained its beginnings with reference to the United States and its awakening of 1967, but Colombia appears to have experienced the rise of a contemporaneous Charismatic prayer group not directly connected to the United States.[4] Better documented is the impact of a team of American Protestant Charismatics, including Harald Bredesen and Samuel Ballesteros, who came to Colombia in October 1967 and won over Father Rafael García Herreros of the Minuto de Dios ministry in Bogotá and Father Diego Jaramillo, then working for the Colombian bishops' conference. In 1968 Ballesteros wrote García Herreros, "God wants me to go to Colombia to work in the name of Our Lord Jesus Christ" and asked if he and his wife could work with the Minuto de Dios ministry. At first, García Herreros wondered what a Protestant minister could contribute to a Catholic ministry, but he too sensed that God was at work. At a time when Protestants and Catholics had little to do with each other, Ballesteros impressed the Colombians during his six-year ministry in Bogotá. "With love and openness," said Jaramillo, "he worked with the parish priests and preached Jesus Christ tirelessly, without any trace of proselytism." In 1969 students began Charismatic prayer groups at a Minuto de Dios school and at a seminary where Jaramillo served as rector. In 1971 the priests of Minuto de Dios asked the Colombian bishops to support what they saw as "a true explosion of the Holy Spirit" that had the potential to enliven the church in the whole nation. In 1972 García Herreros established contact with the Word of God Charismatic community in Ann Arbor, Michigan, and asked for help. A string of North American Charismatics, including Protestant pastor and author Henry Frost, visited Minuto de Dios in the next few years. By 1973 young lay Colombian Charismatics were evangelizing throughout Latin America.[5]

Meanwhile, an American Dominican priest named Francis Mac-Nutt played an important role in spreading the renewal. In 1967, independent of the Duquesne revival, MacNutt had had his own experience of spirit baptism at a Protestant conference where he met Agnes Sanford (1897–1982), an important Protestant Charismatic leader in the 1960s and 1970s. After she gave him a prophetic "word" that he would help to restore the ministry of healing in the Catholic Church, MacNutt became one of the leaders of the CCR in the United States and wrote the seminal book *Healing*. In addition to many retreats, conferences, and lectures in the United States, he visited Bolivia and Peru in 1970, the Dominican Republic in 1971, and Chile, Colombia, Costa Rica, Guatemala, and Mexico in 1972.[6] These visits, on which MacNutt was accompanied by a team that included both Catholics and Protestants, usually centered around a "Life in the Spirit" retreat that introduced Latin Americans and missionaries to baptism in the Spirit, speaking in tongues, and divine healing. For many participants, the powerful personal experience of the Holy Spirit served as a sort of second conversion that propelled them into a higher level of spiritual commitment and into new ministries in the church. Many participants became advocates and teachers of the renewal in their own parishes, starting with small groups devoted to prayer. In MacNutt's last major contribution to the renewal in Latin America, he worked with Father García Herreros to organize the first Encuentro Carismático Católico Latino Americano (ECCLA, Latin American Catholic Charismatic Conference) for the leaders of the incipient movement in Bogotá in February 1973. Mac-Nutt himself soon faded from the picture after marrying a Protestant named Judith Sewell and ending his public ministry, but ECCLA continued to hold biennial meetings for thousands of participants across the region.[7]

The CCR took on different characteristics in different countries, but it grew quickly almost everywhere. Mexico, for example, took a somewhat different path from Brazil and from the mainstream of the movement, mostly due to its emphasis on catechesis and evangelization through the Sistema Integral de Evangelización (SINE) and Escuelas de Evangelización San Andrés (mentioned in Chapter 2). In Colombia, largely through the Minuto de Dios ministries, the CCR put more of an emphasis on social action. In the Dominican Republic, Canadian priest Emiliano

Tardif played a major role in popularizing the movement and won such acclaim for teaching and healing that President Lionel Férnandez called for a national day of mourning at his death in 1999.

The CCR's ability to revitalize Catholicism and to bring in weary and marginal Catholics eventually outweighed the qualms that the Latin American bishops had about the movement. Although few bishops personally participated in the movement, all the national bishops' conferences eventually endorsed it or created national coordinating bodies, although the Brazilian bishops, the most progressive national group in the 1970s and 1980s, did not do so until 1994. The Argentine bishops had their own fears, but still decided to support the renewal in 1989:

> In considering the phenomenon of the Charismatic Renewal, one important issue is its context, the spread of the sects, which is a serious matter for which the Church still lacks an adequate pastoral response. In this situation the Charismatic Renewal can provide a significant service because it uses a similar vocabulary: highly religious language, openness to the transcendent, faith in the gift of healing in the fullest sense of the term, etc.[8]

Many bishops across the region shared this rationale. Even bishops with doubts about Charismatic theology and practice offered some support to the renewal because of its success at resisting the specter of Pentecostal growth. The bishops might not have loved the CCR, but they liked it far more than the prospect of losing millions more Catholics to the Pentecostals. This sometimes tepid support sufficed—the CCR thrived and recently became, numerically at least, more successful than Pentecostalism itself. The CCR made the bishops' support easier by gradually becoming more consciously Catholic, less ecumenical, and more tied to the hierarchy. After a period of experimentation in the 1970s, the CCR increasingly emphasized Catholic distinctives like the Virgin Mary, the Eucharist, and submission to ecclesiastical authority.

Our particular focus here is on Brazil and Bolivia. In a manner similar to the rise of Argentine Pentecostalism, the Brazilian and Bolivian Charismatic movements began humbly but became influential in their own countries, throughout Latin America, and around the world. As these examples show (and as Chapter 10 demonstrates at greater length), the Pentecostal and Charismatic movements were not just exotic religious phenomena. They were a major way—surpassed, perhaps, only by migration, telenovelas, popular music, and trade—in which Latin American populations interacted with each other and with the rest of the world.

## Brazil

Brazil's CCR, today the region's largest and most vibrant, started largely because of the influence of two American Jesuits, Edward Dougherty and Harold Rahm, and a Brazilian priest, Jonas Abib. In the early 1970s Rahm organized a series of retreats called "Prayer Meetings in the Holy Spirit," a Brazilian equivalent of the "Life in the Spirit" retreats taking place in the Spanish-speaking countries, and in 1972 he wrote the influential book, *Sereis Batizados no Espírito* (You will Be Baptized in the Holy Spirit). He also had a long and successful ministry to drug addicts that incorporated spiritual aspects of the CCR into the recovery process.[9]

Dougherty, convinced of the great value of the Charismatic experience in his own life, tried to share it with as much of Brazil as he could. In 1972 and 1973 he held retreats in every state capital, hoping that participants could then pass on what they had learned. He then focused on the media, recognizing the potential especially of television for propagating the Charismatic message. His early efforts stirred the ire of liberationist priests and bishops, who felt that he was minimizing the social aspect of the gospel, but he persevered, eventually building up a group of 70,000 financial supporters called the Associação do Senhor Jesus (ASJ, Association of the Lord Jesus) and starting the Século 21 television network and *Brasil Cristão* magazine. His studio produced a five-hour Sunday afternoon show called "Praise the Lord" and several soap operas with Catholic themes, among its many offerings.[10]

In 1979 Abib started Comunidade Canção Nova (New Song Community), which combined two important features of the CCR: covenant communities and popular Catholic worship music. Covenant communities, groups of mostly lay Catholics who live in some sort of communal arrangement to pursue holiness and mission together, allowed participants in the CCR to grow in their faith in a protective and nurturing environment. Canção Nova hoped to build communities of trained and committed Catholics who would produce and disseminate contemporary-style Catholic music. Within a few years of Canção Nova's founding, artists such as Francisco José dos Santos (known professionally as Dunga) were selling millions of CDs and the community was sponsoring radio stations across the country. By 2004 the community had 254 television stations and a huge church, the Centro de Evangelização "Dom João Hipólito de Moraes," which could seat 70,000 people—the largest Catholic church in Latin America.[11]

With the help of the groundwork laid by Dougherty, Rahm, and Abib, the CCR slowly but steadily grew into a major force in Brazilian life. Starting with a handful of people in 1969, the movement grew to 10,000 adherents in 1970, 2 million in 1989, and as many as 33 million in 2008.[12] The combination of the relational approach—retreats, small groups, and covenant communities—with extensive use of the mass media, proved to be a winning formula for modern, urban Brazil. More than other sectors of the church, and much more than their progressive critics, Charismatics saw the potential of radio, music, magazines, and television to reach mass audiences who craved spiritual direction—both people outside the movement and those already in it. The relational side of the movement then met some of the deep needs for connection and intimacy created by the fragmentation and dislocation of urban modernity.

After its steady growth in Brazil throughout the 1970s and 1980s, some non-Charismatics began to take note of the CCR in the early 1990s, but it was Father Marcelo Rossi who brought the movement to a much broader audience. Born in 1967, and thus part of the second generation of Catholic Charismatics, Rossi was inspired by Pope John Paul II and by two untimely deaths in his family to pursue a deeper Christian life and, eventually, the priesthood. After his studies at a seminary influenced by Father Abib and Canção Nova and his ordination in 1994, Rossi began to attract so many people to Mass that he received permission from his diocese to turn an old factory in Sâo Paulo into one of Brazil's first Catholic megachurches, the Santuario Terço Vizentino (Sanctuary of the Byzantine Rosary), which could seat 30,000 people. Because crowds quickly overwhelmed the church and its surrounding neighborhood, Rossi had to build an even bigger church, Santuario Mâe de Deus (Sanctuary of the Mother of God) in 2001. It soon boasted a weekly attendance of 190,000.[13] In the Mass itself Rossi followed the rubrics (mandatory directions for the celebrant) but afterward he often began what he called "the Lord's aerobics," a combination praise service, exercise class, and prayer session.[14]

Starting in 1998 Rossi made a steady stream of CDs (including several multi-million selling albums), movies, and radio and television shows. In 2007 he organized a music festival and Mass that attracted 4 million people.[15] Rossi's appeal proved somewhat elusive for many non-Charismatics, but it seemed to stem from his youthful appearance, his athleticism, his confident Catholic message, and his indigenization of that message in the form of popular music and culturally relevant language. Whatever his secret, his celebrity made the CCR almost unavoidable in Brazil.

## *Bolivia's Mansion*

*The heart of the meeting is the outpouring of the Holy Spirit, which is prayed for by all who want it. This is achieved by the laying on of hands, as everyone prays aloud seeking the presence of the Holy Spirit, first in Spanish and then in tongues. At the end of the meeting there is a time of silence for hearing messages from God (prophecies).*

—Description of Friday Mass at La Mansión, Santa Cruz, Bolivia, 1978.[16]

Bolivia, with its indigenous majority and high rate of poverty, did not seem like the ideal spot for the development of the CCR, which tended to appeal to middle-class Catholics. In fact, during the 1950s and 1960s, the trend among educated Bolivians was toward progressive Christianity. The former seminarian Nestor Paz Zamora, for instance, became increasingly radicalized during the 1960s, and joined the guerrillas of the Ejercito de Liberación Nacional (National Liberation Army) in 1970. Statements such as "It is the right of every Christian to be a revolutionary—it is the right of every revolutionary to join the revolution" and "Taking up arms is the only effective way of protecting the poor from their current exploitation and of creating the new man" took on lasting resonance when he died just three months after joining the guerrillas. Many members of the middle class and many missionaries came to believe that "to be a Christian is to be on the left."[17] Nevertheless, or perhaps as a reaction against the trend toward progressivism, the nation became one of the regional centers of the Charismatic movement. Starting with Francis MacNutt's first retreat in May 1970, the Charismatic experience found fertile ground among North American Dominican missionaries, such as priests Patrick Rearden, Ralph Rogawski, Daniel Roach, and Crisóstomo (Cris) Geraets and Sister Helen Raycroft. These Dominicans brought the revival to several of Bolivia's main cities, but the ministry of Geraets and Roach in Santa Cruz had the most influence.[18]

Geraets and Roach had a powerful encounter with the renewal in January 1971 but at first struggled to see how the CCR fit with the Dominican approach to liturgy and spirituality or how it would work with traditional Bolivian religiosity. They started a Charismatic prayer meeting at the university where they worked in the city of Santa Cruz, the leading city in eastern Bolivia, but a revolution ended classes for several months and most students went home. The priests took advantage of the lull at the university to devote themselves to prayer and to reading Protestant and Catholic perspectives on the Charismatic movement. When Pentecostal evangelist Julio Cesar Ruibal became a national sensation in January 1973, provoking even Catholics to think about spiritual gifts, Geraets and Roach responded with their first retreat, during which many Charismatic phenomena appeared. With a corps of adherents from their prayer meetings and the recent retreat, the two priests then began celebrating Charismatic Masses outdoors on the grounds of La Mansión, a mansion in downtown Santa Cruz that a wealthy family had given to the local diocese.[19] After the group grew quickly from fifty to 120 people, they built the "Pahuichi," a rustic structure with a thatched roof and no walls that could seat 600.[20]

Meanwhile, Geraets had been devoting several hours of every day to studying and writing, as he tried to build a synthesis of Dominican rationality and Charismatic spirituality that would work in Bolivia. By the late 1970s he had arrived at a basic formula that attempted to respect liturgical norms while still giving free rein to the Spirit. Mass started with contemporary style praise songs and spontaneous prayer by members of the congregation. After the first reading, there would be testimony in which a few people related what God had done in their lives. Because Geraets preached for twenty-five minutes, longer than most priests at the time, and allowed spontaneous songs, prophecies, and speaking in tongues to break out at certain points, and because the exchange of the peace could last for twenty minutes, Mass generally lasted for two and a half hours, much longer than non-Charismatic Masses.[21]

As early as 1976 Geraets began to argue that the renewal had had a profound impact beyond La Mansión and beyond the walls of the city's churches. Responding to the stereotype that Santa Cruz and eastern Bolivia were happier and calmer than the rest of the country, Geraets said it was the result of "the new awakening of the Catholic faith by the New

Pentecost," which had changed people's lives, marriages, and families.[22] As Cleary has noted, the belief that interior renewal could spark exterior social and political changes, common within the CCR, marked a significant change for Geraets, who had spent his early years as a missionary fighting for social justice. La Mansión did not ignore the poor—most of its adherents were poor—and its classes did teach the preferential option for the poor, but it did not emphasize social or political action. Instead, it promoted the evangelization and catechization of the poor and their mobilization as evangelists, catechists, and leaders in the church.[23] In the words of one participant in the 1970s: "We know that the church in Bolivia is poor and we trust that God acts precisely in poverty; we are humble witnesses of the Holy Spirit's work in our people and we want to share our experience with all Bolivians of good will."[24]

Such an attitude, more in line with the approach soon to be taken by Pope John Paul II than with the leading bishops of the 1970s, made liberation theologians suspicious if not downright antagonistic, but it clearly appealed to the poor themselves. By 1978 Sunday Mass was attracting 2,000 people every week, but that was just the beginning of La Mansión's activities, which included a schedule of daily Masses that focused on a specific topic or practice: prayer for the dead on Monday, marriage and family on Tuesday, penance and deliverance on Wednesday, conversion on Thursday, and speaking in tongues and other spiritual gifts on Friday. Also taking place throughout the week were small prayer groups, with forty-two in action in 1977.[25]

## Charisma and Catechesis

A distinctive element of La Mansión was its emphasis on education and leadership development. Because of the Dominican commitment to study, teaching, and evangelization, Geraets and Roach soon saw that it was not enough that the two of them understood how the renewal related to classical Christian doctrine. They needed to teach their people and, even more important, to train new teachers to multiply the effect of that teaching. In 1980 they opened the Saint Thomas Aquinas Pastoral Institute, which slowly developed into a four-year program of thirty-five different courses, starting with the "Life in the Spirit" seminar and including courses such as Moral Theology, Church History, and the Social Teaching of the Church. Starting with 150 students, the institute soon grew to over 700, a large number for a predominantly lower-class city. In fact, so many Catholics who could not read wanted to participate that the Institute had to start a literacy program as well. In later years the institute took up the Vatican's "new evangelization" program, expressing its purpose as "teaching Catholic doctrine to lay people committed to evangelizing their parishes to fulfill Pope John Paul II's call for 'new ardor, new expressions, and new methods' in evangelization." Geraets also encouraged the development of several teams of musicians, numbering fourteen in 2007, who not only performed at the various Masses and meetings but also began to write and record their own songs.[26]

The emphasis on evangelization was not merely theoretical. In the early 1980s Geraets and three younger Bolivian priests who spoke indigenous languages began evangelistic campaigns in the villages around Santa Cruz, at times going head to head with Pentecostals doing the same thing. Geraets could no longer go into the villages after he developed some health problems in the 1990s, but he, other priests, and the musical teams continued to evangelize the neighborhoods of Santa Cruz.[27]

Teams and individuals from La Mansión also traveled to Bolivia's other cities to spread the CCR. In 1975, for example, Ricardo Suárez Selum and a friend, who had experienced the renewal in Santa Cruz, came to La Paz to attend a university. Their attempts to interest local priests in Charismatic prayer meetings met with some interest in the Don Bosco School, but eventually the meetings were shut down over the issues of tongues and prophecy. A few months later Geraets brought a team of twelve from La Mansión to help Suárez and others start prayer groups. By early 1976 a few groups were meeting regularly and one local priest had embraced the renewal to such an extent that he traveled to Santa Cruz for two weeks of training. He returned to La Paz and worked diligently to build up various prayer meetings and Masses, but in 1977 the other priests of his parish turned against the renewal and forced him to end all Charismatic activities. Some of the disappointed Charismatics left the Catholic Church and joined Pentecostal bodies; others simply moved to Charismatic groups in other parishes, such as the ones led by Juanita de Garafulich, a widow who had entered the renewal movement after attending a retreat sponsored by La Mansión in 1974.[28]

In another example of La Mansión's influence, in 1976 five religious sisters from Colombia, who had experienced the CCR in their country, invited Geraets and a team of lay catechists to Oruro to conduct a series of meetings on the renewal. A prayer meeting at the Vetania school, where the sisters taught, soon began.[29]

La Mansión also spread the Charismatic message through retreats and the mass media. In 1980 La Mansión began to draw thousands of Catholics from around the country and the region to Santa Cruz for annual conferences on themes such as "Virgin Mary, Mother of Hope, teach us to evangelize" (1987) and "Jesus Christ, abundant life for all" (1996). Large groups from Paraguay, Argentina, and Peru and speakers from Venezuela, Mexico, and Ecuador demonstrated both the influence of La Mansíon on the larger Latin American Charismatic movement and La Mansión's connectedness to that larger movement.[30] In the 1980s the center also started producing radio and television shows and both Geraets and Roach had daily shows on local channels. In 1996 Geraets and Roach built a studio that produced a wide variety of music and television programs, including children's shows and ecological shows, as well as more straightforward Catholic preaching. By 2011 the studio was broadcasting Sunday Mass in Santa Cruz, as well as in Guayaramerín, Riberalta, Trinidad, Tarija, and other communities, and a national television network had picked up the annual conference. "In an age as influenced by television as our own," argued the center's website, "evangelization, catechesis, and efforts to mature the faith cannot avoid this medium. Put at the service of the Gospel, it can extend the word of God to all creation without limits."[31]

Of course, many Bolivians harbored suspicions about La Mansión's growth and influence. For liberationists in the church and for the political left in general, the rise of the CCR seemed like a step backward. During an era in which indigenous rights and socialist politics were prospering, as typified by the victory of Aymara coca farmer Evo Morales and his Movimiento al Socialismo (Movement to Socialism) in the presidential election of 2005, some activists saw La Mansión as a source of distraction and reaction. For example, one observer of the 2007 annual conference characterized it as a sort of factory for the production of false consciousness. "Not once during the entire week was the economic misery of millions of people around the world questioned," he noted. Instead, the various speakers took poverty for granted and subtly supported the nation's business class. "The principal goal of this kind of event," he said, "is to alienate people from reality, to make them blame themselves for their problems, and to make as many Charismatics as possible."[32]

Such criticisms had little effect on La Mansión. Despite the death of Geraets in 2001 and Roach's poor health in the 2000s, La Mansión continued to prosper. In 2011, there were 141 prayer groups affiliated with the center meeting in Santa Cruz. At the center itself the daily schedule contained a full slate of prayer meetings, Masses, and training sessions and the pastoral institute continued to train hundreds of new students each year. After seven additions, the original Pahuichi had been torn down and replaced by a new one, which could (and did) seat 4,000 on normal Sundays and could be stretched to accommodate 7,000 during Holy Week.[33]

## Conclusion

"Pentecostalism was born in the United States," says Donald Dayton, "but it is discovering its destiny in Latin America."[34] More than in any other region of the world, Spirit-filled Christianity in its Protestant and Catholic versions has thrived in Latin America. In the Protestant world, although non-Pentecostal churches still exist, there is very little doubt that Pentecostalism is the new mainstream. Pentecostals not only outnumbered other Protestants but also heavily influenced non-Pentecostal churches. Many historic and fundamentalist churches used Pentecostal music and musical styles to such an extent that their singing was "indistinguishable" from that of Pentecostals. Sometimes the influence went far deeper, with many churches that would not have described themselves as Pentecostal adopting practices such as the laying on of hands and the anointing of the sick, to the extent that it was increasingly difficult to tell who was and who was not a Pentecostal.[35] In the Catholic world, the Charismatic movement was not as dominant, but it was better able to compete with Pentecostalism.

Perhaps most important, the CCR restored the confidence of Catholics. In contrast to the Mexicans who guarded their homes with signs that rejected "Protestant propaganda," Brazilians influenced by Marcelo Rossi and the CCR started adorning their homes and cars with stickers that said, "I'm happy because I'm Catholic."[36] This confident public Catholicism was poised to become a major force, not just in the religious marketplace but in the political and social spheres as well. The CCR's facility with mass media and urban popular culture, in combination with its institutional base in the church, put it in an excellent position to influence Latin American society in a way that the region had not seen since the colonial period. Liberation theology and the progressive church had hoped to do this, but their almost folkloric view of popular culture, their tense relations with the hierarchy and the Vatican, and their failure to deliver the kind of profound religious and spiritual experiences craved by the popular classes undermined that effort. Protestant Pentecostals came much closer, primarily because they provided spiritual goods that Latin Americans wanted, but their alienation from the Catholic Church, into which the vast majority of the continent was still born and which had shaped the culture of the region for five centuries, presented more of a barrier than many supposed. The CCR's simple ability to provide both divine healing *and* the Virgin Mary gave it a huge advantage.

The Pentecostal/Charismatic story highlights again the Protestant influence on Latin American Catholicism. The dramatic rise of Pentecostal churches in the second half of the twentieth century shocked the Catholic hierarchy. Having just begun to come to terms with historic Protestantism—a result of the ecumenism promoted by Vatican II—they found themselves face to face with something totally different. Dealing with Lutherans and Methodists—still seen by many as "sects"—had seemed difficult enough, but to take seriously independent churches led by untrained men from the popular classes who prophesied, healed, and spoke in tongues seemed outrageous. How could such unorganized, undisciplined, impoverished churches pose a serious challenge to an institution that had made Latin America? Slowly, however, it dawned on even the most unobservant bishops that these Pentecostal churches were popping up everywhere, especially in the poorest neighborhoods. The rise of Pentecostalism thus served as a wake-up call: these new churches had something that the people wanted and that the Catholic Church was not delivering.

Protestants also had a more direct influence, helping spark nearly every instance of the Catholic Charismatic movement in Latin America. Francis MacNutt came to Latin America for the initial conferences with Protestants as part of his team; in Colombia, the Baptist Samuel Ballesteros played a major role in bringing the renewal to the priests at Minuto de Dios; in Bolivia, Geraets devoted years of his life to studying Protestant writings on the renewal. In the end, both rivalry and cooperation contributed to the CCR. It is, of course, unclear what will happen next, but if the CCR does help Catholicism reemerge as the dominant religious force in Latin America, it will be a Catholicism with Protestant roots.

Another important aspect of the rise of Spirit-filled Christianity in Latin America was its restoration of the emotional, spiritual, and supernatural elements of religion in the region. Especially in comparison to liberation theology and the progressive church, Pentecostalism and the CCR made clear that many people needed more than political plans and moral urgency. As pressing as economic and social issues were in their lives, the poor still wanted miracles and ecstatic experience. This is not to say that the progressive church could not prosper or that social criticism has faded from the church, but it did imply that progressive Christians would need to provide at least some access to miracles and emotional release if they wanted to hold onto the poor. A religion without the supernatural simply could not compete with religions that provided healing, exorcism, and direct contact with the divine.

Finally, the growth of the CCR pointed to the importance of bishops but also to the limits of their influence. There is little doubt that if the Latin American bishops had uniformly opposed the renewal—in the sense of prohibiting it in their dioceses—it would not have prospered, at least not as a movement inside the Catholic Church. Their approval, sometimes amounting to little more than grudging acceptance, meant that the CCR could grow and develop as an authentic Catholic movement. On the other hand, it is also clear that for the vast majority of bishops, the CCR was problematic in its liturgy, theology, and general ethos. It was a movement that they did not initiate, a movement that began and developed outside of the episcopal palaces, the chanceries, and the seminaries. It came rather from small prayer groups, new communities, and odd priests. It displayed a facility with mass media and friendliness to consumer culture that seemed crass and superficial when compared to the sacrificial witness of the prophetic church. The bishops accepted it because of its substantial orthodoxy, its evident popular appeal, and its approval by the Vatican. In short, the most successful Latin American Catholic movement of the twentieth century came not from the bishops but from the people—and the Protestants.

# 7

# *Rise of the Laity: Catholic Action and Base Ecclesial Communities*

"I WANT TO meet each one of you to tell you, 'Return to the bosom of the Church, your Mother!'" said Pope John Paul II in Mexico in 1990. "Come back, then, without fear! The Church is waiting for you with open arms to reintroduce you to Christ. Nothing would make the heart of the Pope happier during this pastoral trip to Mexico than the return to the bosom of the Church of those who have left." The pope mentioned the dangers of "sects" eleven times in the course of his visit.[1] Nevertheless, it was clear to the pope and to most concerned Catholics that playing defense would not be enough to revive Catholicism in Latin America. The Catholic laity faced real problems, even crises, for which Protestantism provided genuine answers; only by revitalizing lay spiritual life in ways that dealt directly with those problems and crises could the church reverse the tide. Urbanization, secularization, and economic distress required new ways of being Catholic.

For the inhabitants of urban shantytowns, the challenge was especially daunting. Deprived of the rich communal religion of their rural homes, they confronted religious deserts in which institutional Catholicism had almost no presence—often no church, no priest, and no school—and in which migrants from different regions of a given country had no common folk religion to embrace. In rural areas they had experienced poverty, but as part of a community, and in cultural and religious contexts that provided them with support and a religious lens through which to make sense of their struggles. In the urban "zones of misery" they were alone, not just separated from family and friends but also from the sacred geography and spiritual practices of their hometowns.

To make matters worse, from the Catholic perspective, these poor neighborhoods offered religious alternatives that were attractive to millions of Catholics. "In my *bairro* of 40,000 inhabitants where I am the only priest," said French missionary Dominique Barbé, "at a conservative estimate there are twenty cult [religious] centers of which only six are Catholic; activities of mystical type outstrip *futebol* and *pinga* (fermented sugarcane) in their power to bring people together." Around him he found voodoo, Pentecostalism, spiritualism, the schismatic Brazilian Catholic Church, animism, fortune tellers, astrologers, and Jehovah's Witnesses, among others, but only 400 practicing Catholics. "All this is not to be laughed at," he concluded, for "when people live in an unhappy world, they celebrate in a thousand ways the world they wish to have."[2]

In addition to the Charismatic Renewal and the new evangelization, lay Catholics developed two main responses to the challenges of the time: base ecclesial communities (comunidades eclesiales de base, or CEBs) and new ecclesial movements (NEMs). The CEBs appealed mainly to the poor, the NEMs mainly to the urban middle and upper classes. Although the two approaches differed considerably, both emphasized community and the training of the laity. They gave Catholics a sense of belonging, significance, and solidarity similar to that provided by Protestant churches. And through classes, retreats, institutes, and other programs they turned ordinary men and women into active Catholics who took ownership of their faith in a manner approximating the way that conversion experiences created dynamic Protestant believers. Together, these new kinds of organization represented a resurgence of lay Christianity, not just in terms of intensity of belief and commitment but also in agency, leadership, and confidence. The crisis of priestly vocations was partially solved, therefore, not by the introduction of thousands of foreign missionaries, as John Considine had proposed in *Call for 40,000*, but by millions of lay Latin Americans who devoted themselves to personal growth, evangelization, catechesis, political action, and societal transformation. One might even say that the Protestant approach to the laity provided the model for what Catholics tried to accomplish.

## *The Liberation of the Laity*

Although Catholic sources—including the New Testament, Thomas Aquinas, and Francis de Sales—support the idea of an active laity, lay action has often been seen as a danger to the hierarchy. John Henry Newman, for example, found his tenure as rector of the Catholic University of Ireland (1851–58) continually undermined by Paul Cullen, archbishop of Dublin, who objected to Newman's insistence on hiring lay professors for the new university.[3] In Latin America, an insistent clericalism at times seemed to suggest that the laity's job was "to pay, pray and obey." Lay brotherhoods and confraternities served as prominent exceptions to the idea of a passive laity, but the bishops of CELAM at Medellín were not exaggerating when they lamented the many baptized Catholics whose "participation in official worship is almost null and whose connection to the Church as an organization is very slim."[4]

Pope Leo XIII's encyclical *Rerum Novarum* (1891) asserted repeatedly that Catholics had the right and the responsibility to form "associations" to advance their interests in various ways and especially to humanize the often brutal industrial workplace. His *Graves de Communi Re* (1901) endorsed lay organizations such as "the popular bureaus which supply information to the uneducated, the rural banks which make loans to small farmers, the societies for mutual help or relief, the unions of working men and other associations or institutions of the same kind," and various other efforts "to comfort and elevate the mass of the people." He made clear, however, that "the action of Catholics, of whatever description it may be, will work with greater effect if all of the various associations, while preserving their individual rights, move together under one primary and directive force," that is, "under the authority and direction of the bishops."[5] Pius XI (1922–39) shifted from Leo's generic "action of Catholics" to his own "Catholic Action," a specific form of lay organization that he hoped would spread across the world as part of "the participation of the laity in the hierarchical apostolate of the Church."[6] In nations such as France and Italy, Catholic Action groups, including specialized groups for workers and students, exercised significant influence not just in social and charitable work but also in politics. Nevertheless, Pius XI's successful advocacy of Catholic Action could not disguise the limits of his conception of the lay role in the church. He saw the layperson as an adjunct to the mission of priests and bishops. His attempt to funnel almost all lay activity into the confines of Catholic Action restricted lay involvement and made it appear that the laity did not have a mission of their own.

Although Pope Pius XII (1939–1958) spoke, like his predecessor, of "the collaboration of the laity in the apostolate of the hierarchy," in the 1950s he laid the groundwork for a broader lay role.[7] "It would be a misunderstanding of the Church's real nature and her social character," he said, "to distinguish in her a purely active element, Church authorities, and a purely passive element, the laity. All the members of the Church, as We Ourselves said in the Encyclical *Mystici Corporis Christo*, are called upon to cooperate in building up and perfecting the Mystical Body of Christ. They are all free persons and should therefore be active."[8] John XXIII (1958–63) similarly endorsed the need for all Catholics to engage in "active apostolic work" and seemed to be more in favor of Catholic *action* than Catholic *Action*, that is, in favor of a lay apostolate that included a wide variety of groups and activities that did not necessarily use the Catholic Action label.[9]

It was, however, Vatican II that gave full expression to the idea that the laity had a mission of its own, distinct from the mission of the hierarchy. The central document of the council, *Lumen Gentium*, emphasized the nature of the church as "the new People of God," in which "every disciple" had the obligation to spread the faith and to strive for holiness.[10] Beyond these universal mandates, which applied to all Catholics, the laity had a specific vocation: "They live in the ordinary circumstances of family and social life, from which the very web of their existence is woven. They are called there by God that by exercising their proper function and led by the spirit of the Gospel they may work for the sanctification of the world from within as a leaven."[11] Lay Catholics should have "freedom and room for action" and they should be able to undertake tasks "on their own initiative."[12] In short, Vatican II both liberated the laity and challenged them to a higher level of commitment and participation. The council threw open the doors of the church and sent the laity into the world to take up both the general mission of the church and their own specific mission, in whatever ways they thought most appropriate. In later years the post-conciliar popes repeatedly emphasized the council's view of the laity. Pope John Paul II (1978–2005), for example, urged the laity "to take up again and reread, meditate on and assimilate with renewed understanding and love, the rich and fruitful teaching of the Council" on the lay vocation so that they could take "an active, conscientious and responsible part in the mission of the Church." "It is not permissible," he said, "for anyone to remain idle."[13]

## *Catholic Action*

Vatican II sounded the death knell of Catholic Action, at least as the preferred and official venue for lay evangelization, catechesis, and social action. Catholic Action organizations existed in Latin America after the council, but most had shrunk in size and impact by the 1970s. This did not mean, however, that Catholic Action failed to play an important role in the rebirth of lay Christianity in Latin America. In many ways, Catholic Action and its spiritual child, the Cursillo movement, began the mobilization of lay Catholics that culminated in the rise of the CEBs and the new ecclesial movements.

In Brazil, for instance, Catholic Action played a major role in mobilizing thousands of lay Catholics. After its foundation in 1935, Brazilian Catholic Action spread quickly to most dioceses in the country but then entered a period of lethargy. In the 1950s, however, Catholic Action took up several challenging and influential projects. A new approach to organization that created groups in specific social milieus led to the formation of specialized groups for university students, rural youths, working class youths, and other populations. The university groups became active in social issues under the guidance of some of the nation's most talented priests, most of them from the progressive wing of the church. By 1960 the student groups in particular had taken a radical turn and were talking more about politics than about spirituality, with the word "revolution" occupying a key place in their vocabulary. Meanwhile, members of Catholic Action provided most of the leaders of the Movimento de Educação de Base (MEB), which educated and "conscientized" adults in northern Brazil.[14]

The problem for Catholic Action was that its increasingly radical politics went beyond what most bishops could accept. Starting in 1961 the bishops tried to pull the various groups back to more moderate political positions, based on the traditional view of Catholic Action as a facet of their own ministry rather than an independent organization. Many of the most active members rejected the idea that Catholic Action belonged under clerical direction and created Ação Popular (Popular Action), a movement outside the control of the hierarchy that was committed to the "struggle against the double domination of capitalism (international and national) and feudalism."[15] Ação Popular could not function after the military coup of 1964 and the university and high school organizations of Catholic Action were disavowed in 1965. yet the revitalization of Catholic Action in Brazil between 1950 and 1965 contributed to the growth of the mission of the laity, in that Catholic Action militants gained valuable leadership experience, developed a national vision for the church, and came to see the necessity of a politically, socially, and evangelistically involved laity. Many former militants from Catholic Action went on to found or support base ecclesial communities and other lay organizations.

Perhaps even more important, Catholic Action's "see-judge-act" methodology infused the emerging CEBs.[16] "See-judge-act" emerged from Belgian Cardinal Joseph Cardijn's work with students and young workers and focused on "using active methods, which move to action the elite and the masses." He taught them first "to see the problem of their temporal and eternal destiny," then "to judge the present situation, the problems, the contradictions, the demands of an eternal and temporal destiny," and then "to act with a view to the conquest of their temporal and eternal destiny."[17] Helder Camara, national advisor to Catholic Action, and later Brazil's leading progressive bishop and a prominent supporter of CEBs, said that Cardijn led Brazilians "to see in the most objective way possible; to judge events in the light of the gospel; and to act in consequence." To Camara, Cardijn was "without any doubt, an apostle" who "came to help young workers to know themselves as human persons, as sons of God, charged with a mission that only they could fulfill."[18] The Cardijn method's power lay in its combination of reflection—not always the first reflex of the young—with its expectation of action. It thus avoided the twin pitfalls of analysis without action and action without analysis.

In Chile, Catholic Action also played an important role in organizing, training, and empowering the laity starting in 1931. With 47,000 members by 1936 and 100,000 by 1950, the organization pushed the church toward social commitment. Many of its militants joined the Falange Nacional and its successor, the Christian Democratic Party, which attempted to bring the social teaching of the church into the political arena.[19] The political success of the Christian Democrats, including the election of Eduardo Frei to the presidency in 1964, actually diluted the strength of Catholic Action, as militants accepted positions in the party and the government at the expense of their roles in Catholic Action. Additionally, the failure of the Christian Democratic government to deliver on its promises to solve the nation's underlying economic and social problems led directly to the victory of socialist Salvador Allende in the presidential elections of 1970. Still, despite Catholic Action's loss of momentum and entanglements in electoral politics, as in Brazil it trained thousands of committed, active members of the Chilean laity in the decades before Vatican II.

In Peru, Catholic Action influenced and mobilized many of the lay activists and the progressive theologians who supported liberation theology and CEBs in the 1960s. Gustavo Gutiérrez, for example, had a formative experience as a lay member of Catholic Action in the late 1940s and early 1950s. After studying in Europe and being ordained he became the advisor to Catholic Action's Unión Nacional de Estudiantes Católicos (UNEC, National Union of Catholic Students) in 1959 and led a generation of students, first, into greater commitment to the poor and to political activism and, then, out of Catholic Action and into liberation theology and organizations such as CEBs and his Centro Bartolomé de Las Casas in Lima's Rimac slum. "I joined UNEC," said Rolando Ames, one of Gutierrez's friends during the 1960s, "because I found in Gustavo Gutiérrez, who at that time had only been back in the country for two years, a deeper appreciation of the Catholic Action movement." However, admitted Ames, "I later became critical of a Catholic Action that I found too rooted in the Church and too routine."[20] For Ames and for many students, sociologist Milagros Peña argues, "the need for socialist critiques of capitalism made it increasingly difficult to continue with Catholic Action theology."[21]

The other major achievement of Catholic Action was training and sending out of tens of thousands of what are usually called "lay catechists" but might better be understood as lay missionaries. In the 1950s and 1960s, in Central America and in countries with large indigenous populations, the church was facing a shortage of priests. Catholic Action responded by training community leaders as catechists who formed study and prayer groups and then led various community projects. Although studying the Bible and the basic doctrines of the faith might seem like fairly innocuous activities, their impact on rural villages proved profound and often explosive. Whether intended as such or not, the biblical and doctrinal Catholicism taught by the catechists served as a critique of traditional indigenous religion and of the socioeconomic power structure that supported it. The universal nature of doctrinal Catholicism, for example, could not help but relativize the importance of local religion and local religious authorities; new allegiances to pope, bishop, and priest tended to threaten long-standing local systems of control such as the cargo system cooperatives; and political organizing, often the result of the see-judge-act methodology, introduced new connections to the outside world that could upset village politics.[22] Thus, this doctrinal and politically engaged Catholicism challenged indigenous religion in a manner very similar to the way that Protestantism did, with the added complication that since village authorities characterized themselves as Catholic, they could not directly oppose it.

Despite its strengths at organizing and mobilizing the laity, Catholic Action had three significant flaws. First, as an arm of the hierarchy it minimized the role of the laity even as it was trying to motivate them to greater action. Loss of motivation and conflict with the hierarchy almost inevitably resulted. Second, and often related to the first problem, Catholic Action's tendency to enter partisan politics pulled its most committed members into the electoral arena, where failure and compromise could tarnish and diminish their Catholic identity. Third, in its work with students and workers Catholic Action tended toward radicalization that could leave faith itself behind. For example, the Juventud Obrera Católica (Young Catholic Workers) of Mexico became so committed to the "class option" in the 1960s that they mocked their organization's earlier attention to fiestas and piety as "folkloric."[23] Although Catholic Action gradually lost momentum across Latin America because of its internal contradictions, by the 1960s it had trained two generations of Catholic laity, had mobilized them for various projects, and had given them the expectation of involvement in social, political, and religious affairs.

## CEBs in Brazil

The largest and most famous lay movement in Latin America was the CEB, which started in Brazil and quickly multiplied across the region. At its height, there were as many as 80,000 CEBs and 3 or 4 million participants.[24] By the time of Vatican II Brazil had a strong and vibrant episcopal conference, a homegrown educational and social ideology developed by Paulo Freire, and large numbers of active lay Catholics, many of whom were products of Catholic Action. Brazil also had vibrant Protestant churches that were spreading to every corner of the nation and leading millions of poor Brazilians out of the Catholic Church.

In 1956, a woman confronted visiting bishop Agnelo Rossi with what was happening in her neighborhood in northeastern Brazil: "In Natal the three Protestant churches are lit up and crowded. We hear their hymn-singing . . . and our Catholic church, closed, is in darkness . . . because we don't get a priest."[25] Rossi knew also that in his home diocese of Barra do Pirai Protestant churches were winning converts for the same reasons: pastors without seminary degrees and motivated lay evangelists provided Protestants with an army that went out into the community and then "kept the lights on" for meetings several days a week. Rossi realized that if the Catholic Church wanted to compete, it needed to create a similar kind of pastoral workforce. He decided to train lay catechists, who fanned out into the many neighborhoods of his city to build simple meeting centers, to catechize, and to conduct religious services.[26]

Coupled with the adult education movement and the Movimento de Educação de Base (MEB), Rossi's experiment convinced the Brazilian hierarchy that lay mobilization and the creation of small Catholic communities could provide the solution to many of Brazil's social and religious problems. In the early 1960s, collectively through the CNBB (National Conference of Brazilian Bishops) and in their individual dioceses, Brazilian bishops began to encourage the formation of what were coming to be known as CEBs. It was not always clear how individual CEBs began or how much of a role the hierarchy had, but these groups followed three basic patterns. Sometimes priests, religious sisters, or lay catechists started the communities as a way of living out liberation theology. In other cases Bible study or prayer groups evolved "naturally" into more comprehensive organizations in response to community desires and conditions. In still others people involved in Catholic Action, adult education, or political movements formed communities that took on new attributes, becoming more religious or developing closer connections to the local diocese.[27] The genesis of all these CEBs, numbering 40,000 in Brazil by 1974 and as many as 80,000 by 1979, with another 70,000 in the rest of Latin America, is a complex topic, but it is fair to say that they generally emerged in rural and urban zones of suffering that were underserved by the institutional church but that also had concerned bishops ready to experiment.[28] These bishops often supported liberation theology and saw the CEB as the most obvious way to live out the preferential option for the poor. Brazil's political and economic crises, its rapid urbanization, and its corps of progressive bishops meant that it had both an urgent need for a new kind of lay pastoral strategy and the necessary episcopal support for such a strategy.

In 1962 the Brazilian bishops drafted an "emergency plan" that highlighted the importance of small communities inside parishes; in 1965 they mentioned CEBs by name as an integral part of their new five-year pastoral plan; in the 1970s, after CELAM's 1968 meeting in Medellín had refocused the church's attention on the poor, many bishops endorsed CEBs as one of the primary means of energizing the laity and transforming society.[29] For example, in 1977 Aloisio Lorscheider, bishop of Fortaleza and president of CELAM, argued that CEBs were central to the revitalization of the Brazilian Church along the lines proposed by Vatican II:

We want all Christians to truly feel themselves Christians, to feel themselves the Church. This means that we all have our task within the history of salvation, that we are called to carry forward Christ's saving mission. We are all responsible and therefore we must all *participate*. What we want to obtain with the basic ecclesiastical [*sic*] communities is participation by all in the Church's problems, within a fraternal community where everyone knows each other, all love each other and all give witness to their own faith—a place where faith and life truly form a union.

—Aloisio Lorscheider, "Basic Ecclesiastical Communities in Latin America," *AFER* 19, no. 3 (June 1977): 143–4.

He believed that life in Christian community would slowly free a poor person from the prejudice that entrapped him so that he could become "capable of reflecting, capable of expressing his own ideas and discussing them with others." For Lorsheider and many other bishops the CEBs figured as part of their commitment to "liberation" because even before the CEBs mobilized their members for overt political activism, they were creating political actors. Through Bible study, prayer, and community, the CEB taught people "to think with their own head[s]." This "interior liberation" was "the first and most important phase of liberation."[30] Bishop Ivo Lorscheiter (cousin of Aloisio Lorscheider) agreed: "From the point of view of Church and society, the existence of the [CEBs] is the most important event of our epoch."[31] Another Brazilian bishop, Waldyr Calheiros de Novais of Volta Redonda made the CEB, rather than the parish, the basic administrative unit in his diocese.[32]

During the ascendancy of the progressive bishops and supporters of liberation theology, CEBs stayed near the top of the list of priorities for the Brazilian Church. However, the reign of John Paul II, starting in 1978, slowly pushed the CNBB away from CEBs.[33] The bishops named by John Paul tended to adopt his wariness about CEBs in general and about liberation theology in particular. By the 2000s many CEBs were in decline and many had simply ceased to function. Still, for three decades CEBs played a major role in energizing and mobilizing the laity, most prominently in Brazil but also in other Latin American nations.

## CEBs in Action

In Brazil the basic activities of CEBs included Bible studies, liturgical celebrations, mutual support, and neighborhood improvement projects. Most started with the visit of a pastoral agent such as a priest, religious sister, or lay catechist, who met people in a neighborhood, connected them to each other, developed local leaders, and established some sort of meeting place, often in somebody's home. The emerging community then began meeting together, either to discuss the Bible or for liturgical celebrations, which could be Masses if a priest was present or prayer or communion services if not. Bible study and preaching usually focused on topics such as land, work, poverty, sickness, and oppression—important issues in the life of the poor.[34]

A representative example could be found in a shantytown in Sao Paulo in 1983. First, a lay catechist introduced the Last Judgment passage in the Gospel of Matthew in which Christ separates "the sheep" and "the goats" based on how they had responded to the poor and needy during their lives. Then participants discussed the meaning of the passage, with particular reference to their own situation. "Here it is said that Jesus is among the hungry, the needy, the people who have no houses, the thirsty ones . . . people like us," noticed one woman. Another responded, "And the worst of it is they, the rich, the powerful, give the wrong address [for Jesus] and then we never meet him, although he is among us." The group then made suggestions about how to help various members of their community.[35]

Sometimes the discussion started at an even more basic level. In the early days of a CEB, French priest Dominique Barbé, for instance, liked to begin with questions about people's work, families, and personal histories. Believing that the poor had internalized society's prejudice against them, he taught them to value themselves and their own words and experiences. "It is important," he thought, "for a mother of a family to be able to tell what time she got up; how many times she got up during the night or at dawn to give the bottle to the baby, to heat the coffee for her husband who is going off to the factory, to fix the lunch box for her oldest son who leaves later, to get children ready for school." Although demoralized and inarticulate people could accomplish little, simply telling their own stories could restore the voices of the poor. Once they had the confidence to speak they could begin to take action.[36]

Since most of the pastoral agents embraced liberation theology, they hoped to bring participants around to a more critical view of society, politics, and economics so that they could see poverty as the result of human action, not as the will of God, and so that they could become subjects of history, rather than its objects. They hoped that CEBs would take up the fight against oppression on both the local and national levels, engaging first in neighborhood projects and then in the formal political system. Although many academics and liberationists liked to believe, with Frei Betto, that the CEBs were "effectively bringing about through the practices that they develop . . . a new model of society [which is] popular, democratic, and socialist," in practice people more readily committed themselves to study and worship than to long-term battles for local improvements, especially once they had gained basic services.[37] For example, of the eleven poorest Sao Paulo CEBs studied by sociologist W. E. Hewitt in the early 1980s, six had worked on projects to improve their neighborhoods, but in eleven more prosperous neighborhoods that he studied, no CEBs took up such projects.[38] Activists found it even more difficult to bring CEBs into the national political process in a sustained way.

The Comunidade São José in São Paulo serves as a good example of the activist stage that some CEBs reached. Established in the late 1960s, the CEB operated for nine years on a strictly religious basis. Their first neighborhood project, a common one for CEBs, was an attempt to gain legal title to the land on which their shantytown had been built. (In many cases the urban periphery of Latin America was built on state or private lands without permission and thus without legal title, putting residents in a state of legal limbo even after decades of occupation.) The CEB took the following steps for this and later neighborhood improvement campaigns:

> First, the group's *conselho* called the members together to discuss the particular problem at hand. Second, a petition was drawn up and circulated throughout the neighborhood; and third, a delegation of *conselho* members was selected to meet with the government authorities concerned. At such meetings, a statement of intent regarding the means for resolving the CEB's complaint was normally obtained from the appropriate official and a deadline set for remedial work to begin. This accomplished, group members waited either for the officials involved to take action as promised, or for the negotiated start-up to pass. When the latter occurred, which it frequently did, CEB members would arrive in increasing numbers at subsequently planned encounters, thus applying constant pressure on government agents to resolve their complaint.[39]

After gaining legal title for hundreds of residents of their neighborhood in 1976, the CEB used the same approach over the next few years to gain sewers, running water, streetlights, and a bridge over a busy road. Other

CEBs studied by Hewitt used similar methods to realize neighborhood improvements.[40]

Despite the impressive accomplishments of the Comunidade São José and the other CEBs, they ran into a common set of problems. First, CEB members often became disheartened because neighborhood residents who were not part of the CEBs did not believe that it was actually the CEB that had won local improvements. Even when they did believe, they often objected to the new fees charged by the city for sewers and other services. Second, government officials and political parties tried to take the credit for local improvements and to divide the CEB by offering bribes to their leaders. Third, religious sisters and priests could exercise too much influence on a CEB, stifling the desires and plans of the members in a way that stunted the development of lay leadership. Finally, even when genuine lay leaders did emerge, they often complained that few CEB members seemed motivated to participate in improvement projects.[41] For instance, Hewitt noticed that between 1984 and 1988 the twenty-two CEBs that he was studying were becoming "more and more like the local parish church," with members building "party and Sunday school rooms" and buying sound equipment for their centers. "It would appear," said Hewitt, "that given the choice between initiating bible study or charity circles or reflection and political discussion groups, the former has won out."[42]

Manuel Vasquez's study of a CEB outside of Nova Iguaçu found a similar progression. In 1971 a French priest visited families in the neighborhood and started a Bible study for five women. Using a modified version of Catholic Action's see-judge-act approach, he sent the women out to share the Bible message they had just studied with their neighbors and had them reflect on their experiences and another biblical passage before sending them out again the next week. The women then formed their own small discussion groups, each with as many as thirty participants, and also started a catechism class for children. The priest began celebrating the Mass in the community, but he asked a team of CEB members to do all the liturgical planning. Instead of traditional homilies, he used a discussion format to present themes that community residents could readily understand, as one CEB member related:

> Father Claudio was sensitive to the difficulty people had in reading, people of the Northeast who came here. He would take the gospel reading and write it on a big brown poster and place it in the front

of the room during the mass. And then the people would read each word slowly, discussing it, linking it with our reality.[43]

Through such discussions and through a chapter of Workers Catholic Action started by the priest and supported by his three French successor priests, a core group of CEB members began applying the see-judge-act method to local problems and became increasingly radical. In the mid-1970s they convinced many residents to protest the community's lack of services at city hall. The success of these demonstrations in bringing a school and running water to the neighborhood vindicated the political orientation of the group's leaders and led many residents to join a neighborhood association, founded in 1982, that lobbied for a health clinic and paved streets.[44]

In 1981, however, drastic changes were afoot in the CEB, changes that significantly altered its composition and orientation by the mid-1980s. A team of Irish priests who were more committed to traditional liturgy than to social action and who had a more hands-off approach to involvement in the community replaced the French priests who had supported the CEB for a decade. Meanwhile, Brazil was experiencing an economic downturn that resulted in the loss of employment for some of the more politically minded members in the neighborhood. The combination of the new pastoral approach and the financial crisis led to a shift in power within the CEB. The Society of St. Vincent de Paul, a group of older Catholics devoted to traditional Catholic piety and to charitable person-to-person aid, became the new dominant group, while most of the members of Workers Catholic Action stopped participating, both because they disapproved of the new direction and because they needed to devote themselves to scraping out a living doing anything that they could. Liturgically, the Irish priests insisted on following the rubrics of *A Folha*, a booklet published by the diocese. One of the activists explained the nature of the changes:

With the [French] priests . . . we were the ones who prepared mass. The gospel text was read, but it was reflected on by the people. Each one would speak a little about what the reading meant, what Jesus Christ wanted to say with it. And people linked it with the life of the worker. And when [Irish] Father Jaime arrived he ended all that. He said that we had to organize a liturgy group, take a course to know how to read [*A Folha*] right. So he undid our work, a work that was done for years.[45]

The more traditional liturgy and the decreased attention to politics demoralized the activist corps of the CEB, but to the Society of St. Vincent de Paul, these changes made the CEB more attractive. In short, as in the Sao Paulo CEBs studied by Hewitt, the Nova Iguacu CEB moved from Bible study to liturgy to social activism, but then returned to a more liturgical emphasis.

## CEBs in Nicaragua

An important difference between the Brazilian CEBs and those from most other nations, and probably the reason for Brazil's dominance of the movement, was that the Brazilian CEBs enjoyed extensive episcopal support during the 1960s and 1970s.[46] This was not the case in Nicaragua, but CEBs there did enjoy a season of tacit approval in the late 1970s.

In 1965 Father José de la Jara became the pastor of the Parish of San Pablo in the Colonia Nicarao neighborhood of Managua. He founded a group for married couples and began to lead retreats that introduced a brand of Catholicism that restored the self-respect of many parishioners who had been beaten down by poverty. A new pair of priests from Spain, Father Felix and Father Mariano, and a group of Maryknoll sisters joined de la Jara and formed a CEB in the parish in 1966. The new priests emphasized social themes more than de la Jara did, which alienated some previously active members but attracted a new contingent. "Felix and Mariano organized cursillos too," remembered one participant,

> but now we began to deal with social problems—political things. There certainly was a lot of biblical content, but not in the spiritualistic way that Padre de la Jara had spoken of the Bible. With the new priests, the cursillo's topics seemed to touch our daily reality more deeply. Through their homilies they were awakening, building, making a new consciousness in the people of the barrio.
> —(Kate Pravera, "The Base Christian Community of San Pablo: An Oral History of Nicaragua's First CEB," *Brethren Life and Thought* 29, no. 4 (Autumn 1984): 209)

Another participant added, "The mentality of the old religion was the mentality of the capitalists" and "was used to keep the people asleep," while the message of the new priests allowed the people "to become conscious of our position as an exploited class."[47] The CEB also developed an innovative liturgy, the Misa Popular, that depicted Christ as poor and exploited and was adopted by other CEBs before it was suppressed by the bishops.[48]

By 1968 the CEB had decided that it needed to take a prophetic stance toward the abuses of the corrupt regime of Anastasio Somoza. "First of all," said CEB leader Mercedes, "we had to make people conscious of their duty as Christians. Second, we chose to denounce the atrocities of Somoza, to denounce everything that was against humanity and the dignity of the people." When Somoza raised the Managua bus fare by 50 percent, the San Pablo CEB joined with other CEBs in protests that included barricades in the streets, chanting crowds, and spikes thrown into the street to flatten bus tires. When Somoza planned to raise the price of milk, the CEB organized a boycott and hijacked milk trucks. In the 1970s the CEB began public demonstrations against the dictator and made contact with the Frente Sandinista de Liberación Nacional (Sandinista Front for National Liberation), the socialist revolutionary group that was fighting against Somoza.[49]

After a massive demonstration against Somoza in 1977, CEB members came to believe that they could not save their country "through prayers alone, nor with rosaries" and that they had to join the Sandinistas. "As Christians," Mercedes said, "we were now going to fight for life because God is the enemy of death. Christ overcame death, and we as Christians have to overcome death as well. And we have to do it by struggling, by fighting for life, which is the opposite of death." When the revolution triumphed in 1979, many activists from the CEBs joined the Sandinista leadership.[50] In retrospect, one member of the CEB could readily identify the foundation of San Pablo's growth: "The secret of San Pablo's success was that we gave the lay people in the parish the responsibility which they deserve in the Church. Lay people thus began to participate in classes to interpret the Bible, participating in the Sunday homilies, and helping to evangelize by means of the various classes we gave in people's houses."[51]

For a brief period in 1979 the radicalized CEBs and the hierarchy seemed united in their opposition to Somoza. A pastoral letter just before the success of the revolution in July accepted the necessity of violent opposition to Somoza and another letter in November actually affirmed that "the revolutionary process will be something creative, profoundly original, and in no way imitative" and urged Catholics to work with it, not against it. Although relations between the bishops and the CEBs had been tense in the past, they now endorsed them: "The people of God should renew their vitality by means of the Christian base communities. . . . The Church should both learn and teach the faithful to see things from the perspective of the poor, whose cause is the cause of Christ."[52]

The rapprochement, however, did not last. By 1982 most Nicaraguan bishops had started to criticize the revolution and Archbishop Miguel Obando y Bravo of Managua had become the de facto leader of the opposition, while the CEBs still generally supported the Sandinistas. An auxiliary bishop who called the CEBs "arms of the government—another way to mobilize the youth and women into service for the state" exemplified the distrust that much of the hierarchy felt toward the CEBs.[53] His view was not a total misreading of the situation, for under the Sandinista government (1979–90), many CEB members did dedicate themselves to state programs and the government did tend to view the CEBs as allies who could be mobilized for the state's projects. By the mid-1980s many CEBs had separated themselves from the institutional church, which they viewed as reactionary, or had lost official recognition. In the 1990s, with the Sandinistas out of power, many CEBs experienced an identity crisis. Even after the victory of Sandinista Daniel Ortega in the presidential election of 2006, the remaining CEBs seemed to have lost much of their vitality.[54]

For example, the CEB in Masaya was known as the Movimiento Cristiano "Gaspar García Laviana," which took its name from a priest who joined the Sandinista guerillas in 1977 and died in battle in 1978; this CEB militantly supported Sandinismo during the early 1980s. Many members, for instance, publicly denounced a 1983 letter by the nation's bishops that had criticized the Sandinista government's military draft. As members became more involved in government programs and less involved in the CEB itself, they often channeled their remaining energy toward critiques of the bishops rather than toward liturgy, study, or neighborhood improvement. CEB members who still sought a religious or spiritual experience began to look elsewhere. Bernardo Fuentes, for instance, left the group when it supported Sandinista assaults on conservative priests and joined the local Charismatic Renewal movement. He returned to the CEB only when it reemphasized liturgical practices.[55]

A CEB in Spain attempted to revitalize the Masaya CEB, sending money and a lay leader, Dolores Gómez, in the early 1990s. Gómez drew groups of about thirty people to meetings that included prayer, singing, and Bible study in a building owned by a wealthy supporter and not connected to the local parish. Although the local priests stayed away from the CEB, Jesuits from Managua celebrated Mass whenever possible. The music usually featured songs from the Misa Campesina Nicaraguense, which included lyrics such as "You are the God of the poor/The down-to-earth human God, God who sweats in the street," and referred to Christ as "a working man." Since the Nicaraguan bishops had banned the Misa in 1976, its prominence in the group's celebrations signaled its continuing struggles with the hierarchy, but the group tried to introduce some critical distance between itself and Sandinismo, recognizing that it had lost members through its over-identification with the party. The CEB also renewed its efforts at neighborhood improvement, providing health services to the community and forming cooperative businesses that supported some of its members. Despite its (partially successful) efforts at renewal, the Masaya CEB existed in a state of ecclesiastical limbo since neither its parish nor its diocese recognized it as an official entity.[56]

As had happened to Catholic Action in Chile after the triumph of the Christian Democrats in 1964, the Sandinista victory neither benefited Nicaraguan CEBs nor improved church-state relations as much as militants had expected. As former CEB leaders entered the government, the communities lost many of their most experienced activists; and with the new government embodying some of their most cherished principles, the CEBs lost many of their reasons for political action. Many participants simply could not envision themselves returning to prayer and Bible study after having won an actual revolution.

## Conclusion

The recent history of CEBs in Brazil and Nicaragua disappointed those who had seen the CEB as the vanguard of revolution and the seed of a new popular church. The trajectory of the average CEB, which developed from Bible study and liturgy into neighborhood improvement projects and political action but then dropped its activism, frustrated them. These communities rarely realized or sustained their political potential. In fact, in Hewitt's studies in Brazil, some CEBs showed a definite trend toward religious conservatism: by the mid-1980s some CEB leaders were steering their members into the Charismatic Renewal and the conservative Society for Tradition, Family and Property; two thirds of participants used traditional terms for Christ (rather than liberationist terms such as "Liberator"); and while 71 percent of members regularly attended religiously oriented CEB meetings, only 20 percent usually attended political events.

Hewitt concluded that "the strong presence of the religiously conservative element within our sample CEBs does demonstrate that the civic improvement strategy has had and will likely continue to have difficulty in realizing its participation-enhancing potential," and this disheartened those who hoped that the CEBs would usher in the revolution.[57] In the same way, by the 1980s the isolation of the Nicaraguan CEBs from the hierarchy, their loss of members, and the increasing competition from the Charismatic Renewal and other new movements within the church meant that CEBs no longer played the revolutionary role that they had in the 1970s. They did contribute to the rise of Sandinismo and the success of the Sandinista revolution in the 1970s, but they could not hold onto their militants or their prophetic energy in the midst of the complex religious politics of the 1980s and 1990s.

However, the Brazilian and Nicaraguan examples do offer strong evidence that CEBs played a significant role in reaching, training, and empowering lay Catholics. That such Catholics might demonstrate more interest in prayer, Bible study, traditional understandings of Christ, and even in the Charismatic Renewal, than in political action, signified not that CEBs had less importance than previously thought, but that their importance was primarily religious. Typical was the case of a Guatemalan man who started to weep when asked his opinion during a CEB Bible study. No one had ever invited him to answer such a question before—but the CEB addressed him personally, engaged him in dialogue, and ultimately empowered him. This "interpersonal and sacramental valuing of members" transformed them and made them "co-subjects with God" in a way that made them more active politically but was not strictly political. At base it was a religious and spiritual transformation.[58] The fading of the CEB as a political force, therefore, does not indicate the overall failure of the CEB experiment, for politics cannot serve as the measure of the success of a religious movement. Rather, the impact of the CEB was evident in the millions of Latin Americans—often people in the most desperate situations—who encountered scripture for the first time, cast off their passivity, and became active, thoughtful Catholics, or, as they liked to say, the church itself.

# 8

# *Rise of the Laity: The New Ecclesial Movements*

THE WORKING, MIDDLE, and upper classes had their own religious problems. Those who had secure employment and who enjoyed electricity, running water, paved streets, and other accoutrements of urbanization often had hectic and disjointed lives. The classic Catholic parish served a specific geographical locale, but an urban Latin American family could have parents who worked in one part of city, children who went to school in another, and friends and family spread around several different neighborhoods. As population density increased faster than priestly vocations, Catholics could not expect to receive much spiritual care from the parish priest or to feel any real sense of community with the thousands of other residents of their parish.[1] Meanwhile, the pervasive mass media broadcast challenging messages that attacked Catholicism directly or, more likely, presented alternative visions of the good life in the forms of materialism, secularism, and various political ideologies. How to live as a Catholic became both a logistical issue about where, when, and how to grow in the faith and a philosophical question about what Catholicism meant in urban industrial modernity.

Many Catholics found the answers to these questions in the new ecclesial movements (NEMs)—organizations, each with a specific "charism" (spiritual gifting or calling), that trained and equipped lay Catholics for evangelization, catechesis, and other ministries. Typically, members of a NEM, such as the Sant'Egidio community of Buenos Aires, found spiritual formation, friendships, and religious activities within the movement but still participated to one degree or another in a local parish.

Despite being a major form of lay empowerment, the new ecclesial movements have attracted less scholarly and popular attention than the CEBs for a variety of reasons. First, these new movements often lacked the drama inherent in the CEBs. Rather than the impoverished and the desperate fighting for the basic necessities of life, the usually middle-class members of NEMs were struggling not to survive but to make sense of their place in the world and the church. Second, scholars interested in NEM phenomenon itself tended to do their research in Europe, where most NEMs began and where they had the most influence; scholars interested in Latin American religion tended to give more attention to the CEBS since they were the region's lay movement par excellence. Third, the many different kinds of NEMs made them more difficult to grasp in a collective sense, since each NEM had a different "charism," or founding principle, that gave it a distinctive character. The Neo-Catechumenal Way, for example, emphasized intensive catechesis in small groups that stayed together for decades. Focolare, on the other hand, saw its charism as the "spirituality of communion," with an emphasis on compassion, unity, and service to the poor. Finally, the NEMs tended to be more theologically orthodox than the CEBs, which made them more suspect and less interesting to scholars of Latin America, who tended to favor more progressive religious movements. For the average historian or social scientist, the CEB, with its poor members, its connections to liberation theology, its resistance to dictators, and its revolutionary potential, proved more attractive than NEMs. When the NEMs' bourgeois constituency was coupled with orthodoxy, moral conservatism, and allegiance to the papacy they became even less attractive objects of study. The new ecclesial movements, however, deserve serious attention because they and the CEBs are part of the same general explosion of lay Catholicism in Latin America and because, as of 2012, they still exhibited the growth and dynamism that most CEBs had lost.[2]

A partial explanation of the continued vitality of the NEMs comes from sociologists Roger Finke and Patricia Wittberg. Pointing to the work of Ernst Troeltsch and Richard Niebuhr, Finke and Wittberg highlight the tension between sect and church. A sect, in this sense, is a breakaway movement that fosters religious fervor at odds with the spirit of the age, while a church is a settled body more at ease with the culture around it. The problem for a church is that it lacks the dynamism and excitement generated by sects; revitalization movements within a church can easily lead to schism and the formation of a sect, as the intensity of the new group collides with the mainstream's desire for stability. Finke and Wittberg posit that the Catholic Church has operated for 2,000 years with relatively few major schisms because religious orders offer "a formal structure that allows for sectarian expression." In other words, the founding of a new religious order allows the call for renewal to function inside the Catholic Church but outside the regular structure of parishes and dioceses. "By channeling the most radical calls for change into religious orders," Finke and Wittberg argue, "the Church prevented frequent schisms and could selectively incorporate the proposed changes into the larger church."[3] Although Finke and Wittberg deal primarily with traditional religious orders, they do mention NEMs such as Italy's Communion and Liberation as examples of the same phenomenon.[4]

Over the last fifty years in Latin America, the NEMs, more than either the traditional religious orders or the CEBs, have provided a "sectarian" option within Catholicism. CEBs, after all, were usually set up as parts of parishes or as alternatives to parishes, as *local* communities of the faithful that emphasized their identity as the church. In Brazil, for example, CEBs functioned best when they worked most closely with their bishops. Religious orders played an important role in Latin America, especially in supplying missionaries and teachers, but they rarely had mass appeal. They served the poor, but they never saw large numbers of the poor actually joining their orders. Of course, many millions chose Protestantism as a truly sectarian option, but most Latin Americans were too attached to the religion of their birth to make such a drastic jump. They wanted a deeper and more meaningful way to be Catholic, not an alternative to Catholicism. They wanted to understand the sacraments more deeply, to learn more about doctrine, and to find the resources for greater faithfulness, not to start something completely new. For such people, the new ecclesial movements provided the answer.

"The movements, it seems to me," said Cardinal Joseph Ratzinger, "have this specific feature of helping the faithful to recognize in a world-wide Church, which could appear to be no more than a large international organization, a home where they can find the atmosphere appropriate to the family of God and at the same time remain part of the great universal family of the saints of all times."[5] For Latin America, the issue of finding a "home" and an "atmosphere appropriate to the family of God" assumed special relevance, given the ongoing priest shortage. While Europe, for instance, had about 1,500 Catholics to each priest in 2011, Latin America had more than 7,000 Catholics to each priest, which meant that lay Latin Americans faced the prospect of isolation and inertia if they did not embrace alternatives to the traditional parish.[6] On the most basic level NEMs allowed committed lay Catholics to find each other and to create educational, cultural, devotional, and service opportunities beyond those normally offered in a parish. Similarly, the NEMs encouraged a level of specialization that parishes could not. Especially in the area of culture—both in terms of producing art and literature and in terms of cultural criticism—the NEMs provided a venue for like-minded lay Catholics to work together in a way rarely seen elsewhere. Finally, the NEMs served as a spur to the rest of the church, making clear to clergy and laity alike that the lay vocation really could be lived out in the urban, industrial world.

## *The Cursillo*

Just as Catholic Action prepared the ground for the rise of the CEBs, the Cursillo (literally "short course") movement played a transitional role for the NEMs. In 1948, on the island of Mallorca, "Cursillos for Pilgrim Scouts" who were preparing for a national pilgrimage to Santiago de Compostela attracted new members to Catholic Action. The format, involving "chats" by laymen, lectures by priests, prayer, discussion, and periods of silence, gradually evolved into a highly scripted three-day "Cursillo de Cristiandad" that challenged those who went on the retreat, cursillistas, to a greater commitment to Christ and to the church. Using emotionally intense methods, such as letters from friends and family members who said they were fasting for the cursillista, the Cursillo encouraged its participants to become engaged, serious Catholics.[7] A priest who led the retreats in Bolivia affirmed, "Nothing is left to improvisation: there is not a detail that does not have a precise and intentional aim to reach the final purpose of the Cursillo: to convert Christians who are lukewarm or self-satisfied to a personal and apostolic religion."[8] Another observer described the retreat as "shock treatment designed to bring individuals into active participation as Catholics."[9] Lest the shock fade away after the retreat, leaders invited cursillistas to weekly reunions known as "ultreyas" that encouraged greater devotion to piety, study, and action. After separating from Catholic Action in 1954, the Cursillo spread to other Spanish dioceses, where it operated as an independent entity. By 1969 it had spread to 466 dioceses in forty-three countries; in 2011 it was operating in sixty countries and more than 1,000 dioceses.[10]

In 1953 a Colombian priest named Rafael Sarmiento Peralta attended the Cursillo. Impressed, he brought the practice back to Colombia and began leading retreats for the young women's branch of Catholic Action. The practice spread to Mexico in 1958 and then to Bolivia, Venezuela, Peru, Cuba, Uruguay, Argentina, Ecuador, Puerto Rico, and Chile. Because of linguistic and cultural affinities, outside of Spain the Cursillo put down its deepest roots in Latin America. Mexico and Venezuela, which established national Cursillo secretariats before Spain itself did, played leading roles, with Mexico hosting the Second World Ultreya in 1970.[11] The Cursillo's rapid success in Latin America was a sign of the spiritual hunger among much of the laity, a hunger that Catholic Action groups sometimes neglected when they became more committed to social and political causes than to spiritual ones. Although the Cursillo did not discourage social action and political involvement (its roots in Catholic Action theoretically encouraged such action) in practice it functioned more as a way of catechizing lay Catholics, offering them more profound spiritual experiences and encouraging active participation in the church.

In Mexico, almost every diocese welcomed the movement, in large part because of the testimonies of participants. Armando Fuentes Aguirre, for example, went to the second Mexican Cursillo in Saltillo in 1959. "The Cursillo was a beautiful experience for me," he said. "In it God was presented in an atmosphere of happiness, without the severe rigor or the solemnity that many think necessary for getting close to God." The Cursillo changed his life: "It helped me to give up completely that old kind of religion that focused on the idea of hell, with a vengeful God as its principal motivation. There I understood that God is love." Almost fifty years later, Fuentes was still singing the Cursillo's praises.[12] For many Mexicans who desired a deeper and more intimate Catholic life but did not know where to find it in the urban, industrial world, Cursillo provided a road map. After their own life-changing experiences, many cursillistas devoted themselves to bringing that same experience to others. For instance, Mexico's leading industrial city, Monterrey, became a major center of the Cursillo. After hosting its first retreat in 1959, over the next fifty years the city hosted more than 1,000 Cursillos, each for thirty-five to forty people. In 1998, when the city welcomed 25,000 cursillistas from around the country to the national Ultreya, it boasted 500 Cursillo leaders in addition to many thousands of local participants.[13]

Cursillistas also took their movement to remote areas of many Latin American countries, with its graduates becoming advocates of orthodoxy in the intense competition between indigenous religion and new versions of Christianity. In the Maya community of San Andrés Xecul, Guatemala, for instance, after the decline of a previously active Catholic Action group and the return of indigenous "costumbre" (traditional religion) in the 1970s and 1980s, the Cursillo emerged in 1992 as one of the major religious alternatives in the village. Its twice-yearly retreats and weekly ultreyas slowly built up a corps of active and committed Catholics who rejected "costumbre" and accepted the orthodox teachings of the church. As Christopher Mackenzie observed, the Cursillo offered "a more or less complete world view" that served as one of the "cosmological alternatives to costumbre which are still palatable to local tastes."[14]

Instead of opting for Protestantism, many Latin Americans found in the Cursillo the opportunity for a challenging universal religion *inside* the Catholic Church. Cursillos, however, did not provide an ongoing and multifaceted approach to spiritual formation because in theory each person attended the Cursillo only once.[15] Although Cursillo leaders wanted those who attended their retreats to attend ultreyas and other follow-up meetings, they would still be pleased if a cursillista simply became a better Catholic. Similarly, the ultreya presented itself as a continuation of the Cursillo experience, not as a separate spiritual activity. Leaders focused more on developing the spiritual maturity of the cursillistas, not on building an organization. This was the movement's greatest strength, because nobody could accuse it of building a little kingdom inside of the church, and its greatest weakness, because it could easily lose contact with those it had most influenced. The NEMs became full-fledged organizations, with both the advantages and disadvantages inherent in such an enterprise. With multiple entry points, various ministries and activities, and a conscious group identity, NEMs could call people to ever deeper levels of commitment, but their visibility and strength also caused tensions in many of the dioceses where they operated.

## Controversies and Disagreements

The NEMs were indeed sources of controversy and division. Because they attracted Catholics interested in lives of greater commitment and deeper spirituality, critics charged them with creating a two-tiered laity. At their worst, they did actually foster such a mentality. Additionally, members of NEMs, confident and committed, could easily come into conflict with priests and bishops, especially those of a more progressive bent. Finally, the NEMs' independence from normal diocesan and parish structures could facilitate doctrinal, liturgical, and moral problems, such as Neo-catechumenal Way's refusal to follow liturgical norms in its conduct of the Mass and Regnum Christi's failure to denounce the sexual abuse and financial fraud practiced by its founder.[16]

One of the most controversial of Catholic movements, Opus Dei, demonstrated both the strengths and the weaknesses of intense, highly committed Catholic organizations. (Technically, Opus Dei is not a new ecclesial movement but rather a "personal prelature," a non-territorial diocese similar to a military archdiocese, but it shares many of the char-acteristics of the NEMs.) Founded by Spanish priest Josemaría Escrivá de Balaguer in 1928, the "Work of God" emphasized "the sanctification of ordinary life" and the dignity of the lay vocation well before Vatican II.[17] Escrivá's firm belief that the laity could live lives of holiness in the midst of their normal secular environment seemed "liberal" in the days before Vatican II because it threatened entrenched clericalism. After the coun-cil, however, the prelature's unflinching orthodoxy, poor public relations skills, hierarchical structure (including priests and various classes of lay members), and success in winning over business and political elites led to denunciations that it was a nefarious society of ultra-rightists intent on returning Latin America to the Middle Ages.[18] The left could some-times descend almost into caricature when expressing their fears about the secret machinations of the Opus Dei cabal. What the group's critics seemed to miss was that most people affiliated with Opus Dei were not chief executive officers or cabinet members, but middle- and upper-mid-dle-class Catholics who were seeking guidance on how to live as serious believers in the midst of urban modernity and who had little if any role in politics. Eric Garces's study of Opus Dei businessmen in Guayaquil, Ecuador, although critical of the group's theology and morality, stands as perhaps the only recent piece of scholarship on the group's role in Latin America to take seriously its stated beliefs and actual practices. His work ultimately rejects what he sees as Opus Dei's overly moralistic approach to charity but makes clear that its members were sincere and commit-ted lay Catholics who devoted much of their time to work with the poor. They might have been misguided, as Garces believes, but they bore little similarity to the shadowy, malignant figures that emerged in the popular press and much of secular scholarship.[19]

In Peru, the cradle of liberation theology, Opus Dei and the Sodalitium Christianae Vitae (SVC, a Peruvian family of NEMs) attracted a great deal of criticism for two main reasons. First, high-profile members and supporters of the two movements, including, by 1989, seven Opus Dei priests serving as bishops in different regions of the country, adopted theologically and socially conservative stances that contrasted sharply with the progressive beliefs that many observers had assumed would soon dominate the church. Most prominently, later Cardinal Archbishops of Lima, Augusto Vargas Alzamora (1990–97) and Opus Dei priest Juan Luis Cipriani (1997–), contrasted sharply with their predecessor, Juan Landázuri Ricketts (1955–90). Vargas Alzamora's support for the vocally orthodox SVC and Cipriani's frequent attacks on abortion, same-sex unions, and other proposals of the secular left shocked an intelligentsia accustomed to the progressive politics of Landázuri Ricketts. The nation's most prominent intellectual, Mario Vargas Llosa, for instance, contrasted Landázuri Ricketts, Gustavo Gutiérrez, and other Catholic leaders with Cipriani. "They, and many others like them among Peruvian believers," he said, "seem to me to represent a modern and tolerant current that is distancing itself more and more from the sectarian and intransigent tradition of the Church, the tradition represented by Torquemada and the tortures of the Inquisition that the old-fashioned Cardinal Juan Luis Cipriani insists on keeping alive against all odds."[20] It was particularly galling to progressives that John Paul II was giving Opus Dei a prominence previously reserved for the older religious orders, which by the 1990s generally sympathized with liberation theology and other progressive concerns. Gutiérrez, previously a priest of the archdiocese of Lima, went so far as to join the Dominican order, where he would not be under the direct control of Cipriani.

A second flash point in Peru came when the SVC's Luis Fernando Figari developed a "theology of reconciliation" as an alternative to liberation theology. With support from Opus Dei and from like-minded bishops around the region, including Vargas Alzamora and CELAM secretary general Alfonso López Trujillo, Figari joined elements of liberation thought, such as its emphasis on the poor, to a traditional theology of sin, grace, and redemption, and to Vatican II's emphasis on "communion" in the church. "This communion," argued Figari, "is obtained through the reconciliation that Jesus Christ brought to us and that we continue realizing through the Church." He called Catholics to be "witnesses of reconciliation" who served the poor and the lost as agents of a church that was "a sacrament of unity among human beings."[21] In 1985, the SVC and Archbishop Fernando Vargas of Arequipa hosted a conference on the new theology that attracted more than 600 priests, bishops, and pastoral agents. To sociologist Milagros Peña, the theology of reconciliation represented "an outlet for traditionalists and conservatives opposed to social activism" because, although it took up the concerns of the poor, it rejected class conflict and the revolutionary spirit of liberation theology. For her and for others on the left, it therefore took a dangerous step backward from what liberation theology and the base ecclesial communities had accomplished.[22]

More recently, in October 2010 in the Sucumbíos region of northern Ecuador, the naming of a bishop affiliated with the Arautos do Evangelho (Heralds of the Gospel, known in Spanish as the Heraldos del Evangelio), a Brazilian NEM known for its orthodoxy and allegiance to the papacy, set off protests by supporters of Gonzalo López, a Discalced Carmelite who had served as bishop of the vicariate for forty years.[23] López had developed a communitarian model of governance, in which a lay assembly effectively administered the vicariate, and had led various public health initiatives. When the new bishop, Rafael Ibarguren, arrived, he did not recognize the authority of the lay assembly and some residents feared that he would suspend the vicariate's social programs. Diocesan priests denounced Ibarguren and the Arautos who came with him as "elitists" who were prejudiced against women and the poor. Matters escalated further when supporters of the Carmelites occupied the cathedral in Logo Agrio and Ecuadoran president Rafael Correa denounced the Heraldos as an "ultrafundamentalist" sect and threatened to "veto" the appointment of Ibarguren and other bishops if the Vatican did not relieve him of his position. Correa's spokesman, Kintto Lucas, said the Arautos were in Ecuador illegally and "in the case of the naming of a member of this ultraconservative sector of the Church, we will use our veto capacity, as given in international treaties." On May 17, 2011, supporters of the two orders came to blows when the Arautos demanded that the pro-Carmelites leave the cathedral premises. Ibarguren resolved the confrontation on May 24, 2011, by renouncing his claim to the bishopric. Both religious bodies promised to leave the vicariate after the Vatican named a new bishop belonging to neither order.[24]

Although the Arautos had seen great success in their home country of Brazil and elsewhere in Latin America, in Sucumbíos they walked into a hotbed of progressive Catholicism that they did not fully understand

and for which they had not prepared. Where, for instance, the equally orthodox Opus Dei had built up a strong support system in Peru for decades before they assumed a prominent public role, the Arautos had no roots in Sucumbíos and therefore had no local allies. They demonstrated how NEMs, in their own minds totally committed to the good of the Catholic Church, could be perceived by progressives as enemies of the faith.

In other words, controversy surrounding NEMs often came more from theological and ideological battles than from actual malfeasance. There were genuine cases of abuse, for instance, in Peru's SVC and in Mexico's Regnum Christi—grave matters that needed to be taken seriously.[25] At the same time, the mere existence of anger and division could be a sign of the movements' intensity and ability to inspire commitment as much as an indication of their failures or shortcomings. Millions of lay Catholics became more committed believers through the NEMs, and that very commitment made them more likely to rub other Catholics the wrong way. In an increasingly secular society that sought to make religion private and innocuous, the negative publicity often surrounding NEMs was frequently the result merely of members sticking to their principles, which happened to be different from those of their critics. And not all NEMs were controversial. Movements such as the Sant'Egidio Community, which worked for ecumenical and interreligious dialogue in Buenos Aires, and Focolare, which campaigned for unity throughout Latin America, generally won the approval of the various sectors of the church and of outsiders.

## *Focolare in Brazil*

*Focolare,* the Italian word for hearth, hints at the warmth and hospitality emphasized by this movement, which started in northern Italy during World War II under the guidance of a young woman named Chiara Lubich and became one of the largest NEMs in the world and in Latin America by the end of the twentieth century.[26] To the puzzlement of her friends and family Lubich insisted that she wanted to dedicate her life to God but that she did not want to become a nun. Instead, she and the other young women who gathered around her committed themselves to working for the church in a lay capacity. At first, neighbors thought the women were communists or Protestants, since their zeal and the way they opened their homes to everyone contrasted with the more reserved nature of local Catholicism. During a stressful period when the region was under frequent aerial bombardment, the women developed a deep commitment to one another:

> We were very young, yet at any moment we could have lost our lives. The shelters we fled to were not safe from the bombs. This made sharp in our minds the ever present possibility of our having to go before God. It was a constant source of meditation, increasing in us the desire to find the way in which God would become truly, and as quickly as possible, our ideal.[27]

They decided that they had to love each other, indeed to be willing to die for each other. In everyday life this meant caring for each other and sharing joys, sorrows, and material goods. In the years after the war, Lubich and her followers, now including men, slowly recognized unity as the focus of their movement: "We were speaking about unity, unity with God and among the brethren; unity which was found at the heart of Jesus' testament and which is an effect of reciprocal love." Although it was not an official policy, the members of the movement (Focolarini) tended to live a communal lifestyle, with all of their goods in common.[28] Devotion to "Jesus forsaken"—based on Christ's cry on the cross, "My God, my God, why have you forsaken me?"—served as a second emphasis of the movement. For Lubich and her followers, that image of Christ utterly abandoned provided the key to achieving the unity they sought: Christ's followers had to trace the same path as their master, giving up everything to serve the lost and the poor.[29]

More and more young people began to join, as did some priests and a smattering of intellectuals, including journalist Igino Giordani, who saw in Lubich someone with "a deep and sure conviction which came from mystical experience," who "put holiness within reach of everyone" and "tore down the grille which separated the laity from the mystical life." The movement incorporated celibates and married couples, sponsored a summer meeting called a "Mariapolis" (City of Mary), and was building several permanent Mariapoli (model towns). All this put the Vatican in a quandary, since Focolare "did not fit into any category of society or community which the Catholic Church had ever had to deal with before." Its evident commitment to holiness and to the universal church eventually proved more important than its novel structure and it won official approval in 1962.[30] In the later years the movement worked with politicians, artists, and health professionals and, because of its emphasis on unity, welcomed Protestants, Muslims, Buddhists, and even atheists to many of its programs. Focolare enjoyed so much favor under Pope John Paul II that in 1982 he asked the movement to build a center on the grounds of the summer papal palace, Castelgandolfo.[31]

The movement entered Latin America in 1958. Encouraged by Brazilian seminarians and bishops who had learned about the movement in Rome, a team of lay missionaries that included Lía Brunet, Marco Tecilla, and Fiore Ungaro left Italy for Sao Paulo without knowing Portuguese or Spanish and without any plans for a place to stay.[32] After finding interest among young people in Brazil, and then in Uruguay, Argentina, and Chile, the Focolarini made their first home in Buenos Aires. Brunet, who had been one of the early followers of Lubich, gathered around her a group of ten young women who reminded her of the early days of the movement in Italy. "They decided," she said, "to leave father and mother, family and property, because the presence of Jesus among us was worth more than any treasure in the world and they had all experienced the power of unity." They vowed always to love each other and to conquer the city with love.[33]

Meanwhile, the Focolarini so impressed a group of Brazilians from Recife, in the impoverished northeastern part of the country, that they decided to travel to Italy to find out more about the movement. In response, Lubich decided to send one of her closest friends, Ginetta Calliari, to Recife to begin a Brazilian branch of the movement. In November 1959 Calliari and seven other Italians arrived with almost nothing. They found jobs, rented an apartment, and, in the spirit of Focolare, pooled their resources and held their goods in common. They had arrived at a volatile time, a period of increased social awareness, of militant action by the various specialized branches of Catholic Action, and of the growing attraction to Marxism among students and workers. Focolare's radical call to love, community, and simplicity attracted some of these young people, including Vera Araujo, a student and militant Marxist, who was captivated by the love she found among the Focolarini.[34]

Starting in 1964, at the request of Archbishop Helder Camara, the Focolarini began reaching out to the residents of the bleak Ilhâ do Inferno (Island of Hell) shantytown. They slowly overcame the mistrust of residents, who could not understand why educated Europeans and middle-class Brazilians were visiting their dangerous *favela* (shantytown). They slowly gathered a group of seventeen people, most of them intrigued by the group's simple insistence that they had come not to start a school or a hospital but to follow the crucified Christ. Over the course of the next few years, some Focolarini moved into the neighborhood and started several improvement projects, including drainage ditches, garbage removal, and a credit union, but they believed that more important than these physical improvements was fostering a sense of trust and solidarity in the neighborhood. The community's collective decision to change its name to Ilhâ Santa Teresinha (Saint Teresa Island), and the fact that by the 1990s most of the members of Focolare working in the neighborhood had grown up there, overshadowed the school and the brick factory that they had built.[35]

From its start in 1959 the movement began holding Mariapoli in Brazil, attracting hundreds of young people. By 1964 Focolare was doing well enough in Latin America for Lubich to visit Brazil and Argentina to make the foundation official; she returned in 1965 and 1966 to encourage the new members. In 1965 they began building a variation on the Mariapolis theme, a "Mariapolis Center" in Igarassu. While the permanent Mariapoli functioned as model cities where people lived and worked, the Mariapolis Centers would impart the values of the movement to new members and offer facilities for briefer visits.[36] In 1964 Calliari brought the movement to Sao Paulo and over the next fifteen years to many other Brazilian states. In 1969 she oversaw the establishment of Mariapolis Araceli, a permanent Mariapolis (today known as Mariapolis Ginetta in her honor), in Vargem Grande.[37] By 1999 the movement boasted over 1 million members in Latin America and permanent Mariapoli in Brazil (three different cities), Mexico, and Argentina.[38]

## Economy of Communion

Because of its charism of unity, Focolare in Brazil paid special attention to the poor from the beginning. On one of Calliari's early days in Recife she had glimpsed a dirty, emaciated man, barefoot and dressed in rags, meticulously cleaning leaf after leaf of a large tropical plant on the immaculate grounds of a large mansion. Shocked by this vivid picture of an upper class that cared more about its plants than its human employees, she realized that not only the physical conditions of the poor that but also the hearts of the rich needed to change. Who could effect such change? Calliari answered, "Not an abstract God, far away in heaven, but the God that we had learned to have living among us, in our love for each other, as we lived out his words."[39] Lubich had a similar vision for Focolare in Brazil and told one of its leaders, "The way to the Ideal of Unity in Brazil is the poor." Even more than in Italy, "the movement needs to think about the poor, the objective of the movement in Brazil is the poor."[40] Thus, from the beginning the destitution that they saw around them led the Focolarini to reach out to the poor, including making them feel at home in the movement. Starting in 1969, for instance, the residents of the new Mariapolis Araceli began visiting the neighboring Bairro do Carmo, a community composed mainly of the descendants of slaves. Calliari and others started spiritual programs for the residents and also secured resources for various community improvement projects.[41]

A new chapter in Focolare's development began in 1991 when, looking down from an airplane on her way to spend a few weeks at Mariapolis Araceli, Lubich caught sight of the ring of favelas around the more prosperous middle- and upper-class areas in the center of Sao Paolo. She already had been meditating on John Paul II's latest encyclical, *Centisimus Annus*, which emphasized the "collective responsibility for promoting development." As previous popes had done, John Paul called Christians to solidarity with the poor, but, more than his predecessors, he also emphasized the ways in which "the creation of ever more extensive working communities" showcased the positive side of human freedom and developed "important virtues" such as "diligence, industriousness, prudence in undertaking reasonable risks, reliability and fidelity in interpersonal relationships, as well as courage in carrying out decisions."[42] On May 29 Lubich challenged the people of Araceli to take up what she called the Economy of Communion (EOC), a new initiative in which the members of Focolare would start businesses that would dedicate their profits to the poor:

> We want to grow here, through our Mariapolis, enterprises that put capital in communion for the poor, after having reserved the capital necessary for the functioning of the business. With this capital, in the twentieth century we will live the reality of the first Christians, who laid everything they had at the feet of the apostles and shared it with the poor so that nobody lacked anything among them. Throughout our whole movement we want our members who have the ability to start a business to make it work according to Christian social doctrine and to put their capital in communion with all to aid the poor by giving an example of a society where there are no poor people. . . . A bit of charity, a work of mercy, some of the excess of a few individuals is not enough; it is necessary that the whole business freely share its capital.[43]

From the earliest years of the movement Lubich had had a sense that God wanted Focolare to build "a real and true little city, with houses, especially little houses, but also larger ones, with pavilions, with factories, with businesses and industries." And she had long sought to help build a "third way" between capitalism and socialism. Catalyzed by the desperation of Sao Paolo's favelas, Lubich began to see Focolare's charism "as a charism which can help to resolve social problems."[44] Specifically, the Economy of Communion would create cooperating business in which profits would be the split three ways, with one part for the poor, a second part "for the formation of a new people, that is, people oriented toward the culture of giving," and a third part for the needs of the business itself.[45] The novelty was not so much that businesses would create jobs or support Focolare and the poor but that "profit generation and redistribution should become parallel considerations within the very core of the business."[46]

The response to the proposal was overwhelmingly positive. "When Chiara told us her fascinating ideas, our hearts rejoiced," said Calliari. "For us it was like the Magnificat, the Magna Carta of the social teaching of the Church that Mary, the patron of this movement, proclaimed to unleash a revolution of love. The approval of the idea was immediate, enthusiastic, and passionate." To Calliari and many others Lubich's words seemed like a clarification of the movement's calling. They had always had a commitment to unity and they had always taken the poor seriously, but the connection between those two aspects of their charism was coming into focus. "Our mission," realized Calliari, "cannot be limited to working to help the poor; we are called to communion, to sharing everything, like a family."[47] Beyond jobs for those who desperately needed them and funds for the movement and community improvement projects, Lubich believed the Economy of Communion had the potential to transform society, creating a new economics based on sharing, unity, and collaboration.

Throughout the summer and fall of 1991 Focolarini in Brazil and around the world began to offer support for the new initiative. A family in Sao Paulo, for example, was willing to donate "an Olivetti typewriter, Olympia calculator, two desks, three seats, one computer table, one stamping machine, one cupboard." The Focolarini of Manaus said that they could provide venues to sell the goods produced by the new businesses. Originally, Focolare planned to build an industrial park next to Mariapolis Araceli so that the park could represent, in the words of Focolare leader Enzo Morandi, "the spiritual reality of the fellowship found in a model city and also so that the business park, although a thoroughly secular enterprise operating in civil society, could be clearly linked to the Mariapolis." Although the planners soon discovered that Araceli's residential zone did not allow industry, in 1992 Espri, an EOC corporation in which 3,300 Focolarini (including many who were quite poor) had invested, purchased a piece of land a few miles from Araceli and created Polo Spartaco industrial park, where EOC firms could rent land and start their businesses. By 2004 nine enterprises were operating there, including a cleaning supply company, a textile factory, a pharmaceutical company, a plastic factory, and an investment firm. Meanwhile, EOC businesses developed in other parts of the country. The ethos so infused the Focolare movement in Brazil that children developed their own projects, such as selling pine cones as tiny Christmas trees and donating the profits to the poor.[48]

Vera Araujo, a sociologist and one of the first Brazilian Focolarini, played a significant role in spreading the vision of the EOC and its "culture of giving," initially in Brazil and Argentina, then in other parts of Latin America, and finally to Europe and Asia. For her, as for many Focolarini, the EOC represented not only a compassionate response to local needs but also a significant reformulation of economics itself. "The new element of giving that was entering the economy," she explained, "involved overcoming the culture of selfishness and accumulation through a culture of relationship that brought communion and sharing into circulation."[49] As Araujo spread the principles of the EOC around the world, she was impressed with how well they worked in places as diverse as Belgium, Italy, Brazil, and the Philippines. In her mind the EOC's successes came from its "correct vision of the nature of man."[50] Businesses that truly embraced the EOC ethic developed a "culture of work" based on "the dignity of the worker," an understanding of business as "an integral and vital part of the political community and civil society," and a "spirituality of work" based on collaboration in the creative work of God.[51]

These new emphases might seem revolutionary, but to Araujo they were simply a restoration of Catholic teaching on the universal destination of goods, the doctrine that "God destined the earth and all it contains for all men and all peoples so that all created things would be shared fairly by all mankind under the guidance of justice tempered by charity." While Enlightenment thinking had made private property absolute, the EOC, in her view, provided a proper corrective to that view, a living example of the Catholic social doctrine that subordinated property rights to the common good.[52] The EOC did not oppose private property but emphasized its social purpose, in accord with Catholic doctrine.

The Aurora school, for example, was a primary school that turned no children away and charged students based on the family's income, with the tuition paid by wealthier families subsidizing the poorer students and helping the school to grow.[53] Founder Ana Maria Nascimento wanted to start a school that could contribute to the goals of the EOC. With Christ's Golden Rule—"do unto others as you would have them do unto you"—as their foundational principle, the teachers and students developed a set of rules that stressed ethical relationships with others, including how to treat "a colleague, a teacher, a government official, a family member, or a visitor," all designed to impart to the students not just academic knowledge but a culture of mutual aid.[54] In other words, the school did not simply provide jobs and use its profits to support Focolare and the poor; it was itself a lay ministry that served rich and poor and that trained the lay leaders of the future. As a "for profit" enterprise it needed to collect enough in tuition to pay salaries and expenses, but that profit was a means to service, not an end in itself.

Another example of a successful EOC business was Prodiet, a pharmaceutical company in Curitiba founded by a Focolare married couple, Armando and Roselí Tortelli, in 1989. Although they were generous with the profits of their small company, in the years before Lubich proposed the EOC the Tortellis were dissatisfied with their own leadership of the business. For instance, they routinely prevaricated on their tax returns, justifying their behavior by telling themselves that the rates were immorally high. Similarly, like almost all Brazilian businesses, Prodiet delayed payment to vendors as a way of letting Brazil's high inflation—as high as 40 percent a month—eat away the value of the bill. Once Prodiet entered the EOC, however, the Tortellis insisted on paying their taxes in full and their bills on time. More important, they began looking at their employees less as cogs in the machine of production and more as personal moral agents, whom they now consulted in regular meetings. These changes in Prodiet caused neither bankruptcy nor dissolution but rather expansion, as the company grew from four employees in 1989 to thirty-nine in 1995, built a new plant, and started marketing their products in new areas. The reasons for this success included the Tortellis' clarified vision for their enterprise, their vendors' great appreciation for being paid promptly, and their employees' satisfaction with their more humane treatment and their greater personal agency in the revamped company.[55] Again, the company's profits aided the poor and the Focolare movement, while creating dozens of decent jobs that provided health care and opportunities for advancement at a time of economic uncertainty. The Focolare charism of unity provided the Tortellis with a practical spirituality that helped them put Christian principles into action.

The Economy of Communion businesses that sprang up in the new industrial park and in other parts of Brazil developed close relationships based on mutual support, both spiritual and commercial. The leaders of the businesses met every year at Mariapolis Araceli for a conference that included both practical and spiritual elements. In this way, executives and managers of the EOC enterprises could share their expertise with each other, encourage each other, and also make contact with like-minded businesses that could meet their various needs. For example, the manager of La Tunica textile factory used EOC firms for accounting, health care, and cleaning products and sold uniforms to the Agape health clinic, the Aurora school, and four other EOC businesses.[56]

By 2012 three industrial parks (the initial Polo Spartaco, and Polo Ginetta in Recife and Polo François Neveux in Belem) had opened and over 100 businesses had affiliated with the EOC in Brazil. It should be emphasized that the EOC was only one aspect of Focolare's mission in Brazil, which included also other work with the poor and the landless, ecumenical dialogue, and a movement for unity among politicians.[57] The EOC had special significance because it brought Catholics and Catholic principles into the marketplace, perhaps the environment most resistant to Christian ethics. But even without the EOC, Focolare had a major impact on Brazil and Latin America. In a region of the world that had seen more than its share of division, inequality, and injustice, the movement's emphasis on unity proved to be a key that unlocked many doors. By connecting rich and poor, the movement served as a living example of Catholicism's practicality. Just as the bishops and activists who fought for justice against the military dictatorships provided evidence for the relevance of the faith, so too the 250,000 lay members of Focolare in Brazil stood as models of how the laity in the late twentieth century could live out their faith, or perhaps on a more basic level, *that* the laity could live out their faith.[58]

## Conclusion

In 1985 Edward Cleary said, "The greatest achievement of the Latin American church has been largely ignored: the church is empowering lay persons to a degree and an extent unknown in most other regions of the world."[59] A quarter century later, he was just as emphatic. As far as the laity was concerned, "Resources and energy only hinted at in the days before Vatican II have been released." There had been "a Copernican revolution" in the Latin American church.[60]

The rise of the laity was not merely important; it was necessary. In the colonial Latin American "Christendom" where everyone was Catholic, lay passivity was unfortunate, but in the religious marketplace of the late twentieth century such passivity would have been deadly. Any form of Catholicism that depended on priests and religious doing all the "heavy lifting" simply had no future. Bombarded by secular radio and television, challenged by muscular Protestantism, and disoriented by the poverty and cultural confusion of urban life, Latin Americans could no longer drift along with the culture and hope to remain Catholic. They needed new forms of religiosity and social organization that would enable them to take ownership of their faith.

The CEBs served as the spiritual lifeline to the urban and rural poor. On the urban peripheries, in particular, small local communities were exactly the form of religious organization that residents needed to escape the deadening poverty and anonymity in which they lived. Bible study, prayer, liturgy, and neighborhood improvement projects all helped to turn isolated individuals into members of a community. The CEB played a particularly significant role in fostering agency among the poor. Despite real failings and the disappointment of many that the CEBs did not reach the hoped-for level of political development, CEBs clearly saved millions of the poorest Latin Americans from disillusionment, despair—and conversion to other religions.

The middle and upper classes had similar needs, but CEBs had less to offer them. Mobile, accustomed to affinity organizations in other spheres of their lives, and more committed to the consumer mentality of urban modernity, they were pickier about what kind of organization they might join but also more able to travel to the meetings of different organizations. The multiplicity of NEMs, therefore, provided a sort of religious marketplace *within* Catholicism. Those with different interests and personality types could find appropriate groups, each one offering a specific path to committed Catholic life.

# 9

# *Universal Christianity: The Internal Dimension*

IN 1982 TWENTY-THREE-YEAR-OLD Rigoberta Menchú, an Ixil Mayan activist from the highlands of Guatemala, sat down in Paris with Venezuelan author Elisabeth Burgos-Debray to record eighteen hours of interviews. Those interviews became *I, Rigoberta Menchú*, a testimonial to her experiences in Guatemala's bloody civil war. Ten years later, Menchú received the Nobel Peace Prize. Her reputation suffered, however, when in 1999 anthropologist David Stoll denounced various discrepancies in the book, including her claim that she had had no formal education, when, he asserted, she had attended several schools. Speaking at the headquarters of the National Council of Churches in New York, Menchú defended the book as "a testimonial that mixes my personal testimony and the testimony of what happened in Guatemala." She had tried to do more than simply recording facts: "I was a survivor, alone in the world, who had to convince the world to look at the atrocities committed in my homeland." In later years Menchú founded a political party and ran for president of Guatemala.[1]

Regardless of the merit of Stoll's charges, Menchú's story was a remarkable one. A poor Mayan girl with little education from an obscure part of a small country succeeded in capturing the world's attention, won the Nobel Prize, toured Europe and the United States, and became a controversial political figure in her home country and around the globe. What makes that story relevant to this book is that Menchú was a product and a protagonist of the revitalization of Latin American Christianity.

Her father, whom she identified as the major influence on her life, was one of the first Ixil Maya catechists trained by Catholic Action as part of the attempt by the Guatemalan church to reintroduce biblical and ethical Catholicism to indigenous populations in the 1950s and 1960s. Menchú herself became a catechist and "Catholic missionary" as a girl: "At first I didn't understand what this Catholic thing was, but I was ready to open myself to it all the same. So I began teaching the doctrine in our community. My work was mostly with the small children. The priest used to come to celebrate Mass, form groups of catechists and leave texts for them to study." Motivated by her Christian commitment and her experience of oppression, at the age of eighteen, she joined a clandestine group working to overthrow the government. Rejecting the non-violent stance of Catholic Action but using the skills that she had learned as a catechist, she began to organize groups of indigenous women, employing the Bible as her "main weapon":

> We began to study the Bible as our main text. . . . It's not something you memorize, it's not just to be talked about and prayed about, and nothing more. It also helped to change the image we had as Catholics and Christians: that God is up there and that God has a great kingdom for we the poor, yet never thinking of our own reality as a reality that we were actually living. But by studying the Scriptures, we did. Take *Exodus*, for example, that's one we studied and analyzed. It talks a lot about the life of Moses who tried to lead his people from oppression and did all he could to free his people.
> —Menchú and Burgos-Debray, *I, Rigoberta Menchú*, 131.

To facilitate her work, Menchú learned to speak Spanish, Mam, Cakchiquel, and Tzutuhil. She also developed close relationships with mestizos whom she had previously seen as part of the oppressor class, and they worked together to organize peasants. When the military threatened her life in 1980, she sought refuge in Mexico, where she became an advocate for indigenous Guatemalans and met progressive Catholics from around the world. Despite the dangers, she soon returned to Guatemala to join the Vicente Menchú Revolutionary Christians, for whom she recruited progressive Catholics. "My job," she said, "is above all carrying papers into the interior or to the towns, and organizing people, at the same time practicing with them the light of the Gospel."[2]

In short, Menchú's story was intertwined with the arrival of a new kind of Christianity in the Guatemalan highlands. Traditional Ixil religion combined elements of Catholicism with a pantheon of indigenous spirits and usually applied only to Ixils living in Ixil communities. The faith brought by Catholic Action, by contrast, had a well-developed ethics and applied universally. Its adoption by the Menchú family led Rigoberta to take up work as a catechist and to embrace ever larger notions of who constituted "her people." Her encounter with the Bible, a collection of writings from Jews and Greeks living on the other side of the planet thousands of years before her birth, opened up a new world for her and for the many women with whom she shared its message. At first she embraced other Ixils, then other Mayas, and then, in her most difficult step, mestizo peasants. Eventually she came to see Guatemala not as an unalterably oppressive entity but as her nation, a community of persons that she and her allies could transform. Her later experiences in Mexico, Europe, and the United States as a spokesperson for indigenous Guatemala only deepened the universal nature of her project. She appealed to people around the world for justice in her home country, counting on, and assuming, a universal ethic of justice.

Menchú's life demonstrated the ways in which a universal version of Christianity could have profound effects when embraced by those who had previously adhered to more localized religions. A religion that claims to apply to everyone—everyone in the community, in the region, in the nation, and in the world—and that has universal standards of conduct is so different from a religion that applies only to a specific place or group that it cannot help but transform the individuals, cultures, and nations that adopt it. To embrace such a religion was to begin a journey whose end could not be known and that could take believers out of remote communities and into dialogue with the whole world. It could even lead from an Ixil village in Guatemala to the Nobel awards ceremony in Norway.

Christianity's rebirth in Latin America was marked by the return of universal Christianity—a religion for all people, everywhere, containing truths and ethical standards applicable to all human beings. It is evident that before this rebirth, much of indigenous religion was not universal in this sense, but it is equally true that much of urban mestizo Catholicism was not truly catholic either. In focusing on saints, rituals, and holy days, many Catholics lost sight of (or never knew) the radical nature of their religion, such as its calls for justice, charity, and world evangelization, all based on the religion's claim, contained in its very name, to apply to all people. This chapter focuses on the indigenous appropriation of universal versions of Christianity in Mexico and the Andes, but a similar process took place among mestizos and other groups in cities and towns across the region. Conversion to Protestantism, involvement in a CEB, or commitment to an NEM brought millions of Latin Americans through a transition from local and parochial religion to universal versions of the faith. Although the birth of universal religion in indigenous communities often led to more visible and dramatic transformations because those communities tended to be socially, economically, and linguistically marginalized, universal religion of course had important ramifications among nonindigenous Latin Americans as well.

There were two agents of the renewal of universal Christianity in Latin America. First, the Protestant missionary movement from the United States and Europe was acting on Christ's command to make disciples "of all nations" and to be witnesses "in Jerusalem, and in all Judea and Samaria, and to the ends of the earth."[3] Second, the Vatican was attempting to save the region from that same Protestant missionary movement and from other threats such as Marxism, secularism, and urban despair. Protestant missionaries consciously and programmatically propagated their religion, even as Catholic popes, bishops, catechists, and missionaries attempted to counter the Protestant advance with a renewed emphasis on the universal nature of Catholicism and with concerted efforts to reevangelize the faithful. At the same time, universal Christianity also responded to the inchoate longing of millions of individual Latin Americans to make sense of massive societal phenomena like urbanization, industrialization, nationalism, and globalization. As powerful as folk religion had been in the "microverse" of rural communities, it simply did not transfer well to the "macroverse" of mass society. Thus, the intentional efforts of Catholic and Protestant elites met a growing popular search for religion compatible with industrial modernity.

When Latin Americans did accept universal versions of Christianity, this had both internal and external effects. Whether they were indigenous converts to evangelical Protestantism, Catholics newly committed to the ethical and missionary dimensions of the faith, or slum dwellers led from functional atheism to Pentecostalism, the new religions changed the way people saw the world and connected them directly to streams of thought, religious practices, and institutional structures that stretched across the globe. Conversion therefore functioned as an opening of the individual to the universal, a liberation from the local, the familiar, and the culturally bounded. As happened for Rigoberta Menchu, in many cases the Bible played a major role in this process, opening the eyes of those who studied it to the ways in which their circumstances related to other peoples and places and historical periods and to larger issues of morality and divine plans. In this way the most obscure, isolated, and impoverished people found themselves at the heart of history, part of God's plan, participating in a divine drama, connected to the great events of their day and to fellow believers around the world. They perceived themselves as equally made in God's image, equally able to hear God's call in their own tongue, and equally equipped with spiritual gifts.[4]

## *Totonac Cosmopolitan*

When he was young boy, Manuel Arenas was laughed out of school. As a Totonac Indian, Arenas knew only a few words of Spanish when he first attended the only primary school within walking distance of his home in central Mexico. The mestizo students, and even worse, the mestizo teacher, looked down on Indians in general and Arenas in particular. When he did not understand simple instructions the class burst into laughter and the teacher singled him out for special humiliation. Embarrassed and angry, Arenas quit school, despite his strong desire to learn to read.[5]

In 1941, when Arenas was eleven years old, Summer Institute of Linguistics (SIL) linguists from the United States asked him to help them translate the Bible into Totonac. Impressed by the message he was learning, Arenas converted to Protestantism and became an indispensable aid to the translation process. In 1946 the linguists arranged for him to learn Spanish and to attend primary and secondary school in Mexico City, after which they also secured him spots at a Canadian Bible college, where he learned English, and at Dallas Bible College, from which he graduated in 1957. He then earned a bachelor of education degree from the University of Chicago in 1960 and did graduate work at the University of Erlangen in Germany. If that had been the end of the story, Arenas might serve as an example of the ways in which conversion could open up vast horizons. However, the important part of Arenas's story was not so much its rags-to-riches element—catalysts other than Christianity surely could pull indigenous people out of their communities and send them around the world—as the part of his life that came after all of his academic achievements.[6]

Arenas returned from Germany in 1968 and started the Totonac Cultural Center in his home state of Puebla to train pastors, to improve agricultural productivity, and to serve the health needs of his Totonac people. Over the next decade he built up a Bible school and pastoral training center, a demonstration farm, and a health clinic. By 1985 the center had graduated sixty students, including thirty-five who were serving as pastors in Totonac churches, all of whom had studied the Bible, theology, and practical pastoral issues in the Totonac language and in a manner sensitive to Totonac culture. Arenas used contacts he had made through the SIL and through his travels in Europe to solicit funds for the center and to bring in a steady string of volunteer nurses, doctors, and dentists to supplement his small full-time staff. The medical clinic provided needed services not just to Totonacs but to any sick and suffering people in the area.[7]

Arenas turned the tables on the usual cultural attitude in Mexico, in which European cultural superiority is often assumed. Although appreciative of what he had learned in the United States, Mexico City, and Europe, Arenas had no difficulty in asserting its inappropriateness for Totonacs or, in some cases, its clear inferiority. For instance, mestizo and foreign visitors gave him advice about how he should run the center. "They come with plans that are good, but not for Totonacs," he said. "I have to say to them, 'These are good plans for your country, but they will not work for the Totonac culture.'" Similarly, Arenas understood the benefits of technology well enough to start an influential Totonac language radio program on a local station, but he simultaneously criticized the devastating effects of North American television programs on traditional Totonac culture. He was worldly enough to have a romantic relationship with a North American woman and to name his dogs Solzhenitsyn and Golda Meir, but he devoted his adult life to serving indigenous people. The universal version of Christianity that Arenas learned from the SIL translators made him a citizen of the world but it also led him home again. It allowed him to learn from people and cultures all over the world, but it also helped him to see the riches of his own culture. "When I was a child," said Arenas, "I hated my Indianness." However, after his conversion and education he could say, "I want to tell you that today, as I speak to you, I am proud of my Totonac Indian heritage. . . . God has given this to me and I also encourage my Totonac friends to be proud of their heritage."[8]

Clearly, some forms of universalism could devalue the local and the particular, but in the Christian case the logic of sin, incarnation, and redemption and the practice of translation tended to revalorize formerly despised cultures.[9] For Arenas and for millions like him, the coming of universal forms of Christianity facilitated an escape from local religion, while simultaneously providing the philosophical and ethical tools to judge Western culture itself.

## *Mission and Liberation*

To prevent exactly the sort of Protestant conversion Arenas experienced, in 1955 Pope Pius XII (1939–58) asked for more missionaries to be sent to Latin America. He followed up in 1958 by setting up the Pontifical Commission for Latin America to coordinate aid to Latin America.[10] He believed that the combination of a severe priest shortage and the challenges of urbanization, industrialization, Protestantism, and Marxism had created a crisis that was too much for Latin America to deal with on its own. His successor, Pope John XXIII (1958–63), who shared Pius's fears, sponsored meetings in 1959 that encouraged bishops from the United States, Canada, and Latin America to work together to help the Latin American church.[11] In 1961 John called for a "prompt, timely, and effective" effort in which each American religious province would "contribute to Latin America in the next ten years a tithe—ten percent—of its present membership."[12] The next pope, Paul VI (1963–78) seemed equally committed, stating in 1964 that the Latin American church had reached "a decisive hour." He called for more European priests to go to the region and challenged North American dioceses to adopt the 10 percent goal that had earlier been applied only to religious.[13] Although these initiatives did not succeed in sending the hoped-for tens of thousands of missionaries to Latin America, they did play a role in bringing 3,391 American missionaries by 1968. Although the numbers declined over the next decade, in 1977 there were still 2,293 North Americans serving in the region.[14]

The growing unity of the Latin American bishops under CELAM, their closer connections to the Vatican, and the presence of North American and European missionaries throughout the region all worked to awaken much of Latin American Catholicism to the universal aspects of the faith. Bishops gained a greater understanding of the universal church and communicated this understanding to their priests, who spread it through their dioceses, as did missionaries.

The Andean highlands of South America illustrate the liberating effect on indigenous communities. Much depended on the bishops. If they somehow found the resources to send missionaries with a universal message expressed in the vernacular language into indigenous communities, they often saw these communities adopt universal Catholicism; if they continued the long-standing policy of sending Spanish-speaking priests to visit communities sporadically, they left the door open for Protestant conversions.

Because of the physical barrier of the region's rugged terrain and the linguistic barrier of priests and pastoral agents unable or unwilling to speak indigenous languages, bishops faced challenges in deciding how to provide pastoral care to the indigenous communities. Unfortunately for those bishops, the default tactic of using monolingual Spanish-speaking priests to provide periodic sacramental ministry in effect conceded the field to Protestantism and syncretic religions. The religion of northern Potosí, Bolivia, provides an example. The Aymara peasants of the region saw themselves as Catholics but practiced a religion that included a non-eternal sun God, blood offerings to mountain gods, the use of sheep droppings from miraculous sites as talismans, and a theology in which Jesus Christ did not play an important role. They attended Mass not to receive communion but because they believed that God and the saints needed propitiation in the form of food (bread and wine) and money. They preferred to pay a priest to celebrate Mass and were angered by foreign priests who refused their offers of payment because they felt that they were thereby being prevented from making an effective offering. Large portions of their religion, they believed, had to be hidden from priests and other outsiders.[15]

Andrew Orta's study of Catholic missionaries who arrived in the Andean highlands in the 1960s and 1970s demonstrates that they quickly became frustrated. The missionaries felt trapped by roles as "functionaries of the sacraments," ministering to a people who had been baptized but seemed to have no interest in being evangelized or catechized.[16] Although such indigenous Andeans considered themselves Christians, their religion was not a universal one. It did not apply to all people in all places and, in fact, emphasized its local nature. Its clandestine aspects *guaranteed* that it could not, in fact, be exported to new areas, since only insiders knew the secret lore, and they were not supposed to share it. Although Andean religion varied by region and ethnic group, Aymara religion is broadly representative of what most indigenous communities practiced: syncretistic, oriented more toward saints than toward Christ, based on a sacred local geography, and using Catholic rituals for idiosyncratic purposes.

For Quichua speakers in central highland Ecuador in the days before the agrarian reform of the 1960s, the old folk Catholic religion was so intertwined with the hacienda system that the hacienda's overseer and other privileged peasants often held the top religious positions of *fundador* and *regidor*, regardless of their knowledge of Catholicism or personal moral qualities. Criminal acts and religious laxity both fell under the fundador and regidor's purview, and both could be punished with whippings. The moral-religious order, therefore, was thoroughly enmeshed in the exploitative nature of hacienda life and placed an emphasis on indigenous traditions and respect for authority rather than on justice or Catholic doctrine. When agrarian reform broke up many of the great estates in the 1960s, it freed indigenous peasants not just from the exploitive labor regime but also from its attendant religious system. By the 1970s, under the leadership of Bishop Leonidas Proaño, priests in the region introduced a liberationist approach to Christianity that identified many aspects of popular religion as oppressive and emphasized the Bible instead. In the 1980s Proaño created the Centro de Formación Indígena (Indigenous Formation Center) to train indigenous catechists to lead Bible studies and to teach Catholic doctrine in their own languages. In most cases these young literate men replaced the largely illiterate older generation of regidors and fundadors as the religious authorities in their communities, an important change because the catechists' authority came not from a social hierarchy dependent on the oppressive hacienda system but rather from the institutional Catholic Church and from their knowledge of Catholic doctrine and practice.[17]

Looking back, one of the catechists laughed at the old system, in which those in authority demanded respect but knew little about the faith: "When they were asked about God, they didn't know where God lives, nothing." In the new system, Bible study conducted in Quichua and using a vernacular translation of the Bible or, if none was available, a spontaneous paraphrase of the Spanish Bible, became the dominant ritual. Barry Lyons notes, "Indigenous Catholics sometimes say of their new access to the Bible that the priests have begun to let them in on the knowledge that the priests previously kept to themselves" and that the Bible studies represented a form of the "democratization of moral authority in relation to ethnic and ecclesiastical hierarchies." Simply interpreting a passage from the Bible meant "assuming a role formerly reserved for priests, who were almost invariably mestizos." Some believers used their study of the scriptures to reject traditional aspects of the cult of the saints, as their progressive pastoral agents often hoped that they would. However, the Aymara students of the Bible did not necessarily follow the liberationist line and often frustrated progressive catechists with more conservative readings of biblical passages.[18] In a real sense, then, the extension of liberationist Catholicism into indigenous communities in the Ecuador highlands expanded the horizons of indigenous peasants, making them religious agents rather than religious recipients.

A similar dynamic took hold in the 1960s in highland Bolivia. Perturbed by the indigenous emphasis on festival and ritual without regard for doctrine, Catholic missionaries began to lay down the law: "We won't come anymore to do the fiestas unless you name a catechist who becomes your delegate responsible for the continuation of the Church community here."[19] Slowly, as the catechists learned the rudiments of the faith, a more universal version of Catholicism began to trickle into highland Aymara communities. Then, in the 1970s and 1980s, in some Bolivian Aymara communities liberationist priests came out against drunkenness and religious practices involving indigenous deities. They proposed instead a form of Catholicism based on prayer, study, and singing. Yatiris, the Aymara shamans, became controversial figures, rejected by those who accepted the new universal version of Catholicism but affirmed by others as protectors of the Aymara religion. Meanwhile, catechists emerged—a new type of religious leader, specialists not in arcane ritual but in a body of doctrine and a method of interpreting scripture.[20]

Even when "inculturation" became the theme of the 1990s and priests tried harder to treat Aymara culture with respect, they still were presenting an outside standard that stood over and above that culture. Thus, when a missionary priest tried to help the Aymara discern "a way of being Aymara the way Jesus would have been Aymara," he was simultaneously expressing his respect for Aymara culture and suggesting that Jesus would have had a certain critical perspective on that culture. Consequently, anthropologist Andrew Orta concludes, "the multiculturalism of inculturation is predicated upon a Christian universalism."[21]

## Andean Protestants

As successful as Catholic evangelization was in many Andean communities, it did not reach all of them. At the same time that Proaño and other proactive bishops were reinvigorating Andean Catholicism, Protestants were attempting their own evangelization project. In fact, something similar to Manuel Arenas's transformation happened on a larger scale in Chimborazo province of the central highlands of Ecuador, the same region where Catholic catechists also were at work. During the period of rapid social change in the 1960s, as agrarian reform laws ended the hacienda system and the Catholic Church let go its alliance with the landholding class, North American Protestants of the Gospel Missionary Union developed culturally sensitive and ultimately successful methods of ministry in the region, leading to over 15,000 Quichua (Ecuadoran Quechua) converts by 1985. The missionaries began bilingual Spanish-Quichua schools, started health clinics staffed by Quichua speakers, used Quichua in worship, and started a Quichua radio station. Most important, in 1973 they finished a Quichua translation of the Bible, which created a new Quichua cultural dynamic. As Christian Gros has written: "Protestantism allowed its followers to construct for themselves a new positive self-image, that of 'civilized' Indians freed from alcoholism, ignorance and vice hitherto sustained by 'folk' Catholicism and the conservative elements within the Catholic Church who encouraged it."[22] Although the universal Protestantism adopted by many Quichua speakers clearly changed their culture, it also provided them with a tool to strengthen and protect their ethnic identity. The doubling of the number of Protestant churches in Chimborazo to 320 in the decade after 1976 was coupled with a sort of cultural takeover, as Protestantism became the dominant religion of the region. By 1992 scholars observed that "in no sense" were converts experiencing their religion as something foreign. They had achieved "a high degree of self-management of their religious, economic, educational and cultural affairs."[23]

The indigenous Protestants of Chimborazo became agents and protagonists, throwing off the passivity and subservience of the old regime. This new stance came partly from the freedom that grew from the new Protestant moral code. Most obviously, Protestants did not drink and therefore had extra resources to devote to their families and to commerce or agriculture. New networks enabled Quichua believers to work together on social and political issues, which in turn increased local autonomy and prosperity. The congregation served as the basic social network and facilitated cooperation and mutual support among believers in a given locale. Then, starting in 1966, different Protestant churches joined together to found the Indigenous Evangelical Association of Chimborazo. At first the association concerned itself mostly with protecting Protestants against persecution. In 1982, with the worst of the persecution over and with 300 churches now members, the association broadened its agenda to include goals such as "to improve the moral, cultural, economic, sanitary, and professional standard of the natives of the Chimborazo Province" and "to struggle for national representation of the peasant sector."[24]

The association lobbied aid and development organizations for improvement projects and created "a savings and credit agency, an agricultural supply store, water technicians who assist with the installation of water wells, and potato 'outlets' in the communities." On several occasions in the 1980s it entered national politics to fight for indigenous and peasant interests. It also took over the radio station that the Gospel Missionary Union had established and ran annual cultural festivals in which musical groups from different villages, wearing indigenous garb, performed and competed. "This event," notes sociologist Conrad Kanagy, "provided an opportunity for the peasants to enact their ethnic identity within the context of Protestant values and norms."[25] In more recent years, indigenous Protestants from Chimborazo participated in the Federación Evangélica Indigena Nacional del Ecuador (FEINE, National Evangelical Indigenous Federation of Ecuador), which represented Ecuador's 2.5 million indigenous Protestants. FEINE played a vocal role in national politics, with one of its leaders becoming the second highest-ranking official in the department of social welfare in 2004.[26] In short, conversion to the universal religion of Protestantism transformed highland Quichua communities in Ecuador, making them more prosperous, autonomous, and assertive, at once more confident in their ethnic identity and more involved in national politics.

## Inculturation in Chiapas

In the last sixty years, perhaps nowhere has indigenous universalism taken hold more powerfully than in the state of Chiapas in Mexico. As mentioned in Chapter 1, the SIL's translation work there catalyzed the Protestant conversions of tens of thousands of Tzeltals, Tzotzils, and members of other indigenous groups. Despite murder, expulsion from their communities, and other forms of persecution, indigenous converts became active proponents of the new faith as witnesses and as medical missionaries throughout the Chiapas highlands. Meanwhile, under the leadership of Bishop Samuel Ruiz (1960–99), almost 8,000 indigenous catechists transformed the nature of Catholicism in hundreds of highland Tzeltal and Tzotzil Maya communities, some of them exactly the same ones that had seen massive Protestant awakenings. (Once again it should be pointed out that Protestant success by no means sounded the death knell of Catholicism—it often acted as a spur to Catholic revitalization.)

In 1960, as a young bishop with only thirteen priests—none of them speakers of indigenous languages—to serve the diocese's many isolated indigenous communities, Ruiz faced a particularly daunting assignment.[27] The religion in most indigenous villages, Ruiz came to realize, was "sandwich religion," with a "pagan filling and Christian outward form." Despite the facade of traditional Christianity, in this sort of religion the saints represented "a new version of the ancestors," the Eucharist involved the reception of "the holy sun," and crosses served as "doors of communication with the ancestors."[28] To make matters worse, Mayan religion as practiced in most indigenous communities had evolved into a system in which local elders, enriched by their control of liquor sales and community land, dominated local politics in a heavy-handed and self-serving manner in the name of "tradition." Ruiz's experience of Vatican II In his early years as a bishop and his participation in a CELAM missions conference in 1968 further developed his view of the relationship between mission and culture. Influenced also by Gustavo Gutiérrez's emerging ideas on liberation, the young bishop came to believe that mission as long practiced in Mexico had gone off track by insisting that Indians adopt mestizo culture as a mark of spiritual maturity. Instead, he proposed, missionaries should work "not to create one great universal monoculture" but "to make the Word flesh . . . according to the particular characteristics of the culture." Properly presented, the gospel would produce "both the development of its individual characteristics and unity with other cultures." The practical means to such "inculturation" was the creation of a corps of indigenous catechists who could speak the languages of the many communities in the diocese.[29]

Starting in 1962, Ruiz sponsored yearly training sessions that brought indigenous catechists to the city of San Cristóbal de las Las Casas. At first the content was "utterly opaque linguistically and socio-culturally" and was presented in Spanish to the largely monolingual catechists-in-training, with rudimentary translation provided by the few among them who knew some Spanish. Despite the deficiencies of the early program, from the start the young men who attended responded positively. The prayers, ethical principles, and introduction to the Bible that they encountered there contrasted with traditional Tzotzil and Tzeltal religion in intriguing ways. Most important, biblical literacy and the emphasis on the immorality of drunkenness (which the catechists interpreted as a total proscription of alcohol) proved to be life-changing innovations. The exploitative social-political system of the highlands hinged on indigenous elders who controlled the alcohol integral to the community's religious practices. The simple concept of abstinence thus proved both religiously shocking and politically provocative. Similarly, the emphasis on the Bible as a focus of religion challenged the supremacy of "costumbre," the supposedly ancient religious customs and rituals that in many cases necessitated drinking and inebriation.[30]

For many catechists, especially when the training sessions became more attuned to their needs during the 1970s and 1980s, the time in San Cristóbal became a transformative experience, a sort of conversion:

> The leisure of time away from milpa [field] and machete, wielding the intellectual tools and experiencing the material privileges marking Ladino space—pens and notebooks, texts and clocks, regular (if simple) meals, and, not least, the hygienic advantages of floored and cemented housing with indoor plumbing—provoked fascination and incited critical thought. During courses, peasant catechists paused from their normally unceasing material labor on a symbolically-constructed platform from which they could reimagine themselves.
>
> —Chojnacki, *Indigenous Apostles*, 112–3.

The inability of the teachers at the school to speak Tzeltal or Tzotzil amplified the experience. In Bible studies, the teachers simply pointed their students to a passage in the Spanish Bible (or the Tzotzil Bible after it became available 1997) and had them discuss it in their own languages. Even before they returned to their villages, then, the catechists were crafting their own Tzeltal or Tzotzil Catholicism, with less input from diocesan officials than might have been expected. Their interaction with biblical texts served at once as an encounter with new ideas and concepts, a means of becoming more bilingual, and an experience in which they "discovered and appropriated their own intellectual resources." Indigenous catechists came to embrace the Bible in a deep way, to such an extent that in daily life they were rarely seen without their personal Bibles and exegesis of its texts became their most valued form of work.[31]

In the 1970s and 1980s, for example, Tzotzil catechists in Santa Maria Magdalenas became increasingly critical of their community's social and religious practices. They noticed both excessive alcohol consumption, with people "lying drunk on the side of the road," and the unexplained existence of plots of unused communal farmland during a "land shortage" so severe that most young men had to seek work on distant coffee plantations or in faraway oil fields. Their previous immersion in the books of Genesis and Exodus, combined with the experience of economic exile in the plantations and oil fields, brought them a new critical perspective. "How is it possible?" they asked themselves, that their people had allowed drink to enslave them, "that so much of what land they did possess was haphazardly tended or given to sugarcane supplying *trapiches* (domestic distilleries) rather than corn," and that much communally owned land was not being used at all? The Bible's story of exodus and liberation gave them the tools to analyze their own servitude and to work for their own freedom. Eventually, through their Bible studies the catechists formed groups of Catholics critical of traditional religion and ready to reject drink and to embrace hard work.[32]

Drinking occupied center stage in the struggle between the old and new religions because of the centrality of rationality in the new religion:

Just as trago [drinking] submerges consciousness in the body, the text, and by extension those who possess it, interpolates between the body and consciousness, giving rise to reflective inquiry. Within the critical space thus opened, the autonomous human agent arises and the world becomes available to critical scrutiny. Put another way, whereas traditional obligation entailed involution and loss of control, the catechist's criticism, directed at ritual coercion, manifests freedom for autonomous, deliberated action in, and more, on the world.

—(Chojnacki, *Indigenous Apostles*, 142.)

In the community of Santa Maria Magdalenas catechists led a successful revolt that freed them from the necessity of taking on onerous ritual obligations. The new group of Catholics, influenced by their study of the Bible, not only rejected the drinking and domination associated with costumbre but also placed more of an emphasis on the traditional Catholic understanding of baptism and the other sacraments. They revolutionized sainthood, rejecting the community's concept of a saint as "an implacable divinity imposing a propitiatory regime," a sort of spiritual feudal lord, and introduced the more orthodox view of saints as historical Christians to be emulated. Where, for example, indigenous traditionalists paid a great deal of attention to the physical image of a town's patron saint—"washing, clothing, censing, carrying, and in general guarding [the] icon against any form of violation"—the new breed of indigenous Catholic had almost no interest in such activities.[33]

This new indigenous Catholicism was not entirely orthodox, however, and in fact adopted Protestant-type beliefs, particularly emphasis on the Bible. The catechists turned so far from the perceived idolatry of the traditional cult of the saints that they no longer prayed to saints as orthodox Catholicism encouraged. The fact was, though, that, although deprived of significant input from the hierarchy because of the language barrier, they nevertheless *desired* to be orthodox and were striving to live their lives by biblical principles.

When combined with the similar process that took place in other Mayan communities in Chiapas through Protestant evangelization, as described in Chapter 1, the indigenous communities of the state were transformed in the second half of the twentieth century. Conversion to universal versions of Christianity, whether Protestant or Catholic, freed thousands of Tzeltals, Tzotzils, and other indigenous people from the petty tyrants who often dominated their communities in the name of tradition. Indigenous Chiapans stood up for religious liberty first, but they opened the way for a political struggle as well. On January 1, 1994, the day when the North American Free Trade Agreement (NAFTA) went into effect, the indigenous rebels of the Ejército Zapatista de Liberación Nacional (Zapatista Army of National Liberation, EZLN) invaded the city of San Cristóbal de Las Casas and launched a campaign against globalization and neo-liberalism that attracted attention around the world. The Marxist leader of the EZLN, Subcomandante Marcos, might have denied it, but decades of Protestant and Catholic evangelization and catechesis at least partially prepared the ground for the revolt. Without the steady spread of universal Christianity throughout the region, it is doubtful that many indigenous Chiapans would have been willing to risk their lives for, as the name of their army phrased it, *"national* liberation."

## Neither Pawns nor Clones

The coming of Protestantism and doctrinal, ethical Catholicism to indigenous communities, often portrayed as a tragedy comparable to genocide, occupied much of the attention and energy of anthropologists and other social scientists in the 1970s and 1980s. In the "Declaration of Barbados," for example, leading anthropologists blasted missionary activity among indigenous people as "ethnocentric," "essentially discriminatory," and "hostile" to indigenous culture.[34] A group of Mexican social scientists devoted a conference to condemning the SIL for "ideological domination" of indigenous communities.[35] An international group of scholars contributed a similar series of denunciations in a book that implied that the SIL was preaching a gospel of Americanism.[36] Without dismissing all such concerns—there were missionary insensitivities, abuses, and injustices— more recent work by social scientists has painted a different picture of mission and conversion in Latin American indigenous life. For many indigenous Latin Americans, such as Rigoberta Menchú, Manuel Arenas, Protestant and Catholic Andeans, and Chiapan catechists, universal religion enabled both a strengthening of ethnic identity and more confident and effective interaction with the world around them.

Social scientists also expressed concerns about the spread of Protestantism more generally. Most famously, David Stoll asked *Is Latin America Turning Protestant?* in a book that featured televangelist Jimmy Swaggart on its cover. Stoll went to great length to link various fundamentalist and right-wing organizations from the United States to the growth of Latin American Protestantism. The clear implication was that Protestantism served as a vehicle for right-wing infiltration of the region. As with the charges against the missionaries working with indigenous Latin Americans, many of the connections that Stoll pointed to were real. Pat Robertson, for instance, did indeed support Guatemalan Pentecostals with unsavory political associations.[37] The reality, though, was that by the time Stoll published his book in 1990, Latin American Protestantism had been thoroughly indigenized. Its explosive growth was coming not from US denominations but from homegrown Pentecostal movements. Additionally, its most prominent evangelical leaders were adopting a critical stance toward the United States and American evangelicalism.

For example, Peruvian Samuel Escobar stated clearly: "There is not a tongue into which the Christian message cannot be translated" and "any language is a good vehicle for the gospel."[38] "This means," he said, "that the gospel dignifies every culture as a valid and acceptable vehicle for God's revelation. Conversely, this also relativizes every culture; there is no 'sacred' culture or language that may be considered as the only vehicle God might use."[39] At the same time, he was critical of the attitudes of North Americans and insistent that Latin Americans should avoid their errors. For Latin Americans it was absolutely necessary to abandon "an imperialist mentality" and the "information, technology, and gospel" mindset that had infected North Americans. Latin Americans could perform a great service to world mission if they underwent a "change of spirit" that recovered "the priorities of the person of Jesus."[40] It was extremely unfortunate, he suggested, that Latin American Protestants were still being influenced by the "quantifying rationality of American technological culture" and "expensive Western models of missionary organization" because the explosion of Christianity in the global South "was only possible when indigenous Christians became free from the stifling control of foreign missionary agencies."[41]

Similarly, Antonia Leonora van der Meer, a Brazilian who had served as a missionary in Angola for ten years, asserted, "In reality, mission is the main reason the Christian church exists. . . . To many of us as Brazilian and Latin American Evangelicals, mission has become a very important issue. We are still very excited in discovering that *we* are called to be involved in mission; that God chooses *us*, enables *us*, and supports *us*; and that he can use *our lives* for his glory to be a blessing to others."[42] However, Van der Meer believed, while the peoples of Africa, Asia, and Latin America displayed "solidarity and amazing generosity and hospitality," the residents of the global North had serious spiritual problems: "They are dominated by evils such as idol-worship of the god Mammon and exclusion of 'have-nots,' and they make people more isolated, defensive, competitive, and egotistic." Some Brazilian missionaries were falling into the same mindset as earlier generations of American and British missionaries, but she and many like her had come to believe that "it is a great privilege to be a missionary who does not come from a country with a powerful economy, whose country does not represent any threat whatsoever, and who cannot be expected to solve all financial problems that arise." Lacking the economic and political trappings of a global superpower, Brazilians had the freedom "to serve as partners, as equals" in the developing world.[43]

Thus, Latin Americans were combining universal Christianity with a distinctive missionary vision that, they hoped, would enable them to make a distinctive contribution to the growth of Christianity around the world. Accepting universal Christianity did not turn Latin American Christians into pawns of the United States or the Vatican; rather, it gave them a voice and empowered them on the world stage. From social activists like Rigoberta Menchú, to educators like Miguel Arenas, to missionaries like Antonia Leonora van der Meer, Latin Americans who accepted universal versions of Christianity did not become tame copies of metropolitan elites. They did not become clones of Pat Robertson or Jerry Falwell. They did not assume an otherworldly passivity. Instead, they became bold and active leaders who were not afraid to challenge the pieties of their brother and sister Christians in the North. Universal Christianity also led them out of Latin America and into the rest of the world as confident heralds of religious beliefs that were by no means stale duplicates of ideas from the United States or Europe.

# Universal Christianity: From Latin America to the Ends of the Earth

"I AM AFRAID I will not be able to express without tears how much I love you Americans. And do you know why?" asked Mexican theologian José Porfirio Miranda. "Well, you all who have come to this meeting did not say to yourselves, 'Can anything good come out of Latin America?' That is why I love you."[1] In August 1975 at the "Theology in the Americas" conference at Sacred Heart Seminary in Detroit, Miranda and eight other Latin Americans, including an Argentine historian, a Peruvian sociologist, and several priests, explained liberation theology to an audience of Catholic and Protestant theologians and activists from around the United States. The week-long conference, organized by Chilean priest Sergio Torres to bring leading Latin American liberationist thinkers into contact with interested North Americans, marked liberation theology's official arrival in the United States. From the start, the Latin Americans directly challenged their American interlocutors. "Any liberation that does not include the elimination of capitalism," Javier Iguíñiz asserted, "will be nothing more than a lovely achievement erected upon the hunger and misery of many races."[2] Hugo Assman went so far as to say that if his audience could not accept that the United States was oppressing Latin America, "We do not have the same reference for our hearing of the word of God; and we do not have the same faith."[3]

Most participants received the new Latin American theology respectfully, but there was a great deal of discussion about how it applied to North America. A panel with black theologians became particularly heated, as Assman asked if they were not developing a "defensive theology" that neglected other oppressed peoples of the world. James Cone, leader of a new generation of black theologians, replied "Most of the North American participants here are people I suspect [and] people I've been fighting against." In that context he had to focus on black-white issues rather than on the global struggle for liberation. Another participant added that black theologians were suspicious of liberation theology as a "white theology" that was as foreign to African Americans as the mainstream theology they were trying to overthrow. A Latin American responded with his own skepticism about black theology: "What is the goal of black liberation and black theology? If the goal of black liberation is to become an American citizen equal to all others, I think that perhaps black theology is an American theology. Are free blacks to be part of an imperial nation that is the oppressor of other nations? That is imperialist theology."[4]

In 1986, at a less contentious conference in Switzerland, Manuel Arenas, the Totonac convert discussed in the previous chapter, spoke about his conversion and his work among the Totonacs. Afterward, a Swiss man confronted him for leaving the traditional Totonac religion and for trying to convince other Totonacs to do the same. All religions were equal, asserted the man, and Arenas was doing a disservice to himself and to any Totonacs he had converted. Arenas responded by outlining some of the negative aspects of traditional Totonac religion but then focused on the man's relativistic assumptions. "I grew up fearing the many evil spirits of the forest, of the stream, the earth, and the trees," Arenas said. "But when the New Testament Scriptures were translated into our language and Totonacs began to believe and accept Jesus Christ into their lives, I saw those fears gradually disappear. That is why I want all Totonacs and everyone to become true believers in Jesus Christ. Only he can take away fear and give hope and peace, for this life and for the life to come." After a conversation of several hours, Arenas led the man to accept Jesus as his savior.[5]

The conferences in Detroit and Switzerland, although quite different, highlighted the ways in which universal religion could propel Latin Americans into the role of international religious protagonists. The new-found maturity and confidence of Latin American Christians reversed the traditional missionary relationship. Instead of merely receiving missionaries and religious messages from the developed world, in the 1970s Latin Americans began sending their own messages, and many of them explicitly embraced Christ's call to be witnesses "in Jerusalem, and in all Judea and Samaria, and to the ends of the earth."[6] The *internal* experience of universal religion led to the *external* project of spreading the message to the far corners of the globe.

## Owning the Mission

Although there had been some Protestant support for missions outside of Latin America since early in the twentieth century, the 1976 missionary congress of the Aliança Biblica Universitaria (University Biblical Alliance) in Curitiba, Brazil, marked the beginning of significant modern Latin American Protestant involvement in world missions. Inspired by a teacher's experience at the Lausanne world evangelization conference, the congress brought together 500 students from Brazil and fifty from other countries to study the missionary identity of the church. The concluding statement, the "Declaration of Curitiba," expressed the students' deep concern about "the lack of missionary vision in the Latin American church" and asserted that "the church that is not missionary is not the church." The conference had a profound effect on those who attended— several students headed off to do missionary work in Italy, Bolivia, Ecuador, and Africa—and started a boom in Latin American missions that sent over 1,000 Protestant missionaries to other regions of the world by 1982.[7]

In 1987 in Sao Paulo, a much larger conference, the Congreso Misionero Iberoamericano (COMIBAM, or Ibero-American Missionary Congress) attracted 3,100 evangelical leaders from around Latin America. As the conference organizers had hoped, the delegates affirmed that Latin America was becoming an active participant in world missions, despite the continued poverty of much of the region. Similarly, in 1992, after two meetings that had focused on evangelizing Latin America, the third Congreso Latinoamericano de Evangelización (Latin American Congress of Evangelization, CLADE) took on a new focus as it became clear that Latin Americans had a responsibility for evangelizing beyond their own continent. As Brazilian missiologist Valdir Steuernagel made clear, if evangelicals affirmed the universal nature of their faith, they could not limit their concern to Latin America alone: "The confession of the universal character of the lordship of Jesus Christ takes a deeply missiological dimension." The conference's final document made an explicit connection between the universalism of Christianity and the need for Latin Americans to engage in missionary activity outside their region. "The universal character of the Christian faith," it said, gave a "missionary dimension" to the church, which had the responsibility to share the gospel with "all peoples, races, and tongues." Therefore, the church in Latin America must commit itself to world evangelization "fully and without delay."[8] These conferences reflected a real change in attitudes and behavior: by 1997 Latin American Protestants had sent almost 4,000 missionaries to other parts of the world.[9]

## *Brazil's Universal Church*

To the chagrin of Steuernagel and other Latin American leaders who had earned the respect of evangelicals around the world by presenting a critical and insightful Latin American voice at various international gatherings, the most successful Latin American Protestant export to the rest of the world was Brazilian Pentecostalism. By 2004, Deus é Amor (God Is Love) churches were planted in 136 different countries around the world, Renascer em Cristo (Rebirth in Christ) in eleven, and Igreja Internacional de Graça de Deus (International Church of the Grace of God) in seven. Most impressive in its rapid expansion outside of Brazil was the Igreja Universal do Reino do Deus (IURD, Universal Church of the Kingdom of God). Founded in 1977 by Edir Macedo, an employee of the state lottery system, the Igreja Universal expanded rapidly in Brazil during the 1980s and soon had global missionary aspirations that came to fruition in its first international church plant in Paraguay in 1985.[10] It now has over 1,000 churches in eighty countries, including Brazil's former colonial master, Portugal.[11]

The IURD represented a particularly combative form of neo-Pentecostalism that directly attacked both the Catholic Church and Afro-Brazilian religions such as Umbanda and Candomblé, asserting that Catholic saints and Afro-Brazilian spirits were demons that needed to be exorcised. The church also excelled at sucking the money of its adherents into the church coffers through the prosperity gospel. Although scorned by the Catholic hierarchy, the mainstream media, the intelligentsia, and in fact by most Brazilians—in 1996 the IURD had the lowest public approval rating of any major institution in Brazil—the IURD grew rapidly, gaining 3 million members in less than two decades and purchasing its own television network.[12] One of the explanations for this surprising combination of public scorn and rapid growth was that the IURD focused on the concerns of its largely poor and marginalized adherents by dealing directly with the spiritual, health, and financial issues that many other churches ignored. It also presented itself as a "most Brazilian religion" that received no foreign support and was "attuned to the religious traditions of the continent."[13] It had its own distinctive theology and ecclesiology that sprang directly from the culture in which it was born. As one of its pastors proudly asserted, "we don't follow the European or American evangelical tradition—we come out of the religious practices of our people."[14]

A notorious and revealing incident occurred in October 1995 on the feast day of Our Lady of Aparecida, the Catholic patroness of Brazil, when an IURD pastor beat and kicked a statue of that saint on his television show. "Can God, who created the universe, be compared to such an ugly, horrible and disgraced doll?" he asked.[15] The resulting controversy, including denunciations by Catholic bishops and government officials, gave the IURD, usually adept at turning controversies into opportunities for publicity and grandstanding, perhaps the only instance in its history in which it received more attention than it wanted, as the federal government responded to public outcry by beginning a series of investigations into the church's finances.

That such an organization would spearhead a new Latin American missionary movement might have embarrassed more sedate evangelicals, but it was not surprising. As Latin America's long Christian history has shown, it was quite possible for most Catholic and Protestant Latin Americans, even those who were serious about their faith, to go about their lives without any apparent commitment to mission outside of their immediate environs. Protestants focused on winning the souls of their neighbors and then their nations, while Catholics, once awakened by Protestant inroads, focused on re-evangelizing nominal Catholics. The revival of evangelization detailed in Chapters 1 and 2 initially concentrated on mission *inside* Latin America because, not without reason, both Protestants and Catholics felt that there remained a great deal to accomplish in their own nations and, perhaps, in other parts of Latin America. It was not illogical, either, for Catholics looking to Rome and Protestants looking to the United States or Europe, to see their own lands as the "ends of the earth." It took a level of spiritual confidence and a detachment from the perspective of the missionaries who brought Protestantism to Brazil or from the Christendom model of Catholicism to see Brazil as a "new Jerusalem" and areas outside of Latin America as new "ends of the earth."[16]

Of course, pockets of Catholics and small numbers of Protestants sometimes had the missionary perspective, but they were small minorities with little influence. The IURD's combination of undeniable Brazilianness, real wealth, and a proudly universal theology, as displayed in its very name, meant that it had an especially strong orientation toward global mission. It saw Brazil as a new center of Christianity; it had a theology that necessitated the conversion of the nations; and it had the financial means to carry out its plans. As if to emphasize its role as a new Jerusalem, inside its "World Cathedral of Faith" in Rio de Janeiro the IURD built a 736 square meter replica of ancient Jerusalem. The church presented the replica, built entirely of material transported from Israel, as a way of "joining Brazilian society to the history of Jerusalem."[17]

"God told us," said IURD founder Macedo, "to go to the center of all the nations in the world as Rome was in the time of Jesus. We want to create a center of evangelism there and then send converts back to their own countries." He moved to the United States in 1986 as part of a plan to start several churches in the New York City area.[18] At first he experienced serious difficulties. In 1991, the lead pastor in New York City, Manuel Silva, admitted that the three local temples had only 500 total members and that "the number of Anglo-Saxons is rather minimal." "We have found," he lamented, "that preaching and making converts in New York is not as easy as it is in Brazil." New Yorkers "think they do not need the help of anybody, much less someone from Brazil." Their prejudice and rudeness were, he believed, evidence of deep spiritual problems, such as "pride, love of money, and a spirit of skepticism."[19] Seemingly interminable IURD worship services that took place three times a day, seven days a week, and blasted loud music and angry sermons out of open doors and windows did not win the IURD many friends in the neighborhoods where they planted their temples. In one case, neighbors in Brooklyn Heights became so incensed that they used their garden hoses to spray water over their walls and into the church's sanctuary.[20] Although the IURD eventually did see success in the United States after switching its focus to the Latino population, opening 161 churches by 2012, it saw quicker and more extensive growth in Portugal and southern Africa.[21]

The IURD began its Portuguese work in 1989 in a Lisbon suburb. Even if it had not been a symbolic target for missionary activity as Brazil's "mother country," Portugal was also attractive in that its people spoke Portuguese and had a Catholic culture similar to Brazil's. Appealing mostly to Brazilian, Angolan, and Mozambican migrants and to lower-class, undereducated Portuguese women, the IURD grew quickly in most of the nation's major cities, opening more than fifty churches in its first five years and more than ninety in its first decade. Shocked not so much by non-Catholic religion—there had been a small Protestant community in the country for decades and Brazilian migrants had long practiced Afro-Brazilian religions—as by the assertive and provocative approach taken by the new church, the nation's intelligentsia reacted angrily to the IURD's inroads, especially when in 1995 the IURD announced plans to purchase the Coliseu do Porto, the city of Porto's historic showcase for the performing arts. José Saramago, the nation's Nobel Prize–winning writer, called the IURD "a criminal organization, a band devoted to crime and robbery." A vociferous public debate about the "invasion of the sects" and the loss of national patrimony, with an undercurrent of xenophobia, led to the formation of a society of artists, politicians, and other public figures that bought the Coliseu to keep it out of the church's hands. An IURD plan to form a political party also met with widespread outrage and opposition, leading to legal challenges that doomed the proposed Partido da Gente (People's Party). Despite these setbacks, the church managed to purchase six radio stations and to grow dramatically in the late 1990s. By the 2000s it seemed to have become a permanent part of the religious landscape in Portugal. An orphanage and the well-publicized provision of food and clothing to the poor even seemed to have earned it a measure of public respect.[22]

## *Brazil in Africa*

IURD's success in Southern Africa was even more impressive: they had almost 400 churches there by 2012, including 314 in South Africa alone.[23] "It is possible," suggests Paul Freston, "that no Christian denomination founded in the Third World has ever been exported so successfully and so rapidly." Also striking to Freston was that the IURD was "an essentially lower-class institution" from a nation with about the same income level as South Africa.[24] Unlike American or European missionary endeavors, the IURD's success in southern Africa could not be explained by Brazil's geopolitical influence; the reasons for that success surely had to be found in the IURD itself.

Although the missionaries of the IURD liked to believe that their identity helped them because Brazil represented "a peaceful country that wins the World Cup," the reality was that the IURD's methods were, if anything, more authoritarian and more confrontational than those of contemporary missionaries from the North.[25] After starting in 1991 in Portuguese-speaking Angola and Mozambique and in 1992 in Luso-phone communities in South Africa, in 1993 the IURD began its first

English-language work in Soweto, Durban, and Cape Town. Despite the language difference, South Africa soon became its most successful mission field, as evidenced by a growing cohort of national pastors, stadium events with tens of thousands of people, and a 4,000-seat cathedral built in 1999. Freston relates that, far from being an example of flexibility or "inculturation," the IURD was remarkably consistent in its clericalism and in its centralized hierarchical system, in which "congregational participation in decision-making is eliminated and strong horizontal ties among members are de-emphasized."[26]

Neither did the IURD's success come from great sympathy for African culture. "Their portrayal of the continent in the church's Brazilian media," argues Freston, "is overwhelmingly negative," consisting often of references to superstition and portraits of "a land of witchcraft and idolatry." The long-time leader of the IURD in Africa said, for example, "the African people do not have the same concept of marriage, home, and faithfulness as Brazilians do." Those Africans who did become pastors could scarcely help becoming "Brazilianized," going to the extreme sometimes of adopting a Brazilian accent in their preaching. In the end, Freston concludes, the general IURD perspective on a given mission field displayed "ethnocentrism and lack of empathy with the host population."[27]

What, therefore, explained the IURD's rapid expansion in southern Africa? It seems that the most attractive aspect of the IURD was its apparent spiritual power, especially in the realms of evil spirits and finances. Having to adapt to a new spiritual climate, which lacked the Afro-Brazilian spirits it was used to dealing with, the church in South Africa broadened its approach, not only attacking traditional African religions and their attendant spirits, but also providing spiritual aid for all sorts of problems that it hardly addressed in Brazil. In crime-ridden Johannesburg, for example, it launched a "Campaign of the Holy Mantle" that supposedly conferred protection from mugging.[28] Its bookstores featured a book by Bishop Marcelo Crivella that denounced traditional African religions and ancestor worship as avenues for demonic possession and claimed that both the local Zion Christian Church and the Catholic Church "preach demonic doctrines."[29] This sort of controversial statement surely angered many of the people who heard it; at the same time, its confidence surely attracted many others who longed for this sort of clarity about spiritual matters.

Coupled with the IURD's perceived spiritual power was what one scholar has called "a strategy of visibility." In its mission work the IURD focused on urban areas with high population density and usually rented high-profile venues such as well-known movie theaters for its services. Enormous signs with the church name and its slogan ("Stop Suffering") simply could not be missed by pedestrians and drivers in these high-traffic areas. Once its work in a given region or country reached a certain level of numerical and financial success it then built a cathedral, an even more eye-catching edifice that, in addition to greater visibility, also projected a sense of stability, prosperity, and legitimacy. For example, in Luanda, the capital city of Angola, the church built a $3.5-million air-conditioned cathedral that was one of the largest church buildings in all of Africa. In a similar vein, as in Brazil, the IURD made mass media a priority, purchasing radio and television stations whenever possible and publishing various newspapers and magazines with high production values. When controversies arose, as they inevitably did, over its finances and its confrontational approach to other religions, the IURD seemed to welcome them as a form of free advertising. It should be noted that this strategy of visibility did not represent a call to commitment to civil society or to dialogue with the surrounding culture, for the IURD specifically told its adherents to avoid conversation with those who disagreed with them. High visibility could thus be married to disengagement from society.[30]

Even in Portugal, where one might expect a certain cultural confidence in the national population, IURD converts underwent a process of "Brazilianization" that included adopting Brazilian accents when they prayed.[31] Neither did the IURD demonstrate a model of the church that empowered grassroots leadership. Rather, the organization thrived because of the confident and highly visible proclamation of a message that the poor of both regions wanted to hear and because it provided spiritual services that met deeply felt spiritual needs.

It is also important to point out what the IURD's success in two quite different regions of the world says about the nature of World Christianity:

> Globally speaking, the Universal Church of the Kingdom of God is almost exclusively a phenomenon of *Christian poverty*. Where Christians are not poor, or the poor are not Christian, it fares badly. In this sense its expansion reflects the new global face of Christianity as more and more a religion of the poor from the global South (and of "southern" immigrants in the global North).[32]

Consequently, although the IURD was not an example that most other Latin American churches wanted to follow, it did serve as a sign of the nature of Christianity in the new millennium. Since universal Christianity has a missionary logic that compels it to expand and since much of today's global Christian population lives in Latin America, it is only a matter of time before new—and not necessarily more culturally sensitive—missionary dynamos emerge from Latin America and make their way to Africa, Asia, and the developed world.

## *Catholic Confidence*

It was not only Protestants who were spreading their influence beyond Latin America. Catholic phenomena as varied as liberation theology, veneration of the Virgin of Guadalupe, and Charismatic Renewal were also moving to other regions of the world. This chapter focuses on the United States and Europe, but Latin American Catholics also had influence in Asia and Africa.

Just as Protestantism had reached a point where believers all over Latin America were ready to bring their faith to other continents, so too by the 1970s Catholics had gained a confidence and maturity that made them ready to share their theological and spiritual treasures. Liberation theology swept across the universities and seminaries, both Catholic and Protestant, of Europe, North America, Africa, and Asia, and filtered down into churches and ecclesial communities. In the realm of popular devotion, Mexican immigrants brought the Virgin of Guadalupe everywhere they went and converted Filipinos, Italians, Poles, Japanese, French, Ethiopians, Swedes, Koreans, Kenyans, and Canadians, among others, to Guadalupismo (devotion to Our Lady of Guadalupe).[33] An organized Catholic mission movement developed and began sending full-time missionaries to Africa, Europe, and Asia. Finally, Charismatics echoed their Pentecostal brothers in seeing international mission as almost inseparable from life in the Spirit.

### Liberation Theology

Liberation theology, as outlined in Chapter 3, presented a new sort of Catholic theology that started from "praxis," used Marxist concepts, and pushed the church toward political action on behalf of the total liberation of the poor and oppressed. In many ways it emerged at an ideal time to spread around the world as Latin America's first major theological export. Because of the cultural and political ferment of the 1960s and 1970s, which included decolonization in Africa, civil rights struggles in the United States, student protests around the world, and a revolution in sexual morals, many theologians were searching for a theological rationale for progressive politics. Even moderate thinkers longed for Christian thought to be on the "right" side of the issues of the day, including especially economic and racial issues.

The Theology in the Americas conference in Detroit in 1975, described at the beginning of this chapter, signaled the importance of liberation theology in North America, even in the early days of the theology. Even the disagreements, as passionate and intense as they were, showed how seriously Christians in the United States were taking liberation theology. In later years, many leading progressive theologians and thinkers participated in Theology in the Americas projects and dialogues, including Jim Wallis, Letty Russell, Elisabeth Schüssler Fiorenza, and Rosemary Radford Ruether. Many also participated in the Ecumenical Association of Third World Theologians, another body of progressive theologians in which liberation theology played a major role.[34]

One example of the influence of Latin American liberation theology in the north was the case of James Cone, one of the leading figures in black theology. Independent of the Latin American theologians, Cone had developed his own liberation theology in his 1969 book, *Black Theology and Black Power*, which focused on African Americans in the United States.[35] While Cone's theology shared much with the Latin American version, including extensive use of the term "liberation," there were also definite differences. Most obviously, where the Latin Americans focused on class and class struggle, Cone looked at race and race conflict. Second, Cone used the social sciences and Marxist categories far less often than the Latin Americans. These differences led to diverging interpretations of the theological project and to deep mutual suspicions.[36] Cone later said of the conference in Detroit, "Blacks came close to saying that the Latin Americans were white racists, and the Latin Americans accused blacks of being North American capitalists."[37]

Nevertheless, after the Detroit conference, Cone continued the dialogue with the Latin Americans. Gustavo Gutiérrez's two semesters as a guest professor at Union Theological Seminary, where Cone taught, and Cone's participation at later Theology in the Americas meetings, including one in Mexico City in 1977, continued his exposure to the Latin American perspective. In the end, he accepted much of what the Latin Americans were proposing, broadening his vision to include the poor and oppressed around the world and developing his own critique of capitalism.[38]

Robert McAfee Brown, a Presbyterian theology professor, did not attend the Detroit conference but eventually accepted Latin American liberation theology more unreservedly than Cone, becoming "a herald and apologist" for the new theology. An active participant in the ecumenical movement and one of the Protestant observers at Vatican II, Brown found in liberation theology the integration of politics and theology that he had been looking for during his work in the civil rights and anti-Vietnam War movements. The liberationist critique of power fit well with his own developing anger at the foreign policy of the United States.[39] Particularly influenced by the thought of Brazilian bishop Helder Camara and of Gustavo Gutierrez, who taught with him at Union Theological Seminary and became a close friend, Brown became convinced that liberation theology was nothing less than a restatement of the gospel in the language of the twentieth century.[40]

Impressed by Gutiérrez, Brown later traveled to Peru to learn more about the theology in its original context. "Personal encounter with him," Brown asserted, "has been an important reality in my ongoing theological journey—a journey whose direction he has drastically rerouted."[41] In both journalism and academic books such as *Theology in a New Key: Responding to Liberation Themes* and two books on Gutiérrez, Brown devoted much of his career after 1974 to explaining liberation theology to North Americans.[42] He responded to various critiques of the theology by asserting that most of them depended on distortion and reductionism, and he defended Gutiérrez against attacks from both inside and outside the Catholic Church.[43] In the end, Brown believed that liberation theology, especially that of Gutiérrez, could provide an antidote to the complacency and complicity of "well fed Christians" in the West.[44]

Of course, not all Christians responded so positively. Catholic leaders such as secretary of the Congregation for the Doctrine of the Faith, Joseph Ratzinger, and Colombian cardinal Alfonso López Trujillo penned strong critiques of liberation theology.[45] Even evangelical Protestants, who rarely had much to say about Catholic academic theology, jumped into the fray. For instance, Peter Wagner, a former missionary in Bolivia and later professor at Fuller Theological Seminary, wrote a book that criticized the theology for its insufficient attention to evangelization. To him, the problem was not that the new theology called Christians to serve the poor or to enter the political arena; rather, it was that it emphasized this over evangelism and study and action over prayer and preaching. Similarly, Carl Henry, the editor of the evangelical magazine *Christianity Today*, rejected liberation theology's use of Marxist analysis and argued that the theology's attention to economics and politics had distracted it from Christ and the Bible. The fact that evangelical Protestant writers were taking the time to write books and articles on the subject demonstrated the impact of the new theology.

## Migrants, Pontiffs, and Guadalupe

Even more influential than liberation theology was the cult of Our Lady of Guadalupe. According to tradition, in 1531, on Tepeyac hill in what is today Mexico City, the Virgin Mary appeared to an indigenous Mexican named Juan Diego and performed various miracles, most notably the creation of a dark-skinned image of herself on Juan Diego's *tilma* or cloak. Her words to Juan Diego, "Am I not here, who is your Mother? Are you not under my protection?" emphasized her maternal care for Juan Diego and for all of his people.[46] After Archbishop Juan de Zumárraga recognized the apparition and built a large shrine at Tepeyac, devotion to Our Lady of Guadalupe, La Virgen Morena (Dark-skinned Virgin) and the Mother of all Mexicans, became one of the essential markers of Mexican identity— at times seemingly the only glue binding the nation together. When the United States took half of Mexico's territory in 1848, Guadalupan devotion naturally continued to be a central part of Catholic life in former Mexican territories such as Texas, New Mexico, and California. Similarly, when the United States annexed Puerto Rico in 1898, the Virgin of Guadalupe was already the patroness of Ponce, the territory's second-largest city.[47] In the twentieth century, as Mexican migration rose and fell according to economic and political conditions, new waves of immigrants carried devotion to Our Lady of Guadalupe to communities throughout the Southwest and then, in the second half of the century, to the Midwest, the Southeast, and the Northeast. Thus, through conquest and migration the cult of Guadalupe gradually spread across the United States.

César Chávez, leader of the United Farm Workers, brought Our Lady of Guadalupe to national attention in the United States in 1965 in his union's first major strike. Marching behind a large banner of Our Lady of Guadalupe and crying out "Justice for the farmworkers and long live the Virgin of Guadalupe," Chávez and the farmworkers introduced many

Americans to the centrality of Guadalupe in Mexican life.[48] Meanwhile, wherever Mexican Americans lived they adorned their homes and their workplaces with statuary, pictures, and murals of their "Virgen morena" and as soon as possible they took her into the local Catholic Church. Catholics living in such areas, whether or not they were Latino, often picked up a devotion to the Virgin of Guadalupe. Since by 2006 "more than 11.5 million Mexican immigrants resided in the United States, accounting for 30.7 percent of all US immigrants and one-tenth of the entire population born in Mexico," and since after 1980 these immigrants congregated less in the Southwest and spread out to almost every region of the nation, devotion to Our Lady of Guadalupe could be found in every state.[49]

For example, Kentucky, which had a very low Latino population well into the twentieth century, saw thousands of Mexican and other Latin American migrants enter the state in the 1980s and 1990s to work in agriculture, construction, and service industries.[50] By 2010 even small cities in the foothills of Appalachia had Mexican populations large enough to support stores and soccer leagues and, of course, to insist on devotion to Mexico's Virgin. In response, both St. Clare Church in Berea and St. Mark Church in Richmond added images of Our Lady of Guadalupe to their sanctuaries and featured Spanish-languages Masses and special services on her feast day.

Even in places in the United States with negligible Mexican populations the Vatican's growing attention to Our Lady of Guadalupe served as an additional impetus to Guadalupan devotion. In 1946 Pius XII declared her Patroness of the Americas and in 1961 John XXIII called her the mother of all the people of the Americas, but it was John Paul II who focused the world's attention on her. Starting with his Mass at the basilica of Our Lady of Guadalupe on his first international pilgrimage in 1979, John Paul repeatedly returned to her in his speeches and writings, and spoke at her basilica in Mexico City in 1990 and 2002. With the encouragement of John Paul, who created a chapel to Our Lady of Guadalupe in St. Peter's Basilica in Vatican City, Juan Diego was beatified in 1990 and canonized in 2002.[51]

In 1999 at the basilica of Our Lady of Guadalupe, in response to the Special Assembly for America of 1997—a synod of bishops from North, South, and Central America—John Paul highlighted the special role he saw for the Virgin of Guadalupe in all of the Americas. Her coming to Juan Diego, he said, had had a "decisive effect" on the conversion of the continent because her mestiza appearance presented "an impressive example of a perfectly inculturated evangelization." He therefore endorsed the bishops' call for a unified celebration of her saint's day:

> With the passage of time, pastors and faithful alike have grown increasingly conscious of the role of the Virgin Mary in the evangelization of America. In the prayer composed for the Special Assembly for America of the Synod of Bishops, Holy Mary of Guadalupe is invoked as "Patroness of all America and Star of the first and new evangelization." In view of this, I welcome with joy the proposal of the Synod Fathers that the feast of Our Lady of Guadalupe, Mother and Evangelizer of America, be celebrated throughout the continent on December 12. It is my heartfelt hope that she, whose intercession was responsible for strengthening the faith of the first disciples (cf. Jn 2:11), will by her maternal intercession guide the Church in America, obtaining the outpouring of the Holy Spirit, as she once did for the early Church (cf. Acts 1:14), so that the new evangelization may yield a splendid flowering of Christian life.[52]

Strikingly, John Paul linked Our Lady of Guadalupe closely to the "new evangelization," a central project of his pontificate. Clearly he saw greater devotion to Our Lady of Guadalupe as an integral part of the church's efforts to engage an increasingly secular culture.

## The New Guadalupanos

The combination of, on the grassroots level, millions of Mexican migrants and Mexican Americans carrying their devotion to every corner of the United States, and, on the institutional level, papal backing for Guadalupe as part of the Vatican's new evangelization initiative, together made Guadalupan devotion more and more a part of mainstream Catholicism in the United States.[53] Already present in daily life in the Southwest, Chicago, and other places with long histories of Mexican migration, Guadalupismo jumped out of the Mexican and Mexican American communities and won over Americans from every walk of life. A few examples will give a sense of how Americans embraced the new devotion, but a book could be written on Guadalupe's northern conquest.

For a long time, non-Latinos most commonly found the Virgin of Guadalupe by living in places where she was hard to avoid. Gene Sager, for instance, had grown up as a Protestant in the Midwest but moved to New

Mexico for college. His immersion in the Mexican American culture of the area introduced him to Our Lady of Guadalupe and intrigued him enough that he accepted a friend's invitation to travel with a group of Mexican American pilgrims to her shrine in Mexico City. Impressed by the devotion he saw at the shrine, Sager became more and more interested in the Catholic culture of New Mexico and in 1982 converted to Catholicism, in large part because of Our Lady of Guadalupe. "By blood, I am a gringo," he said, "but socially and spiritually I became an adopted son of the Mexican American people and an adopted son of La Virgen de Guadalupe." Twenty-five years later he felt no regrets: "By becoming a Guadalupano I entered into a double richness that I value more highly each day."[54]

Carl Anderson, leader of the Knights of Columbus, felt "deeply touched" when he attended the canonization of Juan Diego at the Basilica of Our Lady of Gaudalupe in 2002. He soon came to believe that that event was "one of the most profound events in the Catholic Church" during the pontificate of John Paul and a turning point in his own life. The pope, Anderson decided, had given the Americas "a saint for the future" because "the full radicalness of Our Lady of Guadalupe's apparition can only be understood fully" in the new millennium in the light of John Paul's twin concepts of the "Civilization of Love" and the "Theology of the Body." The Virgin's gentle, maternal words to Juan Diego seemed to both the pope and to Anderson to incarnate perfectly the message that busy, angry, divided twenty-first century America needed to hear.[55]

Anderson's experience at the basilica convinced him that the United States needed to meet the Virgin of Guadalupe and to hear her message. He therefore persuaded the Knights of Columbus to sponsor a tour that would bring a small piece of Juan Diego's tilma to twenty cities across the United States in 2003. Americans of all backgrounds came out to see the cloak. Mary Jane Griffin, for example, drove two hours from Eau Claire and braved the "eighty degree heat" to see the relic at the Shrine of Our Lady of Guadalupe in La Crosse, Wisconsin.[56] Hundreds of Yaqui Indians came out to see it in Arizona and construction workers in Denver stopped their work and bowed their heads when it passed by in a procession.[57] The relic ended its journey at St. Patrick's cathedral in New York City, where Anne Manice went so far as to say, "She's probably the strongest presence of God on this continent."[58] Anderson marveled at the more than 125,000 people who visited the cloak and at the "the number of nationalities and ethnicities represented in each gathering," most of them "people with no connection whatsoever to Mexico." He believed that this widespread interest reflected a deeper spiritual reality that could unite the peoples of the Americas: "every person on this continent shares a mother: Our Lady of Guadalupe." He wrote a book about Our Lady of Guadalupe and transformed the Knights of Columbus into the most influential advocate of Guadalupan devotion in North America. In addition to the tour of the relic of Juan Diego's tilma, the Knights sponsored an international Guadalupan congress that attracted 22,000 people to Phoenix in 2009 and a Guadalupe Celebration in 2012 that brought 100,000 people to the Los Angeles Coliseum to hear singers from Mexico and speakers such as Los Angeles Archbishop José Gómez and Eduardo Chávez, rector of the Institute for Guadalupan Studies in Mexico City.[59]

Devotion to Guadalupe did not confine itself to any particular faction in the church, with progressives, moderates, and conservatives all seemingly equally committed to the Virgin. Notably, conservative Cardinal Raymund Burke, who started building a Guadalupan shrine in La Crosse, Wisconsin, when he was bishop there in 2001, and the traditionalist Priestly Fraternity of Saint Peter, which opened Our Lady of Guadalupe Seminary in Denton, Nebraska, in 2003, appeared to see devotion to Our Lady of Guadalupe as central to their ministries.[60]

Even more remarkable than the adoption of the dark-skinned "immigrant" saint by American conservatives was its adoption by Protestants. For instance, Maxwell Johnson, a Lutheran from South Dakota, first encountered the Virgin of Guadalupe in 1973 when he spent three weeks at a Benedictine monastery in Mexico and then visited the basilica at Tepeyac. Although he felt "perplexed and put off" by what he called the "liturgical-sacramental smorgasbord" taking place there, he found himself "strangely attracted" to the virgin herself. Years later, after becoming a Lutheran theologian and adopting two African American children, he found in the dark-skinned virgin "a valuable, indigenous American, ethnically and racially mixed iconographic alternative" to the Nordic-looking religious images he often encountered. He also discovered in his work as a professor that his students often were drawn to Guadalupan themes in their research and that he himself felt the need to reflect further on Guadalupe and her possible role in Protestant churches. In the end, Johnson concluded that she did have a place in Protestantism and adopted "a Protestant-Catholic *mestizaje*, a synthesis of popular Guadalupanismo and Protestant theological convictions."[61]

Johnson was not alone. In his research he found Protestants all over the United States who celebrated Guadalupe in some fashion. For instance, some Lutheran churches in California, Texas, Chicago, and Pennsylvania celebrated December 12, the feast day of Our Lady of Guadalupe. One Lutheran pastor, whose church in Illinois featured two statues of Guadalupe in its sanctuary, said the feast of Our Lady of Guadalupe was "the celebration in our community that brings alive the spirit of Advent and Christmas to our parishioners." Johnson also discovered a Lutheran college in Minnesota with few Mexican students that nevertheless devoted the Advent season of 1994 to the Mexican Virgin. Finally, Johnson found attention to Guadalupan themes especially pronounced among Episcopalians in California. In one impoverished area of downtown Los Angeles, the Episcopal Advent and Christmas services attracted far fewer people than the Guadalupan service on December 12. After noting that "there is really nothing to distinguish those 'Protestant' celebrations from Roman Catholic ones," Johnson concluded "the Virgin of Guadalupe can be integrated and received into an overall Protestant liturgical context."[62]

Another Protestant scholar, Paul Barton of the Episcopal Theological Seminary of the Southwest, went even further, arguing in 2005 that "Guadalupe represents an authentic revelation of the Gospel that has been kept from Latino/a Protestants due to the anti-Catholic message of Protestant missionaries." Like Johnson, Barton visited Tepeyac as a young man, then pondered Guadalupe's message for many years. At the Perkins School of Theology, a Methodist seminary, his Protestant dissertation advisor encouraged him to go on a spiritual pilgrimage with the Virgin of Guadalupe, as the advisor himself had done. The advisor told him, "She invited me to creative participation in the continuing task of loving the Cosmos. That woman you and I know as Our Lady of Guadalupe of Tepeyac is the Mother of God. She is our cosmic Mother." When Barton spent three weeks at the Mexican American Cultural Center in San Antonio he drew still closer to La Morena after observing the centrality of Guadalupan devotion in Mexican American life there. He put a large painting of her in his office and said "she is a source of divine power and revelation" in whom he saw "the Gospel message." Only anti-Catholicism, he believed, was keeping other Protestants from seeing the same thing.[63]

## Catholic Mission "Ad Gentes"

In addition to the spread of liberation theology and Guadalupan devotion, the decades after Vatican II also witnessed the birth of a genuine Catholic missionary movement from Latin America. Educated Latin American

Catholics of course had long known of the biblical injunctions to make disciples of all nations and to go as witnesses to the ends of the earth, but, as with Protestants, had tended to see themselves as the ones at the "end of the earth." In the 1950s Catholics began to turn their attention to indigenous communities in the Andes, Amazonia, and Mesoamerica that had not been fully evangelized.[64] Vatican II deepened this missionary concern by basing it in the "very nature" of the church, while in 1975 Paul VI's *Evangelii Nuntiandi* confirmed that missionary activity had to be at the center of the church.

At first, this missionary concern focused mainly on the region's many unreached and underserved indigenous and impoverished populations, but the logic of the church's missionary vocation soon extended to other regions of the world. The CELAM conference at Puebla in 1979 served as "the decisive turning point in mission awareness and action."[65] Several parts of the final Puebla document dealt with world missions, but section 368 made the most explicit call for Latin America to renew its commitment to this endeavor:

> Finally the time has come for Latin America to intensify works of mutual aid between local Churches and to extend them beyond their own frontiers, "ad gentes." True, we ourselves are in need of missionaries, but we must give out of our own poverty. By the same token, our Churches have something original and important to offer: their sense of salvation and liberation, the richness of their people's religiosity, the experience of the CEBs, the flourishing of their ministries, and their hope and joy rooted faith. We have already undertaken missionary efforts; they can now be deepened and should be expanded.[66]

Several aspects of this statement deserve attention. First, the bishops recognized that they were entering a new era. Second, they explicitly saw their mission going beyond their borders to the "nations" or "peoples" of the world. Third, they recognized that they could not match the resources of missionaries from the United States or Europe, but they saw that they had special gifts that wealthier nations lacked.

Pope John Paul II paid special attention to Latin America's new missionary commitment, harking back to it in over fifty of the 500 speeches to Latin American audiences analyzed by missiologist Romeo Ballán.[67] Starting at Puebla in 1979, John Paul told the Latin American bishops that the whole world was looking at them "with confidence and hope." Repeatedly over the coming decades he encouraged Latin American groups to live up to their missionary vocation and to devote themselves to ministries "without borders." Bishops, priests, and laity, he insisted, all had missionary vocations that extended to the whole world.[68]

Many Latin American Catholics took this injunction seriously. After six national missionary conferences, Mexico hosted the first region-wide Congreso Misionero Latinoamericano (COMLA, Latin American Missionary Congress) in 1977 and the second in 1983. At the end of the latter, 100 Mexican missionaries were sent off. The third and fourth COMLA congresses, in Colombia in 1987 and Peru in 1991, challenged Latin America to make the universal mission of the church part of every diocese.[69] By 1990, Ballán estimates, about 3,000 Latin American missionaries were serving outside their home countries, including 1,000 Mexicans, 970 Brazilians, 200 Argentines, 200 Colombians, 175 Costa Ricans, and 130 Peruvians. (It was not clear how many were serving outside Latin America.) For instance, members of homegrown Colombian religious orders were serving in Angola, Benin, Mali, and Kenya, while members of Mexican orders could be found in Japan, Hong Kong, Angola, and Kenya. Brazil paid special attention to the Portuguese-speaking nations of Africa and set up a theological exchange program in South Africa. Missionary training institutes sprang up in Mexico, Brazil, and Argentina.[70]

Despite these accomplishments, the sixth COMLA congress, which took place in Argentina in 1999, featured a challenging speech by Cardinal Jozef Tomko, prefect of the Vatican's congregation for evangelization, in which he asked Latin America to assume its role as a mature part of the global church. The region had almost half of the world's Catholics, but what percentage of the world's missionaries *ad gentes* did it contribute? Was it not time for the region to supply half of the world's missionaries?[71] A sign that the missionary challenge was already being taken seriously was a change at the Maryknoll language institute in Cochabamba, Bolivia. For thirty-five years it had served missionaries *to* Latin America, but in the 1990s it began training missionaries *from* Latin America for service in other parts of the world.[72] Similarly, the Catholic University in Bolivia, one of the poorer Latin American nations, had opened a missiological institute that offered degrees.[73] By 2002 there were at least 4,000 and possibly 5,000 Catholic Latin American missionaries *ad gentes*, according to Ballán. He, like Tomko, lamented that this represented a tiny fraction of the region's massive Catholic population. Still, many Latin American Catholics had committed themselves to the global mission of the church and there was every sign that that commitment would increase.[74]

## A New Song in Portugal

One of the more interesting Catholic missionary exports from Latin America came from the Brazilian Charismatic movement. Latin American Catholic missions were largely of the province of religious orders that sent their personnel to Africa and Asia. Brazilian Charismatic missionary work, by contrast, was largely done in Europe by laypeople. In Brazil, a major emphasis of the Charismatic movement was the "community," in which Charismatics lived together and worked on various ministries and apostolates, often musical and evangelistic. Like Catholic religious orders or Protestant denominations, these communities often sent members out from a "mother house" to found new groups in other cities. Thus, communities like Cançao Nova (New Song), Obra de Maria (Work of Mary), Palavra Viva (Living Word), Shalom (Peace), and Sementes do Verbo (Seeds of the Word) spread quickly throughout Brazil in the 1980s and 1990s. The evangelistic commitment of such communities made it almost inevitable that eventually they would start new communities in other Latin American nations and then on other continents.

For instance, Obra de Maria, founded in 1990 "for the evangelization of the poorest of the poor," spread from Recife to seventeen Brazilian cities and sixteen foreign countries, including Israel, Palestine, Portugal, Angola, and Italy.[75] In a similar way, Palavra Viva, founded in 1995 in Diamantina "to announce Jesus Christ to the world, preferentially evangelizing young people and families," had started "casas de misión" (mission houses) in twelve Brazilian dioceses and four European countries within twenty-five years.[76]

Cançao Nova's experiences in Portugal provide a glimpse of how Brazilian missionaries operated in Europe. Founded by Father Jonas Abib in 1979, Cançao Nova quickly became a major media presence in Brazil through its radio and television stations and its popular recording artists. In 1998, three Brazilian women brought the movement to Portugal. After joining forces with a priest and a religious sister, they devoted themselves to worship, prayer, and the evangelization of youth around the country. With the help of a sympathetic bishop, Serafim Ferreira Sousa e Silva of Leiria-Fatima, they obtained a house in Leiria in 2000, where they began working on television, radio, and music production. In 2001 they launched their first radio show and by 2007 they had a radio station, a television station, and two bookstores.[77]

Cançao Nova's Brazilian origin meant that it had to fight against stereotypes about Brazilian immigrants that associated them with telenovelas (soap operas), prostitution, and fanatical religion. The third image, of course, proved the hardest to dispel. Unfortunately for Cançao Nova, Brazilian Pentecostal churches such as the IURD and Deus é Amor had preceded it in Portugal. Many Catholic and secular Portuguese viewed these churches as strange, heretical, or dangerous and, as described earlier, the IURD almost seemed to go out of its way to live up to the criticism. To make matters worse, the symbol of the IURD, a descending dove that represented the Holy Spirit, resembled the symbol of Cançao Nova, a dove intertwined with a guitar. Portuguese unfamiliar with either Pentecostalism or the Charismatic Renewal could easily reject Cançao Nova out of hand as just another one of the "Brazilian sects."[78]

Where the IURD emphasized its cultural differences, Cançao Nova took the opposite tack, seeking to accommodate itself as much as possible to mainstream Portuguese Catholicism. First, the community forged a strong tie to Fatima—the site of a 1917 Marian apparition that rivaled Tepeyac and Lourdes as a site of global pilgrimage and that had strong associations with Portuguese national identity—by locating its Portuguese headquarters there and by broadcasting daily Mass from the Sanctuary of Our Lady of Fátima.[79] Second, after several missteps and social blunders, missionaries adopted more conservative Portuguese religious and social practices, for instance, limiting the role of laypeople in meetings led by priests. Third, missionaries changed their vocabulary and grammar to reflect more formal Portuguese speech. Fourth, they expressed their mission as a form of gratitude to the "mother country" for bringing the Catholic faith to Brazil in the first place.[80] These practices did not eliminate all criticism—one particularly indignant writer called the kind of Catholicism practiced by the group "Jansenist, intolerant, and moralistic"—but they slowly won it a measure of legitimacy and understanding.[81] The community's television shows, in particular, worked well to prove Cançao Nova's Catholic credentials and to expose it to new audiences.[82]

## Conclusion

After almost five centuries of receiving missionaries, theologies, and religious practices from abroad, the decades after 1970 marked the beginning of Latin America's role as a sender of those same religious goods. Having accepted the universal implications of their faiths, both Protestants and Catholics took more active roles as protagonists and agents around the world. Despite continued economic struggles that made financing missions difficult, Latin American missionaries tended to see their poverty and their lack of geopolitical power as assets that helped them to identify with the poor of other countries and to present a message devoid of colonialism.

There were real differences between, say, a Mexican laborer who lobbied for a special Guadalupan ceremony in his church in Kentucky and an IURD missionary building a massive cathedral in Angola, but both of them were Latin Americans who believed their religion was universally valid and both of them were confident enough to share that religion with people of other cultures and nations. Thus, although all the four other forms of Christianity's rebirth in Latin America outlined in this book applied to Latin America itself, this fifth area of rebirth directly affected the rest of the world, since it extended those prophetic, evangelistic, Charismatic, lay-led streams of Latin American Christianity to other regions.

If the developments in Latin American Christianity were simply private, localized phenomena, they might be of interest only to Latin Americans and to scholars who study Latin America. However, such was not the case. The increasing interconnectedness of the world and the increasing weight of Christianity in the global South made the rebirth of Latin American Christianity an issue for the entire world. It was no longer a question of *whether* but of *when*, Latin American Christianity would come to the world beyond its borders, and *which types* of Latin American Christianity would be coming. Why does Latin American Christianity matter to the rest of world? Because today many people outside Latin America already are encountering Latin American Christianity in their home countries and many more will do so in the future.

# Conclusion

*I asked my table companions if any of them had them-
selves ever "spoken in tongues" or "prayed in the Spirit"
as the Pentecostals say. There was an awkward silence.
The priest glanced at his watch. The historian brushed
crumbs from the tablecloth. The rest looked doubtfully at
each other. None, it seemed, ever had. Nor had I, I admitted. They seemed relieved. But then I asked whether
anyone had ever wanted to. Here again, the response was
negative, and most seemed surprised when I revealed that
I at times had wanted to.*

—HARVEY COX, *Fire from Heaven.*

NO PART OF the Latin American religious landscape seemed more foreign
to the academic mind than Pentecostal religious experience. Even scholars who had devoted years of their lives to studying Pentecostalism found
its practices alien and embarrassing. Academics could understand and
even embrace aspects of Latin American Christianity—work for human
rights, the idea of community, and devotion to the Virgin Mary. Very few,
however, saw anything appealing, much less anything they could personally endorse, about spiritual warfare, prophecy, spiritual healing, speaking in tongues, or being slain in the Spirit.

Such is the challenge of Pentecostalism, a movement utterly out of
step with the spirit of the age. Where scholars could treat moral, ethical,
ritual, and liturgical religion on a purely human level, the crass supernat-
uralism of Pentecostalism and the Catholic Charismatic Renewal (CCR)
admitted no such purely academic approach. "Surprising" is probably

too mild a word—Pentecostal experience was simply *shocking*. It was so tied to supposedly supernatural events that scholars could not simply go about their business, studying, analyzing, classifying, and explaining. Sooner or later they had to make personal spiritual and philosophical decisions about the phenomena they were observing. As Cox detailed in the opening epigraph, such personal experiences could be uncomfortable, but surely the encounter with Pentecostalism was a pivotal one for those scholars and for modernity more generally. Between 1950 and the present, tens of millions of Latin Americans did not simply believe in demons but spent much of their time fighting against them, fell to the ground under the supposed influence of the Holy Spirit, had spiritual dreams, gave prophecies, prayed for divine healing, and said that they had experienced it. In other words, the rise of Pentecostalism in Latin America over the last sixty years not only challenged the secularization thesis—the idea that urbanization and industrialization would usher in progressively less religious times—but also provided a philosophical challenge to modernity itself.

Take, for instance, Avivamiento Bogotá (Bogotá Revival), a Pentecostal church that every Sunday welcomed 45,000 people to three services in a converted warehouse.[1] The church's promotional videos featured people swaying, jumping, crying, and shaking as pastors Ricardo and Paty Rodriguez preached and prayed. Apparently on a regular basis, when the pastors waved their hands, individuals and whole sections of the crowd would fall to the ground, as if struck by an invisible force.[2] One visiting pastor, who dropped to the floor violently at an event in 2007, testified that he had received "a transfer of anointing" that enabled him to increase the size of his church in Ambato, Ecuador, and then to plant two new churches in other cities.[3] What was happening to him and to the other people at Avivamiento Bogotá? Was it mass delusion? Were they experiencing genuine supernatural phenomena? Could there be intentional deception? None of these scenarios was obvious, or comfortable. Since history and the social sciences do not have the tools to answer metaphysical questions, the Pentecostalism served as a rebuke to both the clockwork universe proposed by modernity and to the meaninglessness proposed by postmodernity. Pentecostalism has not just helped revive Christianity; it has reintroduced Latin America to mystery on a massive scale. Gabriel García Marquez's Nobel Prize–winning novel *One Hundred Years of Solitude* combined the historical and the fantastic in a dreamlike representation of Latin American history. But Pentecostalism was the true magical realism; it accomplished something much grander than any novel ever could: it brought the supernatural back into urban, industrial Latin America.[4]

Although Pentecostalism posed the most direct challenge to modernity's certainties and postmodernity's uncertainties, the more general history of Latin American Christianity since 1950 similarly highlights the failure of the secularization thesis and the paradoxical, even scandalous, nature of recent religious history. The rebirth of Latin American Christianity confounded not only those Marxists, liberals, scientists, and technocrats who forecast the withering away of religion but also traditional Catholics and Protestants as well. Indigenous evangelicals, Opus Dei businessmen, Brazilian missionaries to Africa, televangelists, and singing priests: all of these new groups of Christians offended modern sensibilities and expectations in some way. Even CEBs, with their more understandable (to the secular left especially and to modernity more generally) political orientation, tended to frustrate expectations as they became more traditionally religious and less politically progressive.

All of these paradoxes, challenges, and disappointments suggest not only the great importance of religion in Latin America but also its relative autonomy. Those who expect religious change to follow some predetermined path and those who assume that economic and political factors will dominate religion are doomed to be disappointed. As the recent history of Latin America demonstrates, religion is a genuine field of human action and decision making that has a life of its own.

The history of Christianity in Latin America since 1950 defied expectations not so much because there was a rebirth of Christianity but because of how that rebirth occurred. On one hand, the Catholic hierarchy's strategy of forming new alliances with the state and inviting a massive infusion of foreign missionaries failed miserably. On the other hand, Protestantism, one of the main threats identified by the hierarchy, not only experienced dramatic growth but also served as a catalyst and example for the revitalization of Catholicism. Moreover, even as Latin America became the worldwide heartland of Pentecostalism and shattered any pretense that it was a "Catholic continent," the region simultaneously became the worldwide heartland of Catholicism in a numerical sense.

In the first half of the twentieth century the Catholic Church in Latin America faced the possibility of irrelevance. After decades of attacks from liberal governments, the hierarchy often assumed an understandably defensive posture that focused more on protection of rights, privileges, and the status quo than on evangelization. The belief that a new alliance with the state could solve the church's problems attracted some Catholics, but it was an illusion—not because the state could not provide real benefits to the church, but because it confused external and internal matters. The attempt to engineer close church-state relations overemphasized the quest for security at the expense of the pursuit of spiritual vitality, an ordering of priorities that flew in the face of centuries of history in which persecuted churches thrived but coddled ones fell into decadence. The example of the Mexican church should have sufficed. No Latin American church experienced more persecution, but Mexican Catholicism stayed strong and vibrant, more resistant to Protestantism than Catholicism in any other large Latin American nation, despite Mexico's long border with the largely Protestant United States.

Protestantism was a blessing in disguise for the Catholic Church. Nothing roused Latin American Catholics more than the spread of Protestantism. Unlike other challenges of the era, such as urbanization and industrialization, Protestantism directly attacked Catholicism, and, unlike Marxism, it had a deep religious appeal that could make it popular in a way that a materialistic philosophy never could be. It was easy, before the rise of Protestantism, to blame Catholic problems on government attacks and foreign machinations. But Protestantism could not be blamed credibly on tyrants and the CIA, although priests and bishops did try to do so. Especially in its dominant Pentecostal incarnation, Protestantism was a movement of poor Latin Americans who consciously rejected Catholicism, often at great cost—sometimes of their lives. Its fervor, its lay leadership, and its vigorous evangelization together served as an ongoing rebuke to the Catholic leaders of the continent for their lethargy, their low expectations of the poor, and, at a deeper level, their failure to believe in the power of the gospel message.

A second stimulus came from the region's dictatorships. Confrontation with these unjust governments not only further awakened the Catholic Church but also showed that it had resources that Protestantism lacked. Most obviously, the Catholic intellectual tradition and social magisterium, as reflected in the documents of Vatican II and papal encyclicals, gave Catholics a framework for theological reflection that proved more fruitful than anything Protestants had. Catholic support of the oppressed and resistance to military governments thus had a theological rationale that helped it spread and endure. Also, Catholic resistance produced its own martyrs and served as a powerful sign that there was, perhaps, more to Catholicism than met the eye. A thoroughly superficial, exhausted religion simply could not have achieved what Catholicism did. Its ongoing witness to truth, its defense of the defenseless, and its long list of martyrs made clear that the old religion still had some life. Some of the leaves might have fallen off and the branches might have sustained serious damage, but clearly the roots were still in contact with deep and nourishing springs.

## *The Invisible Key*

In 1970, to explain the "Latin American Boom" in literature during the preceding decade, Peruvian novelist Mario Vargas Llosa said, "The most propitious moment for the development of prose fiction is when reality ceases to have precise meaning for a historic community because the society's religious, moral, or political values, which once provided the foundation for social life and the master key for perceiving reality, have entered upon a period of crisis and no longer enjoy the faithful support of the collectivity." Great novels, he believed, appeared in societies experiencing "periods of decadence immediately preceding historical collapse." The flourishing Latin American fiction of his day showcased an era in which religious, political, and social values were in flux and the old order was fading away. "Latin America is today," he argued, "a continent that is changing its skin, that is becoming the subject rather than the object of history."[5]

In retrospect, it is clear that Vargas Llosa was right. Politically, the region was entering a time of revolution and dictatorship that would cause untold suffering. Socially, peasants and workers would undergo massive changes over the coming decades. Religiously, the Christendom model of a unified Catholic society in which church and state worked hand in hand was breathing its last gasps. Urbanization, industrialization, secularization, Marxism, and a host of related phenomena were, as Vargas Llosa recognized, leading to profound crises for Latin America.[6] Where he was wrong was in underestimating the role of religion in the coming transformation. Like many of the leading intellectuals and writers of the second half of the twentieth century, Vargas Llosa was not so much anti-Christian as post-Christian. He recognized the important role of the Catholic Church in Latin American history and as an institutional actor in his own time, but he assumed that the new "master key for perceiving reality" would be some sort of secular morality or philosophy. It probably never crossed his mind that Catholicism or any kind of Christianity could provide the sort of "master key" that would transform Latin America into "the subject rather than the object of history."

As I have attempted to show, however, through their engagement with Christianity, millions of Latin Americans, perhaps even the majority, did find a "master key for perceiving reality" and did become subjects rather objects of history. For instance, the cultural renaissance and new political assertiveness of many contemporary indigenous groups is, in many cases, tied closely to evangelization and spiritual renewal. Universal Christianity has fueled the use of Tzeltal, Tzotzil, Totonac, Aymara, Quichua, and many other indigenous languages in liturgy, Bible study, and political organizing. The CEBs provided another avenue for marginalized people to make sense of the world in Christian terms and to take action as agents of their own history.

In the case of foreign missions by Latin Americans the transformation has been even more profound. Latin America in the 1950s was a mission field for both Catholics and Protestants. To the dominant Protestant churches of the United States, the region appeared to be a land of idolatrous Catholics and pagan Indians who needed to hear the gospel. For Catholics, the view was similar. From the Vatican, popes Pius XII, John XXIII, and Paul VI called for Europe and the United States to help Latin America. Many Catholics in Europe and the United States, and even many in Latin America, believed that there were not enough priests and that therefore Europe and the United States had to supply them, that there were not enough schools and that therefore Europe and the United States had to build them, and that there was not enough money and that therefore Europe and the United States had to send it. The underlying assumption was that the solution to Latin America's problems would come from outside.

Today Latin America sends thousands of missionaries, both Protestant and Catholic, not only to Asia and Africa, but also to the United States and Europe. The combined efforts of the IURD and Cancão Nova have changed the religious dynamic in Portugal, while Guadalupismo has significantly altered the religious landscape of the United States. Even more remarkably, the instruments of these transformations were not elite Latin Americans but Catholic migrants and Pentecostal missionaries. No longer is Latin America religiously dependent; its religious liberation has made it influential around the world.

Of all the recent religious developments in Latin America, Edward Cleary saw the liberation and empowerment of the laity as the least noticed and most important. Priests and bishops experienced a change of degree—they became more committed to the poor, to the oppressed, and to evangelization than their counterparts of sixty years ago—but the laity was utterly transformed. The combination of CEBs, NEMs, and the Charismatic Renewal created millions upon millions of active Catholics who were involved in so many different projects, developed so many new institutions, wrote so much, changed so much, and learned so much, that they really did create a new religious environment. The beauty of it all, from the Catholic perspective, was that almost every socioeconomic group was reached in new ways: base ecclesial communities (CEBs) for the urban and rural poor, different new ecclesial movements (NEMs) for various strata of the middle class, and the CCR for the millions of Latin Americans intrigued by Pentecostal experience but seeking to remain Catholic. When Protestants are added into the picture—and they demonstrated costly personal decision making and a great deal of personal agency—it is clear that Vargas Llosa's prophecy of societal transformation and new Latin American agency has been fulfilled.

What is interesting is that Vargas Llosa apparently saw none of this. In 2002, responding to a question about the diminished horizons of the Latin American novel, Vargas Llosa implied that the new philosophy that he had been anticipating in 1970 had not yet arrived. Instead, he saw around him a truncated and superficial view of human existence, a view reflected in the contemporary novel:

> In this age characterized by consumerism and constant change, life seems to revolve around the present moment, and the idea of a *novela total*, an immortal work of art, is scarcely accepted today. In the past, an author wrote to achieve immortality, so that when he died his work would remain and he would continue to live on through it. The author's ambition was to attain this immortality through a perfect work of art. Nobody believes in immortality today, and such a notion has been replaced everywhere by an obsession with the present.[7]

Contemporary morality, in his view, lacked the new "religious, political, and moral values" he had mentioned in 1970. It was trapped in the present, unaware of the past and unable to lift its gaze toward the future. In short, one of the most perceptive and insightful observers of Latin American society and culture, a man whose adulthood spans exactly the years covered by this book, attached little importance to the trends identified in this study, if he saw them at all.[8] The invisibility of the rebirth of Christianity, at least to the region's elites, is the next chapter of this story.

The blindness or indifference of one of Latin America's leading intellectuals to the religious rebirth in the region indicates the need for some kind of reintegration of largely secular elites and their largely religious fellow citizens. If political, economic, and intellectual elites are serious about their commitment to Latin America, they need to take its religious side more seriously. At the very least, it behooves leaders and intellectuals to understand their people, which in this case includes becoming familiar with the religious transformation that has taken place over the past six decades. Saying, as Vargas Llosa did, that Latin Americans are obsessed with consumerism unfairly privileges mass culture over other aspects of society such as the family, church, and civic organizations where consumerism is dwarfed by compassion, piety, solidarity, and spirituality; asserting that nobody believes in immortality anymore discounts the "eternal life" millions of Christians explicitly affirm every Sunday; expecting people to adopt a post-Christian belief system, as Vargas Llosa seems to do, assumes a trajectory for the region that ignores the facts on the ground. The reality of Latin America is that it is more Christian today than it was when Vargas Llosa correctly said that it was "changing its skin." Now that it has done so he and other elites need to adjust their focus so they can see that the metamorphosis has made the region more, not less, religious.

From the other side, Latin American Christians need to understand that they have a problem of coherence and communication. For all their successes at the grassroots level, their divisions and inarticulateness mean that they have less prominence and influence than their numbers would seem to imply and are therefore almost inconsequential to elite observers such as Vargas Llosa. Neither division nor inarticulateness will be an easy problem to solve. Dialogue and cooperation are obvious steps to resolve the issue of division, but, as will be explained later, both Protestants and Catholics have doubts about the value of such a process.

As difficult as ecumenism will be, the problem of effective communication, especially the communication of coherent "religious, political, and moral values" that elites can take seriously and that can serve as a "master key for perceiving reality" will be one of the great challenges for

Latin American Christians in the twenty-first century. The temptation is to think that mass media and the internet have made communication easier than ever before. Obviously, though, the new cultural environment is, as Vargas Llosa correctly observes, almost totally focused on the present. It features cultural products—television shows, films, popular music, internet sites—that are ephemeral and commercial. They are produced in an almost industrial fashion in a process dominated by the demands of the market, with little concern for truth and beauty and without the intention of providing a "master key for perceiving reality."

Although most Christians have faltered in this media environment, Pentecostals and Catholic Charismatics have proven adept at producing and marketing their own music and television shows. It is not clear, however, that these cultural products have any great impact on those who consume them. They do present bits of Christian thought, such as defenses of traditional marriage, examples of forgiveness, or calls to greater devotion to Christ. Nevertheless, they have not proved effective at communicating Christianity as a total way of life, or at communicating Christianity as something to which elites should give any serious attention. Throughout the period under consideration in this book, intellectuals often attacked and sometimes supported the Catholic Church and various priests and bishops in relation to specific moral and political issues, but they seldom engaged Christianity itself. To most of them, Christianity simply did not appear to be a plausible source of "religious, political, and moral values."

In the face of continued challenges, the reborn Christianity described in these pages could fizzle out and become marginal, but if it does continue to grow and develop it will have to meet the challenge of communicating not only bits and pieces of its message but also the kind of comprehensive, reality-explaining message that Vargas Llosa once said Latin America was looking for. Of course, one possibility is that Christian organizations will come to dominate the airwaves, the internet, and the recording studios, in an attempted Christianization of mass culture. This seems unlikely for financial reasons and, more important, less fruitful than other approaches because of the ephemeral nature of manufactured cultural products. Much more difficult but more effective in the long term could be the building of culture-making and culture-preserving institutions that could build up cohorts of well-educated, articulate, culturally entrepreneurial believers. The slow expansion of Protestant education, the revitalization of Catholic education, the birth of something like the

Benedictine monasticism that planted Catholicism in Europe after the fall of Rome—one or all of these could start producing large numbers of living examples of Christianity as a universal value system. Perhaps it will be Focolare or one of the other new Catholic movements, or perhaps it will be a reformed and intellectually rigorous Pentecostalism, but more likely it will be some obscure movement no contemporary observer would expect. Wherever it originates, the next era for Latin American Christianity will have arrived when some element of today's religious ferment presents a "master key for perceiving reality" that even intellectuals and elites cannot ignore.

Two central areas in the Christian struggle for plausibility and influence are Catholic-Protestant dialogue and the relations of indigenous Christians with other Latin American Christians. The two sets of relationships both revolve around the nature of Christianity and the call of Christians to unity. If Christians can resolve these relationships in some clear and obvious manner, they will go a long way toward presenting the idea that despite obvious differences, there is some set of core beliefs and values that Christians share, which would pave the way for the kind of unifying philosophy that Vargas Llosa was awaiting. Conversely, failure in these two areas would represent a further fracturing of Latin American society, both because the different groups of Christians could not cooperate on a practical level and because, at a more philosophical level, it would appear that there was no basis for such cooperation.

## Catholic-Protestant Relations

While Protestant growth spurred the rebirth of Catholicism, this is not to say that many Catholics *recognized* that fact, much less valued it. Unfortunately for both sides, thriving Protestant churches and reinvigorated Catholic movements have experienced tension and conflict.

Many Protestants used to dismiss Catholicism as a superstitious sub-Christian religion. In his early writings, SIL founder Cameron Townsend conflated "Romish" practices with exploitation by "witch doctors" and "saloon keepers."[9] Meanwhile, Catholic bishops labeled Protestants as dupes of the United States who had accepted a religion with little theological content. However, the enlivened religions of the 1990s and beyond should have been harder to dismiss, at least if either side was fair to the other and intellectually honest about itself. Since Latin America has become the region of the world with both the most Catholics and the most

Pentecostals, and since Protestants and Catholics together make up an overwhelming majority in every Latin American nation, and since both versions of Christianity have much to say about social and moral issues, there are compelling reasons for a Protestant-Catholic conversation to be center-stage in Latin America today.

Even if neither side had anything specific to say about democracy, human rights, social justice, sexuality, marriage, abortion, economic development, or poverty, simply as the two major blocs of Christian believers in the region, it would make sense for them to see whether they could work together for peace and prosperity. Given the fact that the Bible and the detailed social and moral teaching of the Catholics have all sorts of implications for public policy and for society in general, it would seem almost mandatory that the two groups get to know one another, clarify their positions, find areas of agreement, and work together where they can. After all, it is indisputable that Protestant and Catholic Latin Americans will make the future of the region. However, in no other large region of the world is the relationship between Protestants and Catholics worse than in Latin America.

There were some ecumenical successes, especially in Chile. There, the archbishop of Santiago and the leaders of Pentecostal churches signed an agreement in which they accepted the validity of baptism in each other's churches.[10] Cooperation that started during the Pinochet dictatorship led to the formation of an ecumenical center in Santiago and continued with Protestant scholars studying with the Chilean Jesuits and Catholic scholars earning doctorates in Pentecostal studies.[11] For Latin America as a region, a high point for Catholic-Protestant ecumenism occurred in 1999, when forty leaders from the Catholic Church and various (mostly Pentecostal) Protestant denominations released a joint statement after spending several days together in Quito, Ecuador. Rejoicing that barriers had dropped as they prayed together and came to know one another, the leaders committed themselves "to search together for new and lasting roads of convergence."[12]

However, despite assurances from the Catholic bishops' council, CELAM, of commitment to continue the dialogue started in Quito, little happened in the next decade. Part of the reason was the loss of the attention of Richard John Neuhaus, who had led a successful attempt to bring Evangelicals and Catholics together in the United States, starting in 1992, and who had spearheaded the attempt to do the same in Latin America. At the Synod for the Americas in 1997 Neuhaus, a Lutheran pastor who became a Catholic priest, lobbied for the Catholic Church to take dialogue with Protestants seriously; the Quito meeting and statement of 1999 were in large part the fruit of his efforts.[13] Because of ill health and other commitments, Neuhaus, who died in 2009, could not continue his efforts in Latin America and no one like him—respected by Catholics and Protestants alike *and* committed to dialogue and cooperation—emerged to pick up the torch.

Ecumenism in Latin America failed for many reasons, but ignorance and prejudice were chief among them. Unfortunately, even at the highest levels Catholics did not understand Protestants and tended to accept simplistic accounts of their origins, history, and beliefs. For instance, the archbishop of Guatemala called Protestants "instruments of rich foreign governments" who had "no social conscience." The papal nuncio in Mexico announced that the "the sects, like flies, need to be thrown out" because they were causing strife and "denationalizing" the country.[14] Cardinal Juan Sandoval of Guadalajara characterized Protestants as generally offensive and said, "They are here on the initiative of the United States, as we know from the Rockefeller Plan," a reference to the widely believed notion that the Rockefeller family had engineered the Protestantization of Latin America. Cardinal Sandoval and other Latin American bishops, asserted Edward Cleary, had "almost no intellectual resources to enter into a dialogue with indigenous Pentecostalism" because Catholics in academia seemed to see Pentecostalism as among the least valuable topics of study. Latin American Catholics, in fact, were much more likely to risk their lives opposing unjust regimes than they were to study Pentecostalism. Without solid academic information about the history and reality of Latin American Protestantism, Catholics who wanted to learn more turned to the only literature readily available: anti-Protestant books that were "polemical and global, lumping all but historical Protestants into the same category of sect, or worse, cult."[15] Sadly, the conspiracy theories and reductionist accounts offered in these materials did not prepare Catholics to understand their Protestant neighbors. Especially when dealing with homegrown Pentecostal movements, a Catholic who paid serious attention to the issues of healing, spiritual warfare, and prophecy would have been much more likely to gain a hearing than one who mentioned foreign governments or "the Rockefeller Plan," but very few Catholics had the knowledge and the interest to do so.

From the Protestant side, theology continued to pose the largest barrier. Protestant converts often consciously rejected Mary's special status, prayer to the saints, and "works righteousness." Unfortunately, in their pre-conversion days, many of these individuals did not know or understand the official Catholic position on these issues, as poor or absent Catholic catechesis often had failed to make it known to them, so they were rejecting positions that the Church actually did not hold. Luis Palau, for instance, saw great success in calling Catholics away from the "dead Christ" of Catholicism to the living Christ of Protestantism, but such an appeal could work only on those with a superficial understanding of Catholicism.

If Protestants could put aside some of the preconceptions about what Catholics believed, they might find more common ground than they had expected. To give just one example, in 1999 the Vatican and the Lutheran World Federation signed a joint declaration on the relationship of faith and works in justification, exactly the issue over which Martin Luther had broken with Rome in the sixteenth century.[16] In 2008, Pope Benedict went so far as to say, "Luther's phrase 'faith alone' is true, if it is not opposed to faith in charity, in love."[17] In other words, on the most contentious issue of the Reformation, Lutherans and Catholics had reached substantial agreement. Latin American Protestants nevertheless seemed oblivious to this, despite its potential to revolutionize Catholic-Protestant relations.[18] If interest in dialogue does grow, the ecumenical work already done in Europe and the United States could provide guidelines and departure points for the Latin American conversation.

For a variety of reasons, it will probably have to be the Catholics who take the initiative.

First, Catholics are still the majority in every Latin American country and, at least on an institutional level, are unified. With the dominant Pentecostals split into countless denominations and in disagreement among themselves and with non-Pentecostal Protestants, there is no obvious ecumenical leader or agenda that could come from that side of the aisle. Second, memories of violence by the Catholic majority against Protestant converts still fester in many, if not most, Protestant bodies. Catholic calls for dialogue and cooperation would go nowhere unless Catholics actually asked for forgiveness from Protestants. Third, Catholics have the theological resources to commit themselves to ecumenical dialogue, including a developed body of doctrine specifically devoted to ecumenism. While some individual Pentecostals surely desire dialogue and cooperation with Catholics, Vatican II and the magisterium of John Paul II have given all Catholics a deep well from which to draw. From a theological perspective, in fact, ecumenism is a requirement, not an option, for Catholics.

There is no doubt that dialogue will be difficult. Pentecostals often see Catholics as "unsaved" idolaters. Catholics return the favor by viewing Pentecostals as fanatical, foreign, and unchristian.[19] Those Pentecostals who do participate in an official dialogue can expect to be criticized and even ostracized by their denominations for doing so; those Catholics who participate can expect disapproval from elements of the hierarchy. Despite these real barriers, there are some steps that Catholics could take to increase the possibility for meaningful dialogue.

First, Catholics could stop using loaded terms, especially the term "sect," when referring to Protestants.[20] As Cardinals Edward Cassidy and Walter Kasper of the Vatican's council for Christian unity have made clear, evangelicals and Pentecostals should not be described in this way.[21] If better relations were truly desired, Catholics could employ less offensive terminology not only during official dialogue but also in everyday life.

Second, Catholics should understand that many Protestants can see serious problems in the Protestant world. For instance, Milton Acosta, a professor at a Protestant seminary in Colombia, recently lamented that many neo-Pentecostals were guilty of "faulty theology," "divisionism," and shamanism. The existence of pastors who demanded financial contributions as proof of parishioners' faith, self-declared prophets and apostles, and "experts" in demonology—all widespread throughout Latin America—showed that these new movements had departed from orthodox Protestantism. In fact, he charged, much of neo-Pentecostalism was actually a syncretistic religion, "neither Protestant nor Catholic" but rather a combination of "popular Catholic religiosity with popular Protestant religiosity."[22] Similarly, David Roldán, a professor at a Protestant seminary in Buenos Aires, criticized neo-Pentecostalism for failing to uphold the authority of the Bible, for inducing a "servile state of mind" in its adherents, and for claiming that only members of a specific church were true Christians. In fact, he said, a neo-Pentecostal church with these characteristics was "almost like a sect."[23] In other words, respected Protestant leaders had serious concerns about the theology and practice of some Pentecostal and neo-Pentecostal groups. Such leaders were ripe for dialogue with thoughtful and respectful Catholics, with whom they probably had more in common than they did with neo-Pentecostals.

Third, Catholic leaders should be reassured that meaningful dialogue is possible. The Vatican's ongoing conversations with the Lutheran World Federation have been especially fruitful, but perhaps even more important for Latin America was the Vatican's dialogue with Pentecostal bodies. Starting in 1972, the Pontifical Council for Promoting Christian Unity started meeting with representatives of Pentecostal denominations, including the Church of God of Prophecy and the Assemblies of God, to build relationships, find areas of agreement, and understand the issues on which they disagreed. The release in 2006 of *On Becoming a Christian: Insights from Scripture and the Patristic Writings, With Some Contemporary Reflections*, the statement from the fifth phase of the dialogue, should encourage Latin American Catholic leaders for four reasons:

1. as in the previous four phases, Catholic and Pentecostal leaders met for intensive and productive meetings in both Catholic and Pentecostal sites, in both Catholic-majority and Protestant-majority nations (Italy, Austria, USA);
2. these top level meetings revealed significant areas of agreement on issues related to conversion, faith, and baptism;
3. when disagreement did emerge it led not to recrimination but to the identification of topics for future dialogue, such as, for instance, hermeneutics (principles of interpretation);
4. the involvement of Father Luis Ramos of Mexico and Monsignor Juan Usma of Colombia on the Catholic side and Marta Palma of Chile on the Pentecostal side demonstrated that Latin American leaders were willing to participate in such a process.[24]

The pessimism of Latin American prelates about Catholic-Pentecostal dialogue is simply not warranted.

One potentially fruitful area for conversation and cooperation, for instance, is the area of sexual morality, where Pentecostals and Catholics had a great deal in common. The political momentum toward the legalization of abortion and the redefinition of marriage, coming not only from progressive Latin American sectors but also from aid agencies, the United Nations, and the developed nations, meant that continued non-cooperation between the two largest groups of traditional Christians would probably guarantee the success of their political rivals. It will be interesting to see what proves more compelling: inaction based on long-standing grievances or the possibility of working together to preserve traditional moral arrangements.

Fourth, Catholic bishops, priests, and lay leaders could educate themselves about the history of Protestantism in Latin America and about the priority of ecumenism in the recent magisterium of the church. As far as history is concerned, today's Catholic leaders simply cannot do their jobs effectively if they do not understand the Protestants who fill their cities. They need to give up conspiracy theories that demean the religious decisions of millions of people and they need to take seriously the Catholic weaknesses and Protestant strengths that facilitated Protestant growth. Since the data indicate that Catholicism has been revitalized in exactly those areas where Protestantism has prospered, they might come to see that religious competition is not a zero-sum game.[25] As far as ecumenism is concerned, the issue is fairly simple: Vatican II requires it.[26]

Of course, even some well-meaning Catholic leaders simply cannot conceive of dialogue with Pentecostals. One Catholic theologian, assessing the prospects for ecumenical dialogue in Latin America, asserted that such dialogue could take place with Baptists, Methodists, and similar "historic" denominations, but that "with the majority of Pentecostal groups dialogue is not possible."[27] Since Pentecostals make up the vast majority of Latin American Protestants, such a view would effectively rule out meaningful dialogue, restricting it to the least dynamic Protestant sectors. This pessimistic assessment has particularly unfortunate implications because dialogue with Protestants and especially with Pentecostals offers more potential benefits for Latin America than for any other region of the world. In no other large region does the Protestant-Catholic relationship promise to shape the future of society. The bishops, who would lead any official ecumenical dialogue, are facing a crisis of faith. They can believe, as John Paul II said in *Ut Unim Sint,* "At the Second Vatican Council, the Catholic Church committed herself irrevocably to following the path of the ecumenical venture," or they can turn away from ecumenism because of their preconceptions about its supposed impossibility.[28]

Of course, this is a two-way street: if Catholics initiate dialogue, Protestants will have to respond. One promising catalyst for that would be for Protestants to start seeing Catholic theology as a resource for serious deliberation and reflection on contemporary moral and social issues. There is a centuries-long Catholic tradition of theological reflection that Protestants could not duplicate because of the fragmentation of Protestant churches. Catholic social teaching—starting with Leo XIII's *Rerum Novarum* and going through John Paul II's *Centisimus Annus* and Benedict XVI's *Caritas in Veritate*—offers an accessible body of doctrine that employs the basic social principles of solidarity and subsidiarity to deal with a host of more specific issues such as working conditions, labor unions, private property, and the role of governments.[29] Without having to accept the authoritative nature of these documents, Protestants could use them as sources for reflection. Eventually, study and dialogue based on Catholic documents could enable Protestants to systematize their own social and theological ideas.

## *The Hispanic Captivity of Indigenous Christians*

It might be surprising that one of the main challenges for Latin American Christianity in the coming decades concerns indigenous Christians, since they figured so prominently in the story of Christianity's rebirth. However, there are worrying signs that the Catholic Church and Protestant denominations are pressuring indigenous Christians to conform to the cultural standards of the mestizo mainstream in a way that is damaging not only to indigenous culture but also to the life of faith.

As the work of historians Lamin Sanneh and Andrew Walls has made clear, the mother tongue plays a pivotal role in the development of Christianity in a given culture.[30] When the faith is understood and practiced in the vernacular, and particularly when the Bible and other religious documents are translated into the vernacular, Christianity can put down deep cultural roots. On the other hand, when Christians must learn the faith and practice it in languages other than their mother tongue, it is difficult for Christianity to take hold in a meaningful way. Sanneh describes two corresponding forms of missionary activity: diffusion, in which the missionary culture is the "inseparable carrier of the message," and translation, in which the receiving culture is the "true and final locus of the proclamation." In the first form the recipient culture assimilates the culture of the missionaries, while in the second form the recipient culture engages in "conscious critical reflection" that accepts the new religion but relativizes the missionary culture.[31] Clearly, "mission as translation" brought the unprecedented rebirth of indigenous Christianity in recent decades. Reached in their own tongues, often by means of vernacular scriptures, indigenous peoples from Mexico to South America accepted universal versions of Christianity in large numbers and experienced deep transformations in lifestyle and social participation that strengthened ethnic identity at the same time. It seems, however, that a new attempt at "mission as diffusion" by mestizo Latin Americans is endangering the fruits of successful "mission as translation" among indigenous Latin Americans.

On the Protestant side, mestizo-run denominations in Latin America have little appreciation for indigenous language or culture. With a few exceptions they tend to look down upon indigenous languages (which they pejoratively call "dialects") and are attempting to impose Spanish or Portuguese in indigenous areas. In some cases they have prohibited the use of vernacular Bibles. For instance, after SIL translator William Bivin worked as a consultant for a Bible translation into the language of an ethnic group with about 250,000 speakers (in a Latin American nation he did not name for political reasons) he observed that four Protestant denominations with about 300 churches among that ethnic group had almost no interest in the new indigenous Bible. The Spanish-speaking mestizos who ran these denominations wanted the indigenous churches to use the Spanish Bible, despite the fact that many if not most of the people would be unable to understand it. "The growing hegemony of Spanish-speaking churches over indigenous churches," lamented Bivin, "is producing an identity crisis on the part of many indigenous believers." The root of the problem was the "naïve assertion of entitlement to dominate culturally and spiritually on the part of the national or Latino leaders."[32]

The irony is that the Bible that the mestizo Protestants wanted the indigenous to use was, of course, also a translation and the mestizo culture deemed superior was only one of many cultures practiced by Christians around the world. Mestizo Protestants had lost sight of the basic facts that Jesus spoke Hebrew and Aramaic, not Spanish, and lived his earthly life as a Jew, not a Latin American mestizo. The mistake of elevating mestizo language and culture came from the maturity and confidence of a group that had internalized the gospel to such an extent that it seemed natural to their own culture. Nevertheless, this mestizo cultural myopia had become a danger to indigenous believers because it denied to them the same opportunity to respond to the gospel in their own culture. This is an area where educated and influential Protestants, such as leading pastors, theologians, and professors, need to make their voices heard. As the ambivalent spiritual offspring of North American missionaries, Latin American Protestants should know the dangers of cultural prejudice too well to let their own countrymen dominate and disfigure indigenous Christianity. The danger, however, is actually greater in this case because even at the height of missionary influence mestizos always vastly outnumbered the handful of missionaries, while today's indigenous Protestants have no such advantage over mestizo Protestants.

From the Catholic perspective, the situation is distinct but similarly grave. On an official doctrinal level, the Catholic Church affirms the value of different cultures. *Ad Gentes*, for instance, said, "whatever good is found to be sown in the hearts and minds of men, or in the rites and cultures peculiar to various peoples, not only is not lost, but is healed, uplifted, and perfected for the glory of God" when people from that culture came into the church.[33] Paul VI had called for "full evangelization of culture, or more correctly of cultures" so that each one could be "regenerated by an encounter with the Gospel."[34] Some bishops, such as Samuel Ruiz in Chiapas and Leonidas Proaño in Ecuador took such teaching seriously and tried to translate the gospel into the indigenous languages and cultures of their dioceses. In many cases such bishops saw remarkable spiritual growth in local indigenous groups, as cultures truly were "regenerated"—not as copies of mestizo society but as indigenous Catholic cultures.

The negative side for Catholics is that, even after more than 500 years of Catholicism in Latin America, most of the hundreds of different indigenous languages lacked any sort of vital vernacular Catholic witness. There were a few cases, such as in Chiapas, where dioceses sponsored translation projects and there were a few places where Catholics and Protestants had worked together on unified translations of the New Testament or the whole Bible. However, far too many indigenous Catholics, perhaps millions, had to worship in foreign languages and had no way to read about their faith in their mother tongues. After an intense period of linguistic and translation work in the early colonial period, the hierarchy simply dropped translation as a priority, effectively consigning indigenous Catholics to second-class spiritual citizenship and unleashing an almost certain process of syncretism.

The objection that translation was a painstaking and labor-intensive process was not irrational: the translation of even just the Bible, the liturgy, and the Catechism of the Catholic Church into the indigenous languages of Latin America would take decades of work by hundreds if not thousands of linguists. However, one only has to look at recent Protestant history in the region to see that such a project is possible. The Summer Institute of Linguistics, today the world's largest Bible translation organization, could serve as a model and inspiration for Catholic translation work. In 1932 the organization was no more than the dream of a destitute former fundamentalist missionary and Bible salesman named Cameron Townsend. When it actually started to train linguists in 1934 it did so on a shoestring budget in primitive borrowed facilities. It survived only because it won the support of influential fundamentalist leaders in the United States and of Mexican revolutionary nationalists such as Lázaro Cárdenas.[35] Today it has a worldwide network of more than 5,000 linguists working on 2,500 different languages that demonstrates the power not of US industrialists, as Latin American Catholics and American academics tend to believe, but of Townsend's total commitment to the project of translation and his ability to share his vision with fellow fundamentalists and secular Latin American leaders. In other words, existing religious networks and government contacts, of which the Catholic Church has far more today than Townsend ever had, would probably suffice. What appears to be lacking, though, is the conviction that indigenous Catholics deserve to worship and to study the faith in their mother tongues.

Finally, for non-indigenous Protestants and non-indigenous Catholics, relations with indigenous Christians serve as a test of sorts: the extent to which the non-indigenous adopt mission-as-cultural-diffusion will signal the extent to which Christianity has become culturally captive. Enforced cultural and linguistic conformity, if continued, will damage not only the indigenous cultures on which they are imposed but also the newly revitalized mestizo Protestantism and Catholicism, which will gradually confuse Christianity and culture, slowly dimming their missionary zeal.

On the indigenous side, there is a need for intellectuals who can develop and clearly articulate the legitimacy of indigenous Christianity in a way that makes sense to both indigenous and non-indigenous Latin Americans. Too often those indigenous Christians who seek higher education leave their culture and language behind, but today's crisis calls for theologically astute indigenous leaders who know Christian history, theology, and philosophy and who can operate confidently in both the mainstream academy and in the indigenous village. The indigenous churches need to see that such individuals are not superfluous to Christian life, but rather essential to its growth and proper development.

Although the triumphs of Christianity in Latin America over the past sixty years have been great, they do not guarantee future success. The challenges of division and indigenous Christianity cannot be surmounted by business-as-usual approaches. The need for Protestant-Catholic dialogue requires both sides to take drastic steps to prioritize relations with those they have seen as rivals, even enemies. The crisis of indigenous

Christianity demands a similarly difficult change of trajectory. The non-indigenous must give up control over indigenous culture. And leaders must develop theologies of culture and mission that affirm local culture without vitiating the Christian message.[36] For Protestants, this will be an enormous theological challenge, and it is far from clear that Protestant seminaries have the ability, or even the interest, to meet it. Perhaps indigenous Christianity is one area in which Catholic successes—which seem more likely at this point due to the worldwide network of Catholic theological institutions—will reverse the order of the previous six decades and stand as a challenge to Protestants. Whatever happens, the history of Latin American Christianity over the past six decades suggests that the resolution of the issues surrounding indigenous Christianity somehow will involve both Protestants and Catholics.

# Notes

INTRODUCTION

1. Philip Jenkins, *The Next Christendom: The Coming of Global Christianity* (New York: Oxford University Press, 2002), 1–3, 12; "World Christianity, 1910–2010," *International Bulletin of Missionary Research* 34, no. 1 (January 2010): 32–3.

2. Jonathan Bonk, "Africa and the Christian Mission," *International Bulletin of Missionary Research* 33, no. 2 (April 2009): 1–2.

3. Lamin Sanneh, *Whose Religion Is Christianity? The Gospel beyond the West* (Grand Rapids, MI: Eerdmans, 2003), 15.

4. Tony Lambert, "Counting Christians in China: A Cautionary Report," *International Bulletin of Missionary Research* 27, no. 1 (January 2003): 6–10. The range is quite broad because of the difficulty of counting the Christians involved in unregistered house churches.

5. Steve Moon, "The Recent Korean Missionary Movement: A Record of Growth, and More Growth Needed," *International Bulletin of Missionary Research* 27, no. 1 (January 2003): 11.

6. Ernesto Cardenal, *The Gospel in Solentiname* (Maryknoll, NY: Orbis, 2010 [1975]), xi–v, 18–9.

7. Marjo de Theije, "CEBs and Catholic Charismatics in Brazil," in Christian Smith and Joshua Prokopy, eds., *Latin American Religion in Motion* (New York: Routledge, 1999), 111–8.

8. Enrique Marroquín, *El Botín Sagrado: la dinámica religiosa en Oaxaca* (Oaxaca: Del Barro Nuestro, 1992), 11. The Cursillo movement, described in Chapter 8, is a Catholic reform movement that holds retreats and follow-up meetings for lay Catholics.

9. Jeffrey Klaiber, *The Jesuits in Latin America: 450 Years of Inculturation, Defense of Human Rights, and Prophetic Witness* (Saint Louis: Institute of Jesuit Sources, 2009), 129–39.

10. Bartolomé de Las Casas, *A Brief Account of the Destruction of the Indies* (Middlesex: Echo, 2007 [1552]).

11. Klaiber, *The Jesuits*, 127–41.

12. These indigenous religions were not identical to pre-Columbian religion, for most large-scale religious institutional structures had been destroyed by the Spaniards or Portuguese and, clearly, Christianity had significantly influenced beliefs and practices.

13. Juana Inés de la Cruz, "Critique of a Sermon of One of the Greatest Preachers [Carta Atenagórica]," in *Sor Juana Inés de la Cruz: Selected Writings* (Mahwah, NJ: Paulist Press, 2005), 219–49.

14. Brazil had a different trajectory due to its hosting of the Portuguese court when it fled Napoleonic invasion in 1807 and then due to Prince Pedro's decision to stay in Brazil to create an independent Brazilian Empire after the Napoleonic threat to Portugal was gone.

15. José Oscar Beozzo, "The Church and the Liberal States," in Enrique Dussel, ed., *The Church in Latin America, 1492–1992* (Maryknoll, NY: Orbis, 1992), 132–6.

16. Thomas O'Brien, *The Revolutionary Mission: American Enterprise in Latin America, 1900–1945* (New York: Cambridge University Press, 1996).

17. José Enrique Rodó, *Ariel* (Austin: University of Texas Press, 1988 [1900]).

18. Ruben Dario, "To Roosevelt," in *Selected Poems of Ruben Dario* (Austin: University of Texas Press, 1988).

19. Alberto Hurtado, *¿Es Chile un País Católico?* (Santiago: Editorial Splendor, 1941); John Considine, *Call for 40,000* (New York: Longmans, 1946); Tercera Semana Interamericana de Acción Católica: Documentos (Lima, 1953). An English summary of the Chimbote documents is available in William Coleman, *Latin American Catholicism: A Self-Evaluation* (Maryknoll, NY: Maryknoll Publications, 1958).

20. Pius XII, "Ad Ecclesiam Christi," Vatican, http://www.vatican.va/holy_father/pius_xii/apost_letters/documents/hf_p-xii_apl_19550629_ad-ecclesiam-christi_lt.html; John Considine, *The Church in the New Latin America* (Notre Dame, IN: Fides, 1964), 100.

21. Considine, *Call for 40,000*, 103.

22. John O'Malley, *What Happened at Vatican II* (Cambridge, MA: Belknap Press, 2008), 123; Edward Cleary, *Crisis and Change: The Church in Latin America Today* (Maryknoll, NY: Orbis, 1985), 18–20.

23. The "general" conferences of CELAM are massive events that include hundreds of bishops, whereas the "ordinary" or annual meetings include a smaller group of CELAM officers and officers from the national episcopal conferences. Cleary, *Crisis and Change*, 20; O'Malley, *What Happened at Vatican II*, 122.

24. *Lumen Gentium*, 1, 3–5, 9, 11, 18, 25, 31, 33, 36. The numbers following council documents refer to the numbered sections of the documents, which are the same regardless of the volume or site in which the documents are found. The

documents of Vatican II are available at the Vatican website (http://www.vatican. va/archive/hist_councils/ii_vatican_council/index.htm) and in Austin Flannery, ed., *Vatican Council II: Volume I, The Conciliar and Post-Conciliar Documents*, new revised edition (Northport, NY: Costello, 1975). For the role of the laity, see also *Apostolicam Actuositatem*.

25. *Unitatis Redintegratio*, 1, 3, 4, Second Vatican Council, November 21, 1964, http:// www.vatican.va/archive/hist_councils/ii_vatican_council/documents/vat-ii_ decree_19641121_unitatis-redintegratio_en.html.

26. *Dignitatis Humanae*, Second Vatican Council, December 7, 1965, http://www. vatican.va/archive/hist_councils/ii_vatican_council/documents/vat-ii_ decl_19651207_dignitatis-humanae_en.html.

27. John Paul II explains his view of Vatican II in Karol Wojtyla, *Sources of Renewal: The Implementation of Vatican II* (San Francisco: Harper and Row, 1980), but all of his encyclicals and his Catechism of the Catholic Church feature the council's writings so prominently that it is clear that Vatican II was the most important influence on his pontificate.

28. Editors, "Worldwide Increase in Catholic Population, Deacons, Priests, and Bishops," *International Bulletin of Missionary Research* 36, no. 1 (January 2012): 41. Europe had only about 24 percent of the world's Catholics.

CHAPTER 1

1. Lynda Barrow, "Mission in Mexico: An Evangelical Surge," *Christian Century* (February 28, 2001): 24.

2. Edward Cleary, "Shopping Around: Questions about Latin American Conversions," *International Bulletin of Missionary Research* 28, no. 2 (April 2004): 50.

3. Mortimer Arias, "Contextual Evangelization in Latin America: Between Accommodation and Confrontation," *Occasional Bulletin of Missionary Research* 2, no. 1 (1978): 22: Merlin Brinkerhoff and Reginald Bibby, "Circulation of the Saints in South America: A Comparative Approach," *Journal for the Scientific Study of Religion* 24, no. 1 (March 1985): 50–1.

4. Gary Campbell, "Mexican Presbyterians' Adventure of Faith," *International Review of Mission* 64, no. 254 (April 1975): 200.

5. Gary MacEoin, "How the CIA's 'Dirty Tricks' Threaten Mission Efforts," *Christian Century* 92, no. 8 (March 5, 1975): 217–23.

6. Conrad Kanagy, "The Formation and Development of a Protestant Conversion Movement among the Highland Quichua of Ecuador," *Sociological Analysis* 51, no. 2 (1990): 209.

7. Todd Hartch, *Missionaries of the State: The Summer Institute of Linguistics, State Formation, and Indigenous Mexico, 1935–1985* (Tuscaloosa: University of Alabama Press, 2006), 85.

8. Hartch, *Missionaries of the State*, 106.

9. Since the 1980s Protestant missionaries in indigenous communities often have made a concerted effort to avoid controversy by encouraging their converts to donate to fiestas and to do *tequio* (unpaid community work), thus minimizing disruption to village life: Carolyn Galleher, "The Role of Protestant Missionaries in Mexico's Indigenous Awakening," *Bulletin of Indigenous Research* 26, no. 1 (2007): 88–111.

10. Hartch, *Missionaries of the State,* 70.

11. "Acusan a Gobernación de dejar a los protestantes en completo desamparo," *El Popular* (Mexico), September 28, 1948. A similar wave of violent persecution is cited in Kanagy, "The Formation and Development of a Protestant Conversion Movement," 213.

12. Tibursio Maya et al. to Secretario de Gobernación, November 27, 1947, Dirección General de Gobierno, Secretaría de Gobernación, Archivo General de la Nación, Mexico City, file 2/340(72)1 (hereafter cited as AGN-DGG); F. Ocampo Noble to Jefe de la Oficina de Gobierno, January 3, 1948, AGN-DGG.

13. Rafael Vargas Rodríguez to Secretario de Gobernación, October 1, 1954, AGN-DGG.

14. David Ruesga claimed that in 1930 more than 100 Protestants were forced out of the town. David Ruesga to Adolfo Ruíz Cortines, September 16, 1948, AGN-DGG.

15. Gregorio Reyes et al. to Gobernador Constitucional del Estado de Hidalgo, August 26, 1948, AGN-DGG.

16. Presidente Municipal de Tepeji del Rio to Secretario General de Gobierno del Estado de Hidalgo, as quoted in Prospero Macotela Cravioto to Director General de Gobierno, December 16, 1952, AGN-DGG.

17. Unless otherwise noted, the information on Tepeji del Rio comes from Gaudencio Morales, "Informe que la Dirección General de Gobernación del Gobierno del Estado de Hidalgo se permite render a la Secretaría de Gobernación," Archivo General de la Nación, Ramo Ruíz Cortines, file 547.1/11 (hereafter cited as AGN-RC). Agapito Ramos, Alfredo Santín, and Antonio Cabrera to Angel Carvajal, June 17, 1953, AGN-DGG; Comandante de la 18/a Zona Militar to Secretaría de la Defensa Nacional, as quoted in Alberto Violante Pérez to Presidencia de la República, June 17, 1953, AGN-DGG; Roberto Rodríguez Morales to Presidente Constitucional de la República, June 17, 1953, AGN-RC.

18. Pablo Miranda, Antonio Miranda, and José Padilla were mentioned as part of the group persecuting Protestants in Agapito Ramos, Alfredo Santín, and Antonio Cabrera to Angel Carvajal, June 17, 1953, AGN-DGG.

19. Gonzalo Baez-Camargo, "Punish Mob for Attack on Chapel," *Christian Century* 70 (September 2, 1953): 998, as cited in Lindy Scott, *Salt of the Earth: A Sociopolitical History of Mexico City Evangelical Protestants, 1964–1991* (Mexico City: Editorial Kyrios, 1991), 46.

20. Hartch, *Missionaries of the State,* 97.

21. Paul Turner, "Religious Conversion and Community Development," *Journal for the Scientific Study of Religion* 18, no. 3 (1979): 257.

22. Hartch, *Missionaries of the State*, 96–100.

23. Hartch, *Missionaries of the State*, 98–100.

24. Hartch, *Missionaries of the State*, 168.

25. Hartch, *Missionaries of the State*, 168–75; Paul Jeffrey, "Evangelicals and Catholics in Chiapas: Conflict and Reconciliation," *Christian Century* (February 19, 1997): 195–7.

26. Christine Eber, "Buscando una nueva vida: Liberation through Autonomy in San Pedro Chenalhó, 1970–1998," *Latin American Perspectives* 28, no. 2 (March 2001): 48–51; Christine Kovic, "The Struggle for Liberation and Reconciliation in Chiapas, Mexico: Las Abejas and the Path of Nonviolent Resistance," *Latin American Perspectives* 30, no. 3 (May 2003): 58–9.

27. Instituto Nacional de Estadística y Geografía, Censo 2010, "Volumen y porcentaje de la población según profese alguna religión y tipo de religión, 1950 a 2010," http://www.inegi.org.mx/sistemas/sisept/default.aspx?t=mrel01&s=est&c=22443.

28. Virginia Garrard-Burnett, *Protestantism in Guatemala: Living in the New Jerusalem* (Austin: University of Texas Press, 1998), 60, 162.

29. "La religión católica ya no domina Guatemala," *Terra Noticias* (Madrid), August 14, 2009, http://noticias.terra.es/genteycultura/2009/0814/actualidad/la-religion-catolica-ya-no-domina-guatemala.aspx.

30. Garrard-Burnett, *Protestantism in Guatemala*, 81–8, 94.

31. Garrard-Burnett, *Protestantism in Guatemala*, 102–3.

32. Garrard-Burnett, *Protestantism in Guatemala*, 104–5. One exception to this divisive role of the new religions appears to have been the Maryknoll Sisters' medical work in Jacaltenango in the western highlands between 1963 and 1977, but even there the "Romanized" Catholicism introduced by the sisters was quite different from the indigenous traditions that it encountered: Susan Fitzpatrick Behrens, "Maryknoll Sisters, Faith, Healing, and the Maya Construction of Catholic Community in Guatemala," *Latin American Research Review* 44, no. 3 (2009): 27–49.

33. Ruben Beina and Norman Schwartz, "The Structural Context of Religious Conversion in Petén, Guatemala: Status, Community, and Multicommunity," *American Ethnologist* 1, no. 1 (February 1974): 164, 167–9, 178–80,

34. Garrard-Burnett, *Protestantism in Guatemala*, 116–9, 121, 131, 141–2, 155, 161.

35. David Scotchmer, "Symbols of Salvation: A Local Mayan Protestant Theology," *Missiology* 17, no. 3 (1989): 294, 302–3; David Suazo, "¿Es el protestantismo destructor de la cultura indígena?," *Kairos* no. 18 (1996): 78–9.

36. David Stoll, *Is Latin America Turning Protestant? The Politics of Evangelical Growth* (Berkeley: University of California Press, 1990), 131–4.

37. Sydney Rooy, "The Latin American Council of Churches and Missions: An Historical Approach," *Mission Studies* 20 (2003): 117–24, 129.

38. Sydney Rooy, "FTL History, a Bird's-Eye View," *Fraternidad Teológica Latinoamericana*, http://www.ftl-al.org/index.php?option=com_content&view=article&id=5 8&Itemid=60; Stoll, *Is Latin America Turning Protestant?*, 128–34.

39. Pedro Moreno, "Evangelical Churches," in Paul Sigmund, ed., *Religious Freedom and Evangelization in Latin America: The Challenge of Religious Pluralism* (Maryknoll, NY: Orbis, 1999), 60.

40. Stoll, *Is Latin America Turning Protestant?*, 174–5

41. Jeremy Weber, "Something Better than Revival," *Christianity Today* (June 2010): 38–40.

42. Jean-Pierre Bastian, "Violencia, etnicidad y religión entre los mayas del estado de Chiapas en México," *Mexican Studies/Estudios Mexicanos* 12, no. 2 (1996): 302.

43. Karl-Wilhelm Westmeier, *Protestant Pentecostalism in Latin America: A Study in the Dynamics of Missions* (Madison, NJ: Fairleigh Dickinson University Press, 1999), 23.

44. For instance, see Alvin Goffin, *The Rise of Protestant Evangelism in Ecuador, 1895–1990* (Gainesville: University Press of Florida, 1994), 28, 126, and Andrew Chesnut, *Born Again in Brazil: The Pentecostal Boom and the Pathogens of Poverty* (New Brunswick, NJ: Rutgers University Press, 1997), 30.

45. James E. Goff, *The Persecution of Protestant Christians in Colombia, 1948–1958, With an Investigation of Its Background and Causes* (Cuernavaca: Centro Intercultural de Documentación, 1968); Elizabeth Brusco, "Colombia," in Paul Sigmund, ed., *Religious Freedom and Evangelization in Latin America: The Challenge of Religious Pluralism* (Maryknoll, NY: Orbis, 1999), 238–44. A book needs to be written on the violent persecution of Protestants in Latin America.

46. Samuel Escobar, "The Missiological Significance of Latin American Protestantism," *International Review of Mission* 100, no. 2 (November 2011): 241. For the case that Latin America has a religious marketplace, see Anthony Gill, *Rendering unto Caesar: The Catholic Church and State in Latin America* (Chicago: University of Chicago Press, 1998) and Andrew Chesnut, *Competitive Spirits: Latin America's New Religious Economy* (New York: Oxford University Press, 2003).

47. Bastian, "Violencia," 309.

48. "Constitution of the Argentine Nation," Part, Chapter I, Section 2, Senado de la Nación Argentina, http://www.senado.gov.ar/web/interes/constitucion/english. php: "The Federal Government Supports the Roman Catholic Apostolic Religion"; Political Constitution of Peru, Article 50, Congress of the Republic of Peru, http://www.congreso.gob.pe/ntley/Imagenes/Constitu/Cons1993.pdf: "Dentro de un régimen de independencia y autonomía, el Estado reconoce a la Iglesia Católica como elemento importante en la formación histórica, cultural y moral del Perú, y le presta su colaboración."Political Constitution of the Republic of Costa Rica, Article 75, http://www.constitution.org/cons/costaric.htm: "La Religión Católica, apostólica, Romana, es la del Estado, el cual contribuye a su mantenimiento, sin impedir ellibre ejercicio en la República de otros cultos que no se opongan a lamoral universal ni a las buenas costumbres."

CHAPTER 2

1. Quotations and information are from W. Dayton Roberts, "The Legacy of R. Kenneth Strachan," *Occasional Bulletin of Missionary Research* 3, no. 1 (January 1979): 2–3.

2. W. Dayton Roberts and Paul E. Pretiz, "History of the Latin America Mission," *Latin America Mission*, http://www.lam.org/about/history/.

3. Quotations and information are from W. Dayton Roberts, "The Legacy of R. Kenneth Strachan," *Occasional Bulletin of Missionary Research* 3, no. 1 (January 1979): 2–3.

4. "Jesus Is the Light of the World: Evangelism-in-Depth," *Archives Bulletin Board*, Billy Graham Center, Wheaton College, http://www.wheaton.edu/bgc/archives/bulletin/bu0006.htm.

5. Roberts, "The Legacy," 4.

6. Roberts, "The Legacy," 4.

7. David Howard, "My Pilgrimage in Mission," *International Bulletin of Missionary Research* 21, no. 3 (July 1997): 117.

8. Roberts, "The Legacy," 5.

9. "Billy Graham Crusade Statistics: Chronological," Billy Graham Evangelistic Association, www.billygraham.org.

10. "160,000 Hear Graham," *New York Times*, July 4, 1960; "Baptists on the March," *Time*, July 18, 1960; Kristen Burke, "The Week of 840,000 Crusades," *Decision Magazine*, February 1, 2009, www.billygraham.org.

11. "Billy in Catholic Country: He Collides with Clergy," *Time*, February 23, 1962.

12. David Neff, "Fervor, Unity Greet Graham," *Christianity Today*, January 13, 1992.

13. "My Hope," Billy Graham Evangelistic Association, 2011, www.billygraham.org/myhope_index.asp; "My Hope History," Billy Graham Evangelistic Association, 2011, www.billygraham.org/myhope_history.asp.

14. Geremias Couto, "BGEA Bringing Hope of Christ to Brazil," *Decision Magazine*, October 1, 2008, www.billygraham.org; Jeremy Hunt, "God Moves Mightily," Billy Graham Evangelistic Association, http://www.billygraham.org/articlepage.asp?articleid=1581; "Brazil's One of the Largest Christian Evangelistic Efforts in History," *Christian Telegraph*, November 13, 2008, http://www.christiantelegraph.com/issue3850.html; "Minha Esperança Brasil: mais de trezentas mil converses," *Gnoticias, Gospel Mais Comunicação Cristã*, March 25, 2009, http://noticias.gospelmais.com.br/minha-esperanca-brasil-mais-de-trezentas-mil-conversoes.html.

15. Hongnak Koo, *The Impact of Luis Palau on Global Evangelism* (Grand Rapids, MI: Credo, 2010), 39.

16. James Davis, "Globe Trotting Evangelist Not Another Billy Graham," *Fort Lauderdale Sun Sentinel*, March 1, 1986; Martha Sawyer Allen, "Ministry Was Built upon Graham Mold," *Star Tribune* (Minneapolis), November 28, 2003.

17. Koo, *The Impact*, 208.

18. "Luis Palau: A Draw in U.S. and Latin America," *New York Times*, January 1, 1999.

19. "Religion: Palau Power in Latin America," *Time*, November 7, 1977.

20. "Religion: Palau Power in Latin America," *Time*, November 7, 1977.

21. Davis, "Globe Trotting Evangelist."

22. Davis, "Globe Trotting Evangelist"; Koo, *The Impact*, 209.

23. "Religion: Palau Power in Latin America," *Time*, November 7, 1977.

24. "'Luis Who?' Could Replace Graham as Leading Evangelist," *Capital* (Annapolis), May 19, 2007.

25. "Luis Palau: World Evangelist and Author," Luis Palau Association, http://www. palau.org/uploads/cms/files/downloads/about/lp%20long%20bio%20-%20 Aug%2010.pdf; Koo, *The Impact*, 172–5.

26. "Ministry Summary," Luis Palau Association, http://media.palau.org/press_kit/ ministry_statistics; "Luis Palau: World Evangelist and Author"; "Buenos Aires y Argentina, impactadas por el Festival con Luis Palau," Asociación Luis Palau, http://www.luispalau.net/festival_buenos_aires.htm.

27. "Monterrey, el gigante del norte Mexicano fue sacudido por un gran esfuerzo de la Asociación Luis Palau," Asociación Luis Palau, http://www.luispalau.net/ festival_monterrey.htm.

28. "Monterrey, el gigante del norte"; "Videos Festivales: Monterrey 2007," Asociación Luis Palau, http://www.luispalau.net/videos_festivales_iframe.asp?id= 4&idvideo=23

29. "Monterrey, el gigante del norte"; "Videos Festivales: Monterrey 2007"; Koo, *The Impact*, 147–51, 165–8.

30. Mortimer Arias, "Contextual Evangelization in Latin America: Between Accommodation and Confrontation," *Occasional Bulletin of Missionary Research* 2, no. 1 (1978): 23.

31. Jorge Maldonaldo, "Evangelicalism and the Family in Latin America: A Socio-pastoral Approach," *International Review of Missions* 82, no. 326 (1993): 194–5.

32. Paul VI, *Evangelii Nuntiandi* 14, December 8, 1975. http://www.vatican.va/holy_ father/paul_vi/apost_exhortations/documents/hf_p-vi_exh_19751208_ evangelii-nuntiandi_en.html.

33. Paul VI, "Evangelii Nuntiandi," art. 41–6, 52, 54.

34. Antonio González Dorado, "La nueva evangelización en América Latina," *Estudios eclesiásticos* 62, no. 262 (1992): 408.

35. CELAM, "Final Document," Art. 85, 173, 348, 364–6, in John Eagleson and Philip Scharper, eds., *Puebla and Beyond: Documentation and Commentary* (Maryknoll, NY: Orbis, 1979).

36. CELAM, "Final Document," Art. 456–7, 827, 1153.

37. John Paul II, "Address to the Bishops of CELAM, Rio de Janeiro," July 2, 1980, *Addresses and Homilies Given in Brazil*, vol. 2, trans. National Catholic News Service (Washington: United States Catholic Conference, 1980), 1–22.

38. John Paul II, "Discurso del Santo Padre Juan Pablo II a la asamblea del CELAM," March 9, 1983, http://www.vatican.va/holy_father/john_paul_ii/speeches/1983/march/documents/hf_jp-ii_spe_19830309_assemblea-celam_sp.html. Antonio González Dorado points out that the phrase "new evangelization" occurs in the documents of the Medellín (1968) and Puebla (1979) CELAM conferences: "La nueva evangelización en América Latina," *Estudios eclesiásticos* 62, no. 262 (1992): 399.

39. John Paul II, "Discurso Inaugural de la IV Conferencia General del Episcopado Latinoamericano," October 12, 1992, The Holy See, http://www.vatican.va/holy_father/john_paul_ii/speeches/1992/october/documents/hf_jp-ii_spe_19921012_iv-conferencia-latinoamerica_sp.html.

40. Consejo Episcopal Latinoamericano, "Fifth General Conference, Concluding Document, 2007," Art. 20–30, 99, 2007, http://www.celam.org/nueva/Celam/aparecida/Ingles.pdf.

41. John Paul II, *Ut Unim Sint*, May 25, 1995, The Holy See, http://www.vatican.va/holy_father/john_paul_ii/encyclicals/documents/hf_jp-ii_enc_25051995_ut-unum-sint_en.html.

42. Edward Cleary, *The Rise of Charismatic Catholicism in Latin America* (Gainesville: University Press of Florida, 2011), 154, 168; SINE: Sistema Integral de Evangelization, "P. Alfonso Navarro" and www.sinecentral.org/principal.html.

43. Escuelas de Evangelización San Andrés, "Programa de Formación," www.evangelizacion.com/programa.php, "Historia de las EESA," http://www.evangelizacion.com/historia.php, and "Proyecto Pastoral 2008," http://www.evangelizacion.com/documentos/ProyectoPastoral2008.pdf.

44. Guillermo Cook, "Christian Conversion: A Perspective from Latin America," *Mission Studies*10, no. 1–2 (1993): 99.

45. Arturo Piedra, "The New Latin American Protestant Reality," *Journal of Latin American Theology* 1, no. 1 (2006): 45–6.

46. Samuel Escobar, "The Missiological Significance of Latin American Protestantism," *International Review of Mission* 100, no. 2 (November 2011): 242.

47. William Bivin, "Mother Tongue Translations and Contextualization in Latin America," *International Bulletin of Missionary Research* 34, no. 2 (2010): 72–4; Lamin Sanneh, *Translating the Message: The Missionary Impact on Culture* (Maryknoll, NY: Orbis, 1989).

48. Samuel Escobar, "Católicos y evangélicos en América Latina frente al desafío del siglo veintiuno," *Kairós* no. 14 (1994): 75.

49. Edward Cleary, "Shopping Around: Questions about Latin American Conversions," *International Bulletin of Missionary Research* 28, no. 2 (April 2004): 52.

50. Edward Cleary, "In the Absence of Missionaries: Lay Preachers Who Preserved Catholicism," *International Bulletin of Missionary Research* 34, no. 2 (2010): 67–70.

51. Rodney Stark and Buster Smith, "Pluralism and the Churching of Latin America," *Latin American Politics and Society* 54, no. 2 (2012): 35–44.

52. David Stoll, *Is Latin America Turning Protestant? The Politics of Evangelical Growth* (Berkeley: University of California Press, 1990).

CHAPTER 3

1. "3 Chilean Bishops Snub the Military," *New York Times,* September 19, 1984.
2. "Cardinal in Chile Censures Regime," *New York Times,* March 14, 1983.
3. Jerry Knudson, "Chile's Catholic Opposition Press," *Christian Century* (December 10, 1986): 1121.
4. Ernesto Guevara, "Cuba: Historical Exception or Vanguard in the Anticolonial Struggle?" in *The Che Reader* (New York: Ocean Press, 2003), 130.
5. David Stoll, *Is Latin America Turning Protestant? The Politics of Evangelical Growth* (Berkeley: University of California Press), 337.
6. Stoll, *Is Latin America Turning Protestant?,* 182–209.
7. *Gaudium et Spes* 4, 10, 21, 26, 28, Second Vatican Council, December 7, 1965, http://www.vatican.va/archive/hist_councils/ii_vatican_council/documents/vat-ii_cons_19651207_gaudium-et-spes_en.html.
8. *Gaudium et Spes* 66, 68, 71.
9. *Gaudium et Spes* 52, 64, 67, 68, 71.
10. Helder Camara, "The Church and Modern Latin America" [1966] in *Conferencia Episcopal Peruana, Between Honesty and Hope: Documents from and about the Church in Latin America,* trans. John Drury (Maryknoll, NY: Maryknoll Publications, 1970), 36–45. Most of the new think tanks were run by the Jesuits.
11. Edward Cleary, *Crisis and Change: The Church in Latin America Today* (Maryknoll, NY: Orbis, 1985), 35–6.
12. Paul VI, *Populorum Progressio,* 7, 22–6, 44, 49, available at www.vatican.va; *Gaudium et Spes* 26, 52.
13. Paul VI, *Populorum Progressio,* 31.
14. The bishops also met in Bogotá on August 24, 1968 before reconvening in Medellín.
15. "Message to the Peoples of Latin America," in *Conferencia Episcopal Peruana, Between Honesty and Hope: Documents from and about the Church in Latin America,* trans. John Drury (Maryknoll, NY: Maryknoll Publications, 1970), 41–2.
16. "Justice," 3, 10, 14, 20, and "Peace," 22, 32, in *Conferencia Episcopal Peruana, Between Honesty and Hope: Documents from and about the Church in Latin America,* trans. John Drury (Maryknoll, NY: Maryknoll Publications, 1970).
17. "Poverty of the Church," 7–10, 15–18, in *Conferencia Episcopal Peruana, Between Honesty and Hope: Documents from and about the Church in Latin America,* trans. John Drury (Maryknoll, NY: Maryknoll Publications, 1970).
18. Gustavo Gutiérrez, *A Theology of Liberation: History, Politics, and Salvation* (Maryknoll, NY: Orbis, 1973 [1971]), 36–7, 87, 274–5.

19. Luis G. del Valle, "A Theological Outlook Starting from Concrete Events," in Rosino Gibellini, ed., *Frontiers of Theology in Latin America* (Marykoll, NY: Orbis, 1979 [1975]), 98.

20. Cleary, *Crisis and Change*, 15, 100–103.

21. Alfonso López Trujillo, *Testimonios* (Bogotá: Plaza y Janés, 1997), 109, 121–4.

22. Paul VI, "Evangelii Nuntiandi," 18, 29–30.

23. Paul VI, "Evangelii Nuntiandi," 32–5.

24. Cleary, *Crisis and Change*, 47; López Trujillo, *Testimonios*, 137.

25. Marshall Simpkin, "The Politics of 'Puebla 1979,'" *The Month* 240 (January 1979): 39; López Trujillo, *Testimonios*, 159.

26. CELAM, "Final Document," Art. 25–6, 85, 91, 189, 224, 281, 452, 486, 979, 1031, 1183, and John Paul II, "Opening Address at the Puebla Conference," in John Eagleson and Philip Scharper, eds., *Puebla and Beyond: Documentation and Commentary* (Maryknoll, NY: Orbis, 1979).

27. CELAM, "Final Document," Art. 29–43, 306, 317, 354, 1143, 1165, 1223–49, and John Paul II, "Address to the Indians of Oaxaca and Chiapas," in John Eagleson and Philip Scharper, eds., *Puebla and Beyond: Documentation and Commentary* (Maryknoll, NY: Orbis, 1979).

28. CELAM, "Final Document," Art. 827, in John Eagleson and Philip Scharper, eds., *Puebla and Beyond: Documentation and Commentary* (Maryknoll, NY: Orbis, 1979).

29. John Sinclair, "Historical Protestantism," in Paul Sigmund, ed., *Religious Freedom and Evangelization in Latin America: The Challenge of Religious Pluralism* (Maryknoll, NY: Orbis, 1999), 43.

30. Rene Padilla, "Evangelism and the World," in *International Congress on World Evangelization*, and J. D. Douglas, *Let the Earth Hear His Voice: Official Reference Volume, Papers and Responses* (Minneapolis: World Wide Publications, 1975), 134–46.

31. Samuel Escobar, "Evangelization and Man's Search for Freedom, Justice, and Fulfillment," in *International Congress, Let the Earth Hear His Voice* (Minneapolis: World Wide Publications, 1975), 319–26.

32. "Lausanne Covenant," July 25, 1974, The Lausanne Movement, http://www.lausanne.org/en/documents/lausanne-covenant.html.

33. There were even some Protestant revolutionaries, such as Frank Pais of Cuba: Sinclair, "Historical Protestantism," 44.

## CHAPTER 4

1. United Nations, *From Madness to Hope: The 12-Year War in El Salvador: Report of the Commission on the Truth for El Salvador* (New York: United Nations, 1993).

2. The great exception was Argentina, where the bishops played almost no role in the struggle against the military government and even went so far as to ignore

the Nobel Peace Prize given to priest Aldolfo Pérez Esquivel for his human rights work: Paul Freston, "Religious Pluralism, Democracy, and Human Rights in Latin America," in Thomas Banchoff and Robert Wuthnow, eds., *Religion and the Global Politics of Human Rights* (New York: Oxford University Press, 2011), 105.

3. Madeleine Adriance, "Opting for the Poor: A Social-Historical Analysis of the Changing Brazilian Catholic Church," *Sociological Analysis* 46, no. 2 (1985): 136.

4. Helder Camara, *Revolution through Peace* (New York: Harper & Row, 1971), 29, 39, 51, 75.

5. Adriance, "Opting for the Poor," 137; Scott Mainwaring, *The Catholic Church and Politics in Brazil, 1916–1985* (Stanford, CA: Stanford University Press, 1986), 66–8.

6. *Gaudium et Spes*, 26.

7. For instance, Dominican priests imprisoned by the military government specifically cited *Gaudium et Spes, Populorum Progressio*, and the Medellín document on peace as justification for their anti-government attitudes: "Accusation from Prison," *Communio Viatorum* 14, no. 1 (Spring 1971): 30, 60. Madeleine Adriance, "Whence the Option for the Poor," *Cross Currents* 34, no. 4 (Winter 1984): 504.

8. Adriance, "Opting for the Poor," 140–2.

9. Eula Kennedy Long, "Priests with Pricked Consciences," *Christian Century* (January 17, 1968): 82–3.

10. "Accusation from Prison," *Communio Viatorum* 14, no. 1 (Spring 1971): 30, 60.

11. "Brazilian Priest Murdered by Death Squad," *Christian Century* (June 18, 1969): 834.

12. Roberto Barbosa, "Catholic Church Renewal in Brazil: Defending the Oppressed," *Christian Century* (September 5, 1973): 862–3; James Bruce, "Brazil: Muzzling the Outspoken Church," *Christian Century* (October 22, 1975): 940–1.

13. Bruce, "Brazil: Muzzling the Outspoken Church."

14. Paulo Evaristo Arns, "A Preface and an Appeal," in Catholic Church, and Joan Dassin, *Torture in Brazil: A Shocking Report on the Pervasive Use of Torture by Brazilian Military Governments, 1964–1979* (Austin: Institute of Latin American Studies, University of Texas, 1998), xxv–xxvi.

15. Godofredo Deelen, "The Church on Its Way to the People: Basic Christian Communities in Brazil," *Cross Currents* 30, no. 4 (Winter 1980): 385, 396; Adriance, "Opting for the Poor," 140.

16. Quoted in Deelen, "The Church on Its Way to the People," 394.

17. Quotations are from Madeleine Adriance, "Base Communities and Rural Mobilization in Northeast Brazil," *Sociology of Religion* 55, no. 2 (1994): 173–4.

18. Quoted in Scott Mainwaring, *The Catholic Church and Politics in Brazil, 1916–1985* (Stanford, CA: Stanford University Press, 1986), 87.

19. Latifundia are enormous estates.

20. Mainwairing, *The Catholic Church*, 88; Dean Pearman, "The Silencing of Bishop Casaldáliga," *Christian Century* (October 26, 1988): 939–40.

21. Mainwaring, *The Catholic Church*, 93.

22. Quoted in Mainwaring, *The Catholic Church*, 93, 103.

23. Two of the largest Pentecostal denominations, however, championed the military government throughout its time in power: Sinclair, "Historical Protestantism," 46.

24. Paulo Evaristo Arns, *Brasil, nunca mais* (Petrópolis: Vozes, 1985). Also available in English: Catholic Church and Dassin, *Torture in Brazil*.

25. Edward Cleary, *How Latin America Saved the Soul of the Catholic Church* (Mahwah, NJ: Paulist, 2009), 143, 146; Freston, "Religious Pluralism," 107–8.

26. Pedro Zottele, "Chilean Students Ignite Revolt," *Christian Century* (October 16, 1968): 1318.

27. Jacobo Timerman, *Chile: Death in the South* (New York: Vintage, 1987), 77.

28. Pamela Lowden, "The Ecumenical Committee for Peace in Chile (1973–1975): The Foundation of Moral Opposition to Authoritarian Rule in Chile," *Bulletin of Latin American Research* 12, no. 2 (1993): 192–5; Mario Aguilar, "Cardinal Raúl Silva Henríquez, the Catholic Church, and the Pinochet Regime, 1973–1980: Public Responses to a National Security State," *Catholic Historical Review* 89, no. 4 (October 2003): 721–2.

29. Lowden, "Ecumenical Committee," 198–9.

30. Aguilar, "Cardinal Raúl Silva Henríquez," 722, 726; Brian H. Smith, *The Church and Politics in Chile: Challenges to Modern Catholicism* (Princeton, NJ: Princeton University Press, 1983), 318–9; Brian Smith, "Chile: Deepening the Allegiance of Working-Class Sectors to the Church in the 1970s," in Daniel Levine, ed., *Religion and Political Conflict in Latin America* (Chapel Hill: University of North Carolina Press, 1986), 183.

31. Martín Poblete, "Chile," in Paul Sigmund, ed., *Religious Freedom and Evangelization in Latin America: The Challenge of Religious Pluralism* (Maryknoll, NY: Orbis, 1999), 230.

32. Smith, "Chile: Deepening the Allegiance," 183.

33. Aguilar, "Cardinal Raúl Silva Henríquez," 727; Smith, *Church and Politics*, 341.

34. Poblete, "Chile," 231.

35. Pedro Zottele, "Church-State Tension Intensifies in Chile," *Christian Century* (October 24, 1984): 975.

36. Jerry Knudson, "Chile's Catholic Opposition Press," *Christian Century* (December 10, 1986): 1121.

37. Poblete, "Chile," 231.

38. Kenneth Aman, "Fighting for God: The Military and Religion in Chile," *Cross Currents* 36, no. 4 (Winter 1986): 459–63; Orlando Costas, "Church Growth as a Multidimensional Phenomenon: Some Lessons from Chile," *International Bulletin of Missionary Research* 5, no. 1 (1981): 5–6.

39. Madeleine Adriance, "The Paradox of Institutionalization: The Roman Catholic Church in Chile and Brazil," *Sociological Analysis* 53(1992): 60.

40. James Brockman, _Romero: A Life_ (Maryknoll, NY: Orbis, 1989), 46.

41. Quotations and information come from Brockman, _Romero_, 236–8, 241.

42. A summary of the report is available in English: Archdiocese of Guatemala, _Guatemala: Never Again!_ (Maryknoll, NY: Orbis, 1999).

43. Quoted in Cleary, _How Latin America Saved the Soul of the Catholic Church_, 144.

44. Michael Duffey, "Religious Diversity, Societal Change, and Ecumenical Prospects in Guatemala," _Journal of Ecumenical Studies_ 44, no. 2 (Spring 2009): 232, 235.

45. Costas, "Church Growth as a Multidimensional Phenomenon," 5.

46. Cleary, _How Latin America Saved the Soul of the Catholic Church_, 105.

47. John Paul II, _Veritatis Splendor_ (Boston: St. Paul Books, 1993), Art. 92–3.

CHAPTER 5

1. Pablo Bottari, "Dealing with Demons in Revival Evangelism," in C. Peter Wagner and Pablo Deiros, eds., _The Rising Revival: Firsthand Accounts of the Incredible Argentine Revival—And How It Can Spread around the World_ (Ventura, CA: Renew, 1998), 75–7.

2. Bottari, "Dealing with Demons," 81–9.

3. Verónica Roldán, "Formas de religiosidad de fin de milenio: El movimiento carismático católico en Buenos Aires y Roma," _Sociedad y Religión_ 18/19 (1999): 120, 126.

4. Andrew Chesnut, "Conservative Christian Competitors: Pentecostals and Charismatic Catholics in Latin America's New Religious Economy," _SAIS Review of International Affairs_ 30, no. 1 (2010): 92.

5. Luis Lugo et al., _Spirit and Power: A 10-Country Study of Pentecostals_ (Washington, DC: Pew Research Center, 2006), 76, 78.

6. Cecil Robeck, _The Azusa Street Mission and Revival: The Birth of the Global Pentecostal Movement_ (Nashville: Thomas Nelson, 2006), 68–73, 113, 131, 149, 169; 235; Joel 2:23–32; Acts 2.

7. Durham, as quoted in Robeck, _The Azusa Street Mission_, 179–80.

8. Shepherd, as quoted in Robeck, _The Azusa Street Mission_, 181.

9. Allen Anderson, "The Pentecostal and Charismatic Movements," _The Cambridge History of Christianity_, Vol. 9, _World Christianities_ (Cambridge: Cambridge University Press, 2006), 92–3; Robeck, _The Azusa Street Mission_, 187–234.

10. Robeck, _The Azusa Street Mission_, 235–42.

11. Vinson Synan, _The Holiness-Pentecostal Tradition: Charismatic Movements in the Twentieth Century_, 2nd ed. (Grand Rapids, MI: Eerdmans, 1997), 226–33; "Religion: Speaking in Tongues," _Time_, August 15, 1960.

12. David Barrett et al., "Christian World Communions: Five Overviews of Global Christianity, AD 1800–2025," _International Bulletin of Missionary Research_ 32, no. 1 (2009): 32.

13. Gastón Espinosa, "Latino Pentecostal Healing in the North American Borderlands," in Candy Gunther Brown, ed., *Global Pentecostal and Charismatic Healing* (New York: Oxford University Press, 2011), 130–1, 141.

14. Anderson, "Pentecostal and Charismatic Movements," 95; Jean-Pierre Bastian, "The New Religious Map of Latin America: Causes and Social Effects," *Cross Currents* 48, no. 3 (1998): 334.

15. David Bundy, "Unintended Consequences: The Methodist Episcopal Missionary Society and the Beginnings of Pentecostalism in Norway and Chile," *Missiology: An International Review* 27, no. 2 (1999): 220–3; Jan-Ake Alvarsson, "Some Notes on Swedish Contributions to Pentecostalism in Latin America," *Swedish Missiological Themes* 97, no. 3 (2009): 378–81.

16. Alvarsson, "Some Notes," 384–5.

17. Alvarsson, "Some Notes," 388–9.

18. Christian Lalive d'Epinay, "The Training of Pastors and Theological Education: The Case of Chile," *International Review of Missions* 56, no. 2 (1967): 186.

19. d'Epinay, "The Training of Pastors," 188.

20. Emilio Willems, "Validation of Authority in Pentecostal Sects of Chile and Brazil," *Journal for the Scientific Study of Religion* 6, no. 2 (1967): 255–7.

21. This is the argument of Andrew Chesnut in *Competitive Spirits: Latin America's Religious Economy* (New York: Oxford University Press, 2003).

22. Paul Freston, "Researching the Heartland of Pentecostalism: Latin Americans at Home and Abroad," *Fieldwork in Religion* 3, no. 2 (2008).

23. Christian Lalive d'Epinay, "The Pentecostal 'Conquista' in Chile," *Ecumenical Review* 20, no. 1 (1968): 21, 26–8.

24. Ana Langerak, "The Witness and Influence of Pentecostal Christians in Latin America," *International Review of Mission* 87, no. 345 (1998): 176.

25. Paul Freston, "Neo-Pentecostalism in Brazil: Problems of Definition and the Struggle for Hegemony," *Archive de sciences socials des religions* 44, no. 105 (1999): 146.

26. Richard Shaull, "From Academic Research to Spiritual Transformation: Reflections on a Study of Pentecostalism in Brazil," *Pneuma* 20, no. 1 (1998): 78.

27. Pedro Moreno, "Rapture and Renewal in Latin America," *First Things* 74 (1997): 31.

28. Quoted in Lene Sjorup, "Pentecostals: The Power and the Powerless," *Dialog: A Journal of Theology* 41, no. 1 (2002): 19.

29. Thomas Csordas, "Global Religion and the Re-enchantment of the World: The Case of the Catholic Charismatic Renewal," *Anthropological Theory* 7, no. 3 (2007): 295–314. See also James K. A. Smith, *Thinking in Tongues: Pentecostal Contributions to Christian Philosophy* (Grand Rapids, MI: Eerdmans, 2010), 39.

30. Ari Pedro Or and Pablo Semán, "Brazilian Pentecostalism Crosses National Borders," in André Corten and Ruth Marshall-Fratani, eds., *Between Babel and Pentecost: Transnational Pentecostalism in Africa and Latin America* (Bloomington: Indiana University Press, 2001), 188.

31. Paul Freston, "Researching the Heartland of Pentecostalism: Latin Americans at Home and Abroad," *Fieldwork in Religion* 3, no. 2 (2008): 130–1.

32. Michael Burdick, *For God and the Fatherland: Religion and Politics in Argentina* (Albany: State University of New York Press, 1995), 242.

33. Matthew Marostica, "Pentecostals and Politics: The Creation of the Evangelical Christian Movement in Argentina, 1983–1993," PhD diss., University of California, Berkeley, 1997, 131, 143–4; Omar Cabrera, "Vision of the Future," in C. Peter Wagner and Pablo Deiros, eds., *The Rising Revival: Firsthand Accounts of the Incredible Argentine Revival—And How It Can Spread around the World* (Ventura, CA: Renew, 1998), 93.

34. Cabrera, "Vision of the Future," 93, 97.

35. Hilario Wynarczyk, *Tres Evangelistas Carismaticos: Omar Cabrera, Annacondia, Giménez* (Buenos Aires, 1989), 25.

36. Omar Cabrera, "La Maravillosa Ley de la Abundancia" (pamphlet), in Wynarczyk, "Tres Evangelistas," 63.

37. Wynarczyk, *Tres Evangelistas*, 17–21.

38. Wynarczyk, *Tres Evangelistas*, 27–8.

39. Cabrera, "Vision of the Future," 97.

40. Wynarczyk, *Tres Evangelistas*, 5, 28–31.

41. Matthew Marostica, "Learning from the Master: Carlos Annacondia and the Standardization of Pentecostal Practices in and beyond Argentina," in Candy Gunther Brown, ed., *Global Pentecostal and Charismatic Healing* (New York: Oxford University Press, 2011), 218–9.

42. Marostica, "Learning," 209.

43. Carlos Annacondia, "Power Evangelism, Argentine Style," in C. Peter Wagner and Pablo Deiros, eds., *The Rising Revival: Firsthand Accounts of the Incredible Argentine Revival—And How It Can Spread around the World* (Ventura, CA: Renew, 1998), 61–3.

44. Annacondia, "Power Evangelism," 63–4.

45. Annacondia, "Power Evangelism," 64.

46. Marostica, "Learning," 208, 211.

47. Carlos Annacondia, as quoted in Marostica, "Learning," 211.

48. Marostica, "Learning," 216.

49. Marostica, "Learning," 218.

50. Marostica, "Pentecostals and Politics," 98.

51. Wynarczyk, *Tres Evangelistas*, 74–99.

52. Marostica, "Pentecostals and Politics," 102–5.

53. C. Peter Wagner, "Revival Power: God Has Set His People A-Praying," Pablo Deiros, "The Roots and Fruits of the Argentine Revival," and Claudio Freidzón, "The Holy Spirit, the Anointing, and Revival Power," in C. Peter Wagner and Pablo Deiros, eds., *The Rising Revival: Firsthand Accounts of the Incredible Argentine Revival—And How It Can Spread around the World* (Ventura, CA: Renew, 1998), 21, 41, 115–6.

54. Marostica, "Learning," 220–1.

55. Pablo Deiros, "The Roots and Fruits of the Argentine Revival," in C. Peter Wagner and Pablo Deiros, eds., *The Rising Revival: Firsthand Accounts of the Incredible Argentine Revival—And How It Can Spread around the World* (Ventura, CA: Renew, 1998), 41.

56. Wagner, "Revival Power," 12.

57. Wagner, "Revival Power," 12; Anderson, "Pentecostal and Charismatic Movements," 106.

58. Ralph Tone, "Maximum Security Unlikely Setting for Model Church," *Christianity Today* (September 16, 1996): 102–3; Juan Zuccarelli, "God's Kingdom in Olmos Prison," in C. Peter Wagner and Pablo Deiros, eds., *The Rising Revival: Firsthand Accounts of the Incredible Argentine Revival—And How It Can Spread around the World* (Ventura, CA: Renew, 1998), 171–84.

CHAPTER 6

1. Shelley Emling, "Catholic Worship in Brazil Taking on a Livelier Tone," *Atlanta Journal-Constitution*, December 7, 1997, B 5.

2. Gaston Espinosa, "The Pentecostalization of Latin American and U.S. Latino Christianity," *Pneuma* 26, no. 2 (2004): 266.

3. Edward Cleary, *The Rise of Charismatic Catholicism in Latin America* (Gainesville: University Press of Florida, 2011), 1, 27–9, 268. Cleary accepts a similar estimate of the number of Catholic Charismatics in Latin America (73 million) but puts the number of Protestant Pentecostals at only 35 million. His estimate would make the Latin American CCR much more important than Pentecostalism. This chapter is based on Cleary's work: there is no other scholarly book-length treatment in English of the CCR in Latin America.

4. Espinosa, "Pentecostalization," 271–2.

5. Diego Jaramillo, "La renovación carismática en Colombia," March 10, 2008, *Comunidad Agua Viva*, comunidadaguaviva.org; Diego Jaramillo, *Rafael García Herreros: una vida y una obra* (Bogotá: Editorial Carrera 7a, 1984), 196, 199–200; Cleary, *The Rise*, 55–6.

6. Cleary, *The Rise*, 31, 35; Francis MacNutt, *Healing* (Notre Dame, IN: Ave Maria Press, 1974).

7. Cleary, *The Rise*, 22, 30–1, 38. MacNutt regularized his marriage and received a dispensation of his priestly vows from the Catholic Church in 1993. In 2007 and 2008 he returned to active participation in Catholic Charismatic circles. Both Cleary and Jaramillo give 1973 as the year of the first ECCLA, while other sources give the year as 1972.

8. As quoted in Roldán, "Formas de religiosidad," 88–9.

9. Cleary, *The Rise*, 97–9.

10. Cleary, *The Rise*, 100–2, 118–20; Emling, "Catholic Worship."

11. Cleary, *The Rise*, 106–8; Comunidade Canção Nova, "Nossa Sede," http://comunidade.cancaonova.com/nossa-sede/.

12. Cleary, *The Rise*, 102.

13. Cleary, *The Rise*, 139–47; Padre Marcelo Rossi, "Perfil Padre Marcelo Rossi," www.padremarcelorossi.com.br/perfil_padremarcelo.php.

14. Peter Clarke, "Pop-Star Priests and the Catholic Response to the 'Explosion' of Evangelical Protestantism in Brazil: The Beginning of the End of the Walkout?" *Journal of Contemporary Religion* 14, no. 2 (1999): 211.

15. Cleary, *The Rise*, 139–47.

16. Ricardo Suárez Selum, *La Renovación Carismática en Bolivia* (La Paz, 1979), 64–5.

17. Hugo José Suárez, *¿Ser Cristiano es Ser de Izquierda? La Experiencia Politico-Religiosa del Cristianismo de la Liberación en Bolivia en los Años 60* (La Paz: Muela del Diablo, 2003), 84–6, 91.

18. Cleary, *The Rise*, 31–3.

19. Ricardo Suárez Selum, *La Renovación Carismática en Bolivia* (La Paz, 1979), 54–8; Cleary, *The Rise*, 32–5.

20. "Bienvenidos," La Mansión: Centro Católico Carismático de Evangelización, www.lamansion.org.

21. Suárez, *La Renovación*, 59–60; Cleary, *The Rise,* 32–5.

22. Crisostomo Geraets quoted in Saúl Paniagua Flores, "Paciencia," *El Deber* (Santa Cruz, Bolivia), October 9, 2009, http://www.eldeber.com.bo/2009/2009-10-09/vernotacolumnistas.php?id=091009002321. (Geraets literally said the people of Santa Cruz were living life with less "politiquería," a term that indicates political maneuvering and shady dealings.)

23. Cleary, *The Rise*, 34, 49.

24. Suárez, *La Renovación*, 44.

25. Suárez, *La Renovación*, 58–66; Cleary, *The Rise*, 32–5.

26. "Instituto Pastoral Santo Tomas de Aquino," *La Mansión*, www.lamansión.org/historia_ipsta.html; Cleary, *The Rise*, 40–5.

27. Cleary, *The Rise*, 40–1.

28. Suárez, *La Renovación*, 89–93.

29. Suárez, *La Renovación*, 105–9.

30. Roxana Escobar, "Calidad de predicadores marcará el Pentecostés," *El Deber* (Santa Cruz, Bolivia), November 18, 2007, http://www.eldeber.com.bo/2007/2007-11-18/vernotasantacruz.php?id=071117215201.

31. "Encuentros," *La Mansión*, www.lamansion.org/encuentros_anteriores.html; "Estudio de Televisión," *La Mansión*, www.lamansion.org/estudio.html.

32. Feliciano Molino, "Como adormecer a favor de los que más tienen y en desmedro de los marginados," *Bolpress*, December 7, 2007, http://www.bolpress.com/art.php?Cod=2007120702.

33. "Grupos de Oración," La Mansión: Centro Católico Carismático de Evangelización, http://www.lamansion.org/grupos_oracion.html; "Bienvenidos," La Mansión: Centro Católico Carismático de Evangelización, http://www.lamansion.org/.

34. Quoted in Ana Langerak, "The Witness and Influence of Pentecostal Christians in Latin America," *International Review of Mission* 87, no. 345 (1998): 178.

35. Langerak, "Witness," 185.

36. Clarke, "Pop-Star Priests," 210.

CHAPTER 7

1. John Paul II, *Juan Pablo II Habla a México en 1990* (Mexico City: Librería Parroquial de Clavería, 1990), 130, 178.

2. Dominique Barbé, *Grace and Power: Base Communities and Nonviolence in Brazil* (Maryknoll, NY: Orbis, 1987), 96, 132.

3. Ian Ker, *John Henry Newman* (New York: Oxford University Press, 2007), 397–489.

4. II Conferencia General del Episcopado Latinoamericano, "Pastoral Popular," Documentos finales de Medellín, 1968, http://www.ensayistas.org/critica/liberacion/medellin/medellin8.htm.

5. Leo XII, *Rerum Novarum*, 1891, http://www.vatican.va/holy_father/leo_xiii/encyclicals/documents/hf_l-xiii_enc_15051891_rerum-novarum_en.html, and *Graves de Communi Re*, 1901, http://www.vatican.va/holy_father/leo_xiii/encyclicals/documents/hf_l-xiii_enc_18011901_graves-de-communi-re_en.html.

6. Quoted in Gianfranco Poggi, *Catholic Action in Italy: The Sociology of a Sponsored Organization* (Stanford, CA: Stanford University Press, 1967), 23.

7. Pius XII, *Summi Pontifactus*, October 20, 1939, http://www.vatican.va/holy_father/pius_xii/encyclicals/documents/hf_p-ii_enc_20101939_summi-pontificatus_en.html.

8. Pius XII, "Guiding Principles of the Lay Apostolate," Address to the Second World Congress of the Lay Apostolate, October 5, 1957, *Papal Encyclicals Online*, http://www.papalencyclicals.net/Pius12/P12LAYAP.HTM.

9. John XIII, *Princeps Pastorum*, November 28, 1959, *Papal Encyclicals Online*, http://www.papalencyclicals.net/John23/j23princ.htm; Ivan Rohloff, *The Origins and Development of Cursillo (1939–1973)* (Dallas: National Ultreya Publications of the United States National Secretariat, 1976), 21.

10. *Lumen Gentium* 9, 17, 39. Although many interpreted the concept of "the People of God" as minimizing the importance of the hierarchy or even eliminating distinctions between the laity and the hierarchy, such was clearly not the meaning of the document, for directly after the "People of God" section, the document stresses "the sacred primacy of the Roman Pontiff and of his infallible magisterium" and affirms his "full, supreme, and universal power over the Church." Similarly, bishops "govern the particular churches entrusted to them" and the laity "should . . . promptly accept in Christian obedience decisions of their spiritual shepherds." See also *Lumen Gentium* 18, 22, 27, 37.

11. *Lumen Gentium* 32.

12. *Lumen Gentium* 37. See also the council's document on the laity, *Apostolicam Actuositatem*, whose view of the lay role was a "dramatic departure from primarily

juridical approach to the lay apostolate," and was based on the sacrament of Baptism, not on "a juridical concession of power granted by ecclesiastical authority": Robert Oliver, "The Decree on the Apostolate of the Laity, *Apostolicam Actuositatem*," in Matthew Lamb and Matthew Levering, eds., *Vatican II: Renewal within Tradition* (New York: Oxford University Press, 2008), 276.

13. John Paul II, *Christifideles Laici*, December 30, 1988, http://www.vatican.va/holy_father/john_paul_ii/apost_exhortations/documents/hf_jp-ii_exh_30121988_christifideles-laici_en.html.

14. Thomas Bruneau, *The Political Transformation of the Brazilian Church* (London: Cambridge University Press, 1974), 81, 95–9.

15. Ação Popular, Documento de Base, as quoted in Bruneau, *Political Transformation*, 99.

16. Edward Cleary, "The Brazilian Catholic Church and Church-State Relations: Nation-Building," *Journal of Church and State* 39, no. 2 (1997): 253–72.

17. Joseph Cardijn, "The Three Truths," August 26, 1935, *The Cardijn Project*, http://www.josephcardijn.com/the-three-truths.

18. Helder Camara, Preface to Marguerite Fiévez, Jacques Meert, and Roger Aubert, *Cardijn* (London: Young Christian Workers, 1974).

19. Michael Fleet and Brian H.Smith, *The Catholic Church and Democracy in Chile and Peru* (Notre Dame, IN: University of Notre Dame Press, 1997), 41–8.

20. Quoted in Milagros Peña, "Liberation Theology in Peru: An Analysis of the Role of Intellectuals in Social Movements," *Journal for the Scientific Study of Religion* 33, no. 1 (1994): 40.

21. Peña, "Liberation Theology in Peru," 40.

22. Edward Cleary, *How Latin America Saved the Soul of the Catholic Church* (Mahwah, NJ: Paulist Press, 2009), 118–20.

23. José Aparecido Gomes Moreira, "Para una historia de Juventud Obrera Católica (1959–1985)," *Revista Mexicana de Sociología* 49, no. 3 (1987): 210.

24. W. E. Hewitt, *Base Christian Communities and Social Change in Brazil* (Lincoln: University of Nebraska Press, 1991), 7–8.

25. Quoted in Guillermo Cook, *The Expectation of the Poor: Latin American Base Ecclesial Communities in Protestant Perspective* (Maryknoll, NY: Orbis, 1985), 64.

26. Cook, *Expectation of the Poor*, 64.

27. Cook, *Expectation of the Poor*, 65–8.

28. Cook, *Expectation of the Poor*, 68.

29. Gottfried Deelen, "The Church on Its Way to the People: Basic Christian Communities in Brazil," *Cross Currents* (Winter 1980–81): 388.

30. Aloisio Lorscheider, "Basic Ecclesiastical Communities in Latin America," *AFER* 19, no. 3 (June 1977): 143–4.

31. Quoted in Deelen, "The Church on Its Way," 406.

32. Deelen, "The Church on Its Way," 399.

33. In fact, by 1987 the bishops rarely used the term CEB: W. E. Hewitt, "Religion and the Consolidation of Democracy in Brazil: The Role of the Comunidades Eclesiais de Base (CEBs)," *Sociological Analysis* 51, no. 2 (Summer 1990): 148–50.

34. J. B. Libanio, "Experiences with the Base Ecclesial Communities in Brazil," *Missiology: An International Review* 8, no. 3 (July 1980): 331–5. In communion services previously consecrated hosts are distributed.

35. Julio de Santa Ana, "Schools of Sharing: Basic Ecclesial Communities," *Ecumenical Review* 38, no. 4 (1986): 383.

36. Barbé, *Grace and Power*, 97.

37. Frei Betto quoted in W. E. Hewitt, "Strategies for Social Change Employed by Comunidades Eclesiais de Base (CEBs) in the Archdiocese of São Paulo," *Journal for the Scientific Study of Religion* 25, no. 1 (March 1986): 18.

38. Hewitt, "Strategies for Social Change," 20.

39. Hewitt, "Strategies for Social Change," 21–2.

40. Hewitt, "Strategies for Social Change," 22.

41. Hewitt, "Strategies for Social Change," 23–7.

42. W. E. Hewitt, "Religion and the Consolidation of Democracy in Brazil: The Role of the Cumidades Eclesiais de Base (CEBs)," *Sociological Analysis* 51, no. 2 (Summer 1990): 146–7.

43. Manuel Vásquez, "Structural Obstacles to Grassroots Pastoral Practice: The Case of a Base Community in Urban Brazil," *Sociology of Religion* 58, no. 1 (Spring 1997): 56–7.

44. Vásquez, "Structural Obstacles," 56–8.

45. Vásquez, "Structural Obstacles," 59–65.

46. Libanio, "Experiences," 328.

47. Kate Pravera, "The Base Christian Community of San Pablo: An Oral History of Nicaragua's First CEB," *Brethren Life and Thought* 29, no. 4 (Autumn 1984): 206–9.

48. John Kirk, *Politics and the Catholic Church in Nicaragua* (Gainesville: University Press of Florida, 1992), 70.

49. Pravera, "The Base Christian Community," 210.

50. Pravera, "The Base Christian Community," 210.

51. Félix Jiménez, "Historia de la parroquía San Pablo Apóstol a XX años de fundación con Cristo y la revolución, 1966–1986" (Managua: 1986, mimeo.), 6, as quoted in Kirk, *Politics and the Catholic Church in Nicaragua*, 70.

52. Kirk, *Politics and the Catholic Church in Nicaragua*, 101–4.

53. Kirk, *Politics and the Catholic Church in Nicaragua*, 172.

54. Catherine M. Stanford, "Religion and Politics in Nicaragua: A Historical Ethnography Set in the City of Masaya," PhD diss., State University of New York at Albany, 2008, 310–11.

55. Stanford, "Religion and Politics," 311–2.

56. Stanford, "Religion and Politics," 310–6.

57. Hewitt, "Strategies," 25.

58. J. Stephen Rhodes, "Interpreting Reality in Latin American Base Communities," *International Bulletin of Missionary Research* 15, no. 3 (July 1991): 110–2.


CHAPTER 8

1. In 2009 there were 1,487 Catholics per priest in Europe and 1,682 Catholics per priest in North America (not including Mexico), while there were 6,845 Catholics per priest in Mexico and Central America and Catholics per priest in 7,099 in South America: Editors, "Worldwide Increase in Catholic Population, Deacons, Priests, and Bishops," *International Bulletin of Missionary Research* 36, no. 1 (January 2012): 41.

2. There is great need of a general book-length study of NEMs in Latin America and of many book-length studies on the individual movements.

3. Roger Finke and Patricia Wittberg, "Organizational Revival from Within: Explaining Revivalism and Reform in the Roman Catholic Church," *Journal for the Scientific Study of Religion* 39, no. 2 (June 2000): 154–6.

4. Finke and Wittberg, "Organizational Revival," 166.

5. Ratzinger was not entirely positive about the NEMs. He warned against tendencies of the movements "toward being exclusive, toward having one-sided emphases, and, thus being incapable of fitting into the life of the local Church." He also warned against "overemphasis on the specific task" of the NEM and "attributing an absolute value to the movement." Joseph Ratzinger, *New Outpourings of the Spirit: Movements in the Church* (San Francisco: Ignatius, 2007), 21, 56, 91.

6. Editors, "Worldwide Increase," *International Bulletin of Missionary Research* 36, no. 1 (January 2012): 41.

7. Ivan Rohloff, *The Origins and Development of Cursillo (1939–1973)* (Dallas: National Ultreya Publications of the United States National Secretariat, 1976), 25–41, 50.

8. V. Gaudet, "Intensive Courses of Christian and Apostolic Formation in Bolivia," *Christ to the World* 4 (1959): 431, as quoted in Christopher Mackenzie, "Maya Bodies and Minds: Religion and Modernity in a K'iche' Town," PhD diss., SUNY Albany, 2005, 232.

9. Richard Adams, *Crucifixion by Power: Essays on Guatemalan National Social Structure, 1944–1966* (Austin: University of Texas Press, 1970), 299, as quoted in Mackenzie, "Maya Bodies," 232.

10. Rohloff, *Origins*, 41, 74; "Countries," World Organization of Cursillos of Christianity, http://www.orgmcc.org/countries/index.htm.

11. Rohloff, *Origins*, 76–8, 102–3, 124.

12. Armando Fuentes Aguirre, "Cursillos—Grandes Cursos," *Palabra* (Saltillo), June 27, 2005.

13. Vicente Guerrero, "Van tran una meta: Cristificar a México—Ultreya Nacional 1998 en Monterrey," July 29, 1997, *El Norte* (Monterrey); Paulo Alvarado, "Preparan cursillistas fiesta de aniversario," *El Norte*, July 2, 2008.

14. Mackenzie, "Maya Bodies," iii, 235–7, 290. In San Andrés Xecul there was a significant overlap between cursillistas and participants in the Charismatic Renewal, not surprising given that the renewal originally grew out of the Cursillo and the two movements were closely related in the early years of the renewal.

15. Cursillo was organized on the national and international levels, but it attempted to preserve the Cursillo as a method and experience more than a body of people, in theory more similar to the Spiritual Exercises of Ignatius than to the Knights of Columbus or Regnum Christi. In practice, the Cursillo functioned as an intermediate or hybrid entity that shared some of the strengths and weaknesses of Catholic Action and some of the strengths and weaknesses of the NEMs.

16. Desmond Connelly, "A Resurgent Laity in Church Ministry," *Champagnat: An International Marist Journal of Charism in Education* 13, no. 3 (Spring 2011): 73.

17. Alvaro del Portillo, "El camino de Opus Dei," *Scripta Theológica* 13, no. 2 (May 1981): 31.

18. Penny Lernoux, "Opus Dei and the Perfect Society," *The Nation* (April 10, 1989), 481–7; Guillermo de los Reyes and Paul Rich, "Opus Dei and Mexico: Civil but Sinister?" *Review of Policy Research* 22, no. 1 (January 2005): 93–101; Fabián Gaspar Bustamante Olguín, "La formación de una nueva mentalidad religiosa de la elite empresarial durante la dictadura military, 1974–1990: El catolicismo empresarial de Opus Dei," *Revista Cultura y Religión* 4, no. 1 (2010): 105–19.

19. Eric Garces, "Whither Charity? Andean Catholic Politics and the Secularization of Sacrifice," PhD diss., Princeton University, 2009. Although all the NEMs active in Latin America cry out for more serious scholarship, Opus Dei seems especially in need of serious and fair-minded articles and books that focus on what its members actually do, say, and believe, rather than on their supposed plans for political domination.

20. Mario Vargas Llosa, "Cobardía e hipocresia," December 8, 2002, *El Norte* (Mexico).

21. Luis Fernando Figari, "Una eclesiología de communion y reconciliación," January 26, 1996, VE Multimedios, www.multimedios.org.

22. Milagros Peña, "The Sodalitium Vitae Movement in Peru: A Rewriting of Liberation Theology," *Sociological Analysis* 53, no. 2 (Summer 1992): 166; Milagros Peña, *Theologies and Liberation in Peru: The Role of Ideas in Social Movements* (Philadelphia: Temple University Press, 1995), 149–70.

23. A vicariate is Catholic territory administered by a bishop that has not achieved the status of diocese.

24. "El conflicto entre seguidores de dos órdenes católica," Agence France-Presse, May 24, 2011; "Una pugna por el control de un vicariato entre los Carmelitos Descalzos y los Heraldos del Evangelio," Agence France-Presse, May 25, 2011;

"Correa pide a sacerdote español deponer huelga de hambre que lleva 19 días," EFE News Services, June 11, 2011; "El gobierno ecuatoriano dijo el lunes que el papa Benedicto XVI dio una señal para superar el conflicto," Agence France-Presse, March 21, 2011; "Sucumbíos está dividida por el conflicto con los Heraldos," *El Comercio* (Quito), March 17, 2011. The Ecuadoran bishops denied that Correa had any power to veto episcopal appointments.

25. Lina Godoy, "Cancelan proceso de beatificación de líder Sodalicio Germán Doig," *Diario 16* (Lima, Peru) February 1, 2011; Ian Fisher and Laurie Goodstein, "Vatican Disciplines Founder of Order over Abuse Charges," *New York Times*, May 20, 2006.

26. Third orders are the branches of religious orders for laity who do not take religious vows.

27. Chiara Lubich, *That All Men Be One: The Origins and Life of the Focolare Movement* (New York: New City Press, 1969), 10.

28. Jim Gallagher, *A Woman's Work: Chiara Lubich* (Hyde Park, NY: New City Press, 1997), 42, 55, 87, 156.

29. Lorna Gold and Dimitrij Bregant, "Case Study: The Focolare Movement—Evangelization and Contemporary Culture," *International Review of Mission* 92, no. 364 (January 2003): 28.

30. Gallagher, *A Woman's Work*, 70–1, 77, 89.

31. Gallagher, *A Woman's Work*, 197.

32. Lía Brunet, *Tejiendo una red* (Buenos Aires: Ciudad Nueva, 1989), 15; "Lia Brunet: Una elección que ha suscitado una extraordinaria fecundidad," Focolare International Website, February 4, 2011, http://www.focolare.org/es/print.php?lang=& print=24597; Aroldo de Oliveira Braga, *Cais No 10: Histórias dos 50 anos dos Focolares no Brasil* (São Paulo: Cidade Nova, 2009), 59.

33. Brunet, *Tejiendo*, 78–85, 93; Lía Brunet, *Alle radici: Le origini del movimento dei Focolari in Sudamerica* (Rome: Città nuova, 2003), 98–9. One of the early Argentine members, Margarita Bravosi, known as Luminosa, is now in the process of being recognized for sainthood. Nine newsletters outlining her life are available at http://www.focolares.es/es/Testimonio/0809_luminosa.html.

34. de Oliveira Braga, *Cais No 10*, 67–70, 90–3.

35. Lorna Gold, "Making Space for Sharing in the Global Market: The Focolare Movement's Economy of Sharing," PhD diss., University of Glasgow, 2000, 82–3; "Cronologia da vida de Ginetta Calliari," May 12, 2009, www.ginettacalliari. blogspot.com; "Ginetta: Uma Divina Aventura," *Cidade Nova-Ediçâo Portuguesa* (January 1998); de Oliveira Braga, *Cais No 10*, 196–204.

36. Brunet, *Tejiendo*, 88, 98–112, 120.

37. Gallagher, *A Woman's Work*, 156; "Cronologia da vida de Ginetta Calliari."

38. Gallagher, *A Woman's Work*, 149, 219; Gold, "Making Space," 80.

39. Quoted in Matilde Cocchiaro, *Partono i Bastimenti: Vita di Ginetta Calliari* (Rome: Città Nuova, 2009).

40. de Oliveira Braga, *Cais No 10*, 194–5.

41. Maria Aparecida, "O Bairro do Carmo, uma comunidade predileta de Ginetta," Ginetta Calliara (website), March 23, 2010, www.ginettacalliari.blogspot.com.

42. John Paul II, *Centisimus Annus* 32, 52 (Washington, DC: United States Catholic Conference, 1991); Gallagher, *A Woman's Work*, 159–60.

43. Chiara Lubich, "Una sociedad sin pobres," *Economía de Comunión: Una Cultura Nueva* 2, no. 4 (April 1996): 4.

44. Gallagher, *A Woman's Work*, 159–60.

45. Vera Araujo, "The Economy of Communion Project: Presentation Given to the Economic Justice Plenary," *Ecumenical Review* 58, no. 1 (January 2006): 102.

46. Gold, "Making Space," 141.

47. Ginetta Calliari, "Ginetta a empresários e agents da EdC," 1994, www.ginettacalliari.blogspot.com, May 2, 2011.

48. Gold, "Making Space," 138, 264; Gold and Bregant, "Case Study," 24; Lorna Gold, "The Economy of Communion: A Case Study of Business and Civil Society in Partnership for Change," *Development in Practice* 14, no. 5 (August 2004): 636–7; Antonella Ferrucci, "Por todas partes se veía la mano de Dios: entrevista a Enzo Morandi 'Volo,'" March 31, 2011, *Economía de Comunion Online*, www.edc-online.org/es/inicio/especial-brasil-2011.

49. Antonella Ferrucci, "La certeza de que algo tenía que ocurrir en Brasil: entrevista a Vera Araujo," May 6, 2011, *Economía de Comunion Online*, www.edc-online.org/es/inicio/especial-brasil-2011.

50. Vera Araujo, "La empresa, lugar de communion," *Economía de Comunión: Una Cultura Nueva* 1, no. 1 (March 1995): 4.

51. Vera Araujo, "Un empresario nueva par una economía nueva," *Economía de Comunión: Una Cultura Nueva* 2, no. 3 (December 1996): 4; Vera Araujo, "El trabajador y el indigente, actors de Economía de Comunión," *Economía de Comunión: Una Cultura Nueva* 3, no. 1 (April 1997): 4.

52. Vera Araujo, "Destino universal de los bienes, propiedad privada y Economía de Comunión," *Economía de Comunión: Una Cultura Nueva* 4, no. 1 (April 1998): 4; Pontifical Council for Justice and Peace, Compendium of the Social Doctrine of the Church (2004), sec. 171, 177, http://www.vatican.va/roman_curia/pontifical_councils/justpeace/documents/rc_pc_justpeace_doc_20060526_compendio-dott-soc_en.html.

53. Gold, "The Economy of Communion," 639.

54. Ana Maria Nascimento, "El hilo de oro de la EdC en Brasil en estos 20 años," May 26, 2011, *Economía de Comunion Online*, www.edc-online.org/es/inicio/especial-brasil-2011.

55. "La historia de la Prodiet Farmecéutica de Curitiba de Roselí y Armando Tortelli," *Economia de Comunion: Una Nueva Cultura* 1, no. 2 (September 1995): 8–9.

56. Gold, "Making Space," 249–51, 260–2.

57. Nascimento, "El hilo de oro"; de Oliveira Braga, *Cais No 10*, 237–42.

58. In 2009 Pope Benedict XVI endorsed the EOC as one of the best business models for the future: "It would appear that the traditionally valid distinction between profit-based companies and non-profit organizations can no longer do full justice to reality, or offer practical direction for the future. In recent decades a broad intermediate area has emerged between the two types of enterprise. It is made up of traditional companies which nonetheless subscribe to social aid agreements in support of underdeveloped countries, charitable foundations associated with individual companies, groups of companies oriented towards social welfare, and the diversified world of the so-called 'civil economy' and the 'economy of communion'. This is not merely a matter of a 'third sector,' but of a broad new composite reality embracing the private and public spheres, one which does not exclude profit, but instead considers it a means for achieving human and social ends. Whether such companies distribute dividends or not, whether their juridical structure corresponds to one or other of the established forms, becomes secondary in relation to their willingness to view profit as a means of achieving the goal of a more humane market and society. It is to be hoped that these new kinds of enterprise will succeed in finding a suitable juridical and fiscal structure in every country." *Caritas en Varitate* 46, www.vatican.va.

59. Edward Cleary, *Crisis and Change: The Church in Latin America Today* (Maryknoll, NY: Orbis, 1985), 126.

60. Cleary, How Latin America Saved the Soul, 43.

CHAPTER 9

1. Rigoberta Menchú and Elisabeth Burgos-Debray, *I, Rigoberta Menchú: An Indian Woman in Guatemala* (New York: Verso, 1983); David Stoll, *Rigoberta Menchú and the Story of All Poor Guatemalans* (Boulder, CO: Westview Press, 1999); "Guatemala Nobel Laureate Defends Methods," *New York Times*, February 11, 1999.

2. Menchú and Burgos-Debray, *I, Rigoberta Menchú*, 81–5, 120–2, 130–1, 161, 165, 188–94, 242–6.

3. Matthew 28: 19 and Acts 1:8, Holy Bible: New International Version.

4. Lamin Sanneh, *Encountering the West: Christianity and the Global Cultural Process: The African Dimension* (Maryknoll, NY: Orbis, 1993).

5. Hugh Steven, *Manuel: The Continuing Story* (Langley, Canada: Credo, 1987), 20–4,

6. Steven, *Manuel*, 31–7.

7. Steven, *Manuel*, 10–12,

8. Steven, *Manuel*, 10, 18, 102–4.

9. Lamin Sanneh, *Translating the Message: The Missionary Impact on Culture* (Maryknoll, NY: Orbis, 1989).

10. Pope Pius XII, *Ad Ecclesiam Christi*, June 29, 1955 (available in Spanish at Biblioteca Electrónica Cristiana, http://multimedios.org/docs/d000022/); Gerald Costello, *Mission to Latin America: The Successes and Failures of a Twentieth Century Crusade* (Maryknoll, NY: Orbis, 1979), 41–2.

11. Paul Hoffman, "Task in Americas Stressed by Pope," *New York Times*, November 16, 1958; "Church Seeks Latins: Catholic Bishops of Canada, U.S., South America Meet," *New York Times*, November 5, 1959; George Dugan, "Catholics Set Aim in Latin America," *New York Times*, September 14, 1960; James Garneau, "The First Inter-American Episcopal Conference, November 2–4, 1959: Canada and the United States called to the Rescue of Latin America," *Catholic Historical Review* 87, issue 4 (October 2001): 662–88.

12. Agostino Casaroli, "Appeal of the Pontifical Commission to North American Superiors," August 17, 1961, in Costello, *Mission*, 273–82.

13. "Pope Asks for More Priests for Latin American Lands," *New York Times*, February 28, 1964.

14. Costello, *Mission*, 179–81, 210.

15. Olivia Harris, "Christianity in Highland Bolivia," in Fenella Cannell, ed., *The Anthropology of Christianity* (Durham, NC: Duke University Press, 2006), 51–65.

16. Andrew Orta, "Living the Past Another Way: Reinstrumentalized Missionary Selves in Aymara Mission Fields," *Anthropological Quarterly* 45, no. 4 (Autumn 2002): 716, 720–2.

17. Barry Lyons, "Religion, Authority, and Identity: Intergenerational Politics, Ethnic Resurgence, and Respect in Chimborazo, Ecuador," *Latin American Research Review* 36, no. 1 (2001): 7–9, 11–7, 31–4, 39.

18. Lyons, "Religion," 7–9, 11–7, 31–4.

19. Orta, "Living," 723; Andrew Canessa, "Contesting Hybridity: Evangelistas and Kataristas in Highland Bolivia," *Journal of Latin American Studies* 32, no. 1 (February 2000): 133.

20. Andrew Orta, "Converting Difference: Metaculture, Missionaries, and the Politics of Locality," *Ethnology* 37, no. 2 (Spring 1998): 166–79.

21. Orta, "Converting Difference," 166–79.

22. Christian Gros, "Evangelical Protestantism and Indigenous Populations," *Bulletin of Latin American Research* 18, no. 2 (April 1999): 182.

23. Gros, "Evangelical Protestantism," 182–6; Conrad Kanagy, "The Formation and Development of a Protestant Conversion Movement among the Highland Quichua of Ecuador," *Sociological Analysis* 51, no. 2 (Summer 1990): 209–10,

24. Kanagy, "Formation and Development," 211–2, 214–6.

25. Kanagy, "Formation and Development," 211–2, 214–6. A similar process occurred among Aymara communities in the highlands of Bolivia, with the Adventists and Assemblies of God seeing the greatest growth: Canessa, "Contesting Hybridity," 131–40.

26. José Antonio Lucero, "Representing Real Indians: The Challenges of Indigenous Authenticity and Strategic Constructivism in Ecuador and Bolivia," *Latin American Research Review* 41, no. 2 (June 2006): 41, 49.

27. Ruth Chojnacki, *Indigenous Apostles: Maya Catholic Catechists Working the Word in Highland Chiapas* (Amsterdam: Rodopi, 2010), 15, 27–30.

28. Samuel Ruiz, "The Incarnation of the Church in Indigenous Cultures," *Missiology: An International Review* 1, no. 2 (April 1973): 21–3.

29. Chojnacki, *Indigenous Apostles*, 53–5, 87; Jan Rus, "The Comunidad Revolucionaria Institucional: The Subversion of Native Government in Highland Chiapas, 1936–1968," in Gilbert Joseph and Daniel Nugent, eds., *Everyday Forms of State Formation: Revolution and the Negotiation of Rule in Modern Mexico* (Durham, NC: Duke University Press, 1994), 265–300.

30. Chojnacki, *Indigenous Apostles*, 110–12.

31. Chojnacki, *Indigenous Apostles*, 112–3, 162.

32. Chojnacki, *Indigenous Apostles*, 115, 121–5.

33. Chojnacki, *Indigenous Apostles*, 115, 142, 148, 176–80.

34. Miguel Bartolmé et al., "Declaration of Barbados: For the Liberation of the Indians," in Walter Dostal, ed., *The Situation of the Indian in South America: Contributions to the Study of Inter-Ethnic Conflict in the Non-Andean Regions of South America* (Geneva: World Council of Churches, 1972), 376–81.

35. Colegio de Etnólogos y Antropólogos Sociales, *Dominación Ideológica y Ciencia Social: El I.L.V. en México* (Mexico City: Nueva Lectura, 1979).

36. Søren Hvalkof and Peter Aaby, eds., *Is God an American? An Anthropological Perspective on the Work of the Summer Institute of Linguistics* (Copenhagen: International Work Group for Indigenous Affairs, 1982). The Summer Institute of Linguistics was the scientific identity used by the Wycliffe Bible Translators to secure contracts with secular governments. See also Roberto Jaulin, ed., *El etnocidio a través de las Américas* (Mexico City: Siglo Veintiuno, 1976).

37. David Stoll, *Is Latin America Turning Protestant? The Politics of Evangelical Growth* (Berkeley: University of California Press, 1990), 185–217.

38. Samuel Escobar, *Changing Tides: Latin America and World Mission Today* (Maryknoll, NY: 2002), 173–5.

39. Samuel Escobar, "The Global Scenario at the Turn of the Century," in William Taylor, ed., *Global Missiology for the 21st Century: The Iguassu Dialogue* (Grand Rapids, MI: Baker, 2000), 26.

40. Escobar, *Changing Tides*, 173–5.

41. Escobar, "The Global Scenario," 28, 31, 44.

42. Antonia Leonora van der Meer, "The Scriptures, the Church, and Humanity: Who Should Do Mission and Why?," in William Taylor, ed., *Global Missiology for the 21st Century: The Iguassu Dialogue* (Grand Rapids, MI: Baker, 2000), 149.

43. Van der Meer, "The Scriptures, the Church, and Humanity," 158.

CHAPTER 10

1. José Porfirio Miranda, "Statement of José Porfirio Miranda," in Sergio Torres and John Eagleson, eds., *Theology in the Americas* (Maryknoll, NY: Orbis, 1976), 291.

2. Javier Iguíñiz, "Statement of Javier Iguíñiz," in Sergio Torres and John Eagleson, eds., *Theology in the Americas* (Maryknoll, NY: Orbis, 1976), 286.

3. Hugo Assman, "Statement of Hugo Assman," in Sergio Torres and John Eagleson, eds., *Theology in the Americas* (Maryknoll, NY: Orbis, 1976), 303.

4. "The Black Theology Panel," in Sergio Torres and John Eagleson, eds., *Theology in the Americas* (Maryknoll, NY: Orbis, 1976), 351–6.

5. Hugh Steven, *Manuel: The Continuing Story* (Langley, Canada: Credo, 1987), 40–3.

6. Acts 1: 8.

7. Samuel Escobar, *Changing Tides: Latin America and World Mission Today* (Maryknoll, NY: 2002), 157–9.

8. Norberto Saracco, "Mission and Missiology from Latin America," in William Taylor, ed., *Global Missiology for the 21st Century: The Iguassu Dialogue* (Grand Rapids, MI: Baker, 2000), 364.

9. Escobar, *Changing Tides*, 159–60, 164–5.

10. Ari Pedro Oro, "A presença religiosa brasileira no Exterior: o caso da Igreja Universal do Reino de Deus," *Estudos Avançados* 18, no. 52 (2004): 140.

11. Oro, "A presença," 139–40.

12. Ken Serbin, "International Church Builds an International Empire," *Christian Century* 113, no. 12 (April 10, 1996): 398; Nilton Cezar Pereira Pinto, "La Iglesia Universal del Reino de Dios en Europa," *Historia Actual Online* 6 (Winter 2005): 47.

13. Paul Freston, "The Transnationalization of Brazilian Pentecostalism: The Universal Church of the Kingdom of God," in André Corten and Ruth Marshall-Fratani, eds., *Between Babel and Pentecost: Transnational Pentecostalism in Africa and Latin America*, (Bloomington: Indiana University Press, 2001), 213.

14. Pereira Pinto, "La Iglesia Universal," 47.

15. Serbin, "International Church," 398.

16. Paul Freston, "The Universal Church of the Kingdom of God: A Brazilian Church Finds Success in Southern Africa," *Journal of Religion in Africa* 35, no. 1 (2005): 39.

17. "Centro Cultural Jerusalém é inaugurado no Rio de Janeiro," *Centro Cultural Jerusalém*, 2010, http://www.centroculturaljerusalem.com.br/asso3.php?id_noticia=10; "De Jerusalém ao Rio de Janeiro," *Revista Annual* (March 2010): 64.

18. Alan Riding, "A Spirited 'Holy War' in an Easygoing Land," *New York Times*, December 31, 1988.

19. Manuel Silva, "A Brazilian Church Comes to New York," *Pneuma* 13, no. 2 (Fall 1991): 165–5.

20. Mark Cohen, "Loud Church Is Irking Souls," *New York Times*, June 23, 1996.

21. Universal Church of the Kingdom of God, "Our Locations," http://universal.org/who-where-how/our-locations.html; Freston, "Transnationalization," 202.

22. Oro, "A presença," 142–5; Pereira Pinto, "La Iglesia Universal," 45–7. In recent years at least one scholar has detected a less combative stance in the Portuguese IURD and a new emphasis on providing non-threatening "spiritual services": Claudia Wolff Swatowiski, "Igreja Universal em Portugal: tentativas de superação de um estigma," *Intratextos* número especial 01 (2010): 187–91.

23. Universal Church of the Kingdom of God, "Our Locations," http://universal.org/who-where-how/our-locations.html; Universal Church of the Kingdom of God, "South Africa," http://universal.org/who-where-how/our-locations/south-africa.html; Freston, "Universal Church," 39.

24. Freston, "Universal Church," 33.

25. Freston, "Universal Church," 36. The success of Brazilian missionaries could also be seen as evidence of Brazil's development into "a middle-size post-colonial power" that started "to occupy spaces such as those left in Latin America by the United States" after the end of the Cold War: Otávio Velho, "Missionization in the Post-Colonial World: A View from Brazil and Elsewhere," *Tensões Mundiais: Observatório das Nacionalidades* 2, no. 1 (2006): 204–5.

26. Freston, "Universal Church," 41–3, 48–9, 51.

27. Freston, "Universal Church," 46–7, 63.

28. Freston, "Universal Church," 42–5.

29. Freston, "Universal Church," 51–2.

30. André Mary, "Le pentecôtisme brésilien en Terre africaine: L'universel abstrait du Royaume de Dieu," *Cahiers d'Études Africaines* 42, no. 167 (2002): 464–7; "Sectas evangélicas de Angola se muestran indiferentes ante llegada del Papa," Agence France-Presse, March 19, 2009.

31. Pereira Pinto, "La Iglesia Universal," 47; Freston, "Transnationalization," 204.

32. Freston, "Universal Church," 62.

33. Maxwell Johnson, *The Virgin of Guadalupe: Theological Reflections of a an Anglo-Lutheran Liturgist* (New York: Rowman and Littlefield, 2002), 9.

34. Craig Nessan, *Orthopraxis or Heresy? The North American Theological Response to Latin American Liberation Theology* (Atlanta: Scholars Press, 1989), 215–6.

35. James H. Cone, *Black Theology and Black Power* (New York: Seabury Press, 1969).

36. Nessan, *Orthopraxis or Heresy?*, 147–51.

37. James Cone, "From Geneva to Sao Paulo: A Dialogue between Black Theology and Latin American Liberation Theology," in Sergio Torres and John Eagleson, eds., *The Challenge of Basic Christian Communities* (Maryknoll, NY: Orbis, 1981), 269, as quoted in Nessan, *Orthopraxis or Heresy*, 151.

38. Nessan, *Orthopraxis or Heresy*, 151–7.

39. Nessan, *Orthopraxis or Heresy*, 173–6.

40. Robert McAfee Brown, *Makers of Contemporary Theology: Gustavo Gutiérrez* (Atlanta: John Knox, 1980), 10–1.

41. Brown, *Makers*, 11.

42. Robert McAfee Brown, *Theology in a New Key: Responding to Liberation Themes* (Philadelphia: Westminster Press, 1978); Robert McAfee Brown, *Spirituality and Liberation: Overcoming the Great Fallacy* (Philadelphia: Westminster Press, 1988); Robert McAfee Brown, *Gustavo Gutiérrez: An Introduction to Liberation Theology* (Maryknoll, NY: Orbis Books, 1990); Robert McAfee Brown, *Liberation Theology: An Introductory Guide* (Louisville: Westminster/John Knox Press, 1993).

43. Nessan, *Orthopraxis or Heresy*, 181–5.

44. Brown, *Makers*, 78.

45. Alfonso López Trujillo, *Liberation or Revolution?: An Examination of the Priest's Role in the Socioeconomic Class Struggle in Latin America* (Huntington, IN: Our Sunday Visitor, 1977); Congregation for the Doctrine of the Faith, "Instruction on Certain Aspects of the Theology of Liberation," August 6, 1984, http://www.vatican.va/roman_curia/congregations/cfaith/documents/rc_con_cfaith_doc_19840806_theology-liberation_en.html.

46. Antonio Valeriano, *Nican Mopohua* (Mexico, 1649). An awkward English translation is available at Our Lady of Guadalupe, http://www.sancta.org/nican.html.

47. Carl Anderson and Eduardo Chávez, *Our Lady of Guadalupe: Mother of the Civilization of Love* (New York: Doubleday, 2009), 188.

48. Gastón Espinosa, "Today We Act, Tomorrow We Vote: Latino Religions, Politics, and Activism in Contemporary U.S. Civil Society," *Annals of the American Academy of Political and Social Science* 612 (July 2007): 156.

49. Jeanne Batalova, "Mexican Immigrants in the United States," Migration Policy Institute, April 2008, http://www.migrationinformation.org/feature/display.cfm?ID=679.

50. Todd Hartch, "Kentucky," in Mark Overmyer-Velázquez, ed., *Latino America: A State-by-State Encyclopedia* (Westport, CT: Greenwood Press, 2008), 337–9.

51. Timothy Matovina, "Theologies of Guadalupe: From the Spanish Colonial Era to Pope John Paul II," *Theological Studies* 70, no. 1 (March 2009): 85–8; Anderson and Chávez, *Our Lady*, 190–1.

52. John Paul II, "Ecclesia in America," January 22, 1999, http://www.vatican.va/holy_father/john_paul_ii/apost_exhortations/documents/hf_jp-ii_exh_22011999_ecclesia-in-america_en.html.

53. Another factor in the spread of Guadalupismo was its widespread appropriation and reinterpretation by Mexican American theologians and scholars such as Father Virgilio Elizondo: Matovina, "Theologies of Guadalupe," 79–85.

54. Gene Sager, "A Gringo's Devotion," *Commonweal* 134, no. 21 (December 7, 2007): 10–11.

55. Anderson and Chávez, *Our Lady*, ix–xi, xv–xvii. John Paul II's "Civilization of Love" emphasized a cultural renewal that put the human person at the center of society, while his "Theology of Body" offered a view of sexuality based on "the gift of self."

56. Meg Jones, "Scrap of Cloth Draws Flock of Faithful to La Crosse," *Milwaukee Journal Sentinel*, June 23, 2003.

57. Stephanie Innes, "Saint's Relic Draws Thousands," *Arizona Daily Star*, October 31, 2003; Rhina Guidos, "Utah Catholics Greet Venerated Relic," *Salt Lake City Tribune*, November 7, 2003.

58. Daniel Wakin, "At St. Patrick's, a Fragment of an Aztec Saint's Cloak," *New York Times*, December 6, 2003.

59. Anderson and Chávez, *Our Lady*, 157, 168–9; "Guadalupe Message Resounds at Los Angeles' Massive Marian Festival," *National Catholic Register*, August 6, 2012, http://www.ncregister.com/daily-news/guadalupe-message-resounds-at-los-angeles-massive-marian-festival/.

60. Shrine of Our Lady of Guadalupe, "History," http://www.guadalupeshrine.org/about/history; Our Lady of Guadalupe Seminary, http://www.fsspolgs.org/.

61. Johnson, *The Virgin of Guadalupe*, 12–5.

62. Johnson, *The Virgin of Guadalupe*, 122–6.

63. Paul Barton, "Guadalupe in Theology and Culture: A Hispanic Protestant Response to Nuestra Señora de Guadalupe," *ATLA Proceedings* 59 (2005): 142–8.

64. John Gorski, "How the Catholic Church in Latin America Became Missionary," *International Bulletin of Missionary Research* 27, no. 2 (April 2003): 60.

65. Gorski, "How the Catholic Church," 62.

66. CELAM, "Final Document," Art. 368, in John Eagleson and Philip Scharper, eds., *Puebla and Beyond: Documentation and Commentary* (Maryknoll, NY: Orbis, 1979). Other missionary aspects of the document are listed in Romeo Ballán, *El Valor de Salir: La aperture de América Latina a la misión universal* (Lima: Ediciones Paulinas, 1990), 104–5.

67. Ballán, *El Valor de Salir*, 10.

68. Dozens of John Paul's missionary exhortations to Latin America are excerpted in Ballán, *El Valor de Salir*, 31–53.

69. Gorski, "How the Catholic Church," 63; Ballán, *El Valor de Salir*, 147.

70. Ballán, *El Valor de Salir*, 138–49.

71. Jozef Tomko, "Mensaje de aperture de VI COMLA-I CAM," September 28, 1999, sedos.org.

72. Stephen Judd, "Journey of Immersion into Liminality: Forty Years of the Maryknoll Language Institute, Cochabamba, Bolivia," *U.S. Catholic Historian* 24, no. 3 (Summer 2006): 106.

73. Francisco McGourn, "Palabras de Bienvenida al Simposio," in *La Misión en el Umbral del Tercer Milenio: Simposio Latinoamericano de Misionología* (Cochabamba: Editorial Verbo Divino, 2002), 6.

74. Romeo Ballán, "Misión 2000: Retos y prioridades para la misión en América en el siglo XXI," in *La Misión en el Umbral del Tercer Milenio*, 139.

75. "Casas de Missão," Obra de Maria, http://www.obrademaria.com.br/.

76. "Histórico," Comunidade Católica Palavra Vida, http://www.palavraviva.com/portugues/historico.html.

77. "Missão em Portugal," Cançao Nova, http://www.cancaonova.pt/index.php?option=com_content&view=article&id=1&Itemid=2.

78. Eduardo Gabriel, "Catolicismo carismático brasileiro em Portugal," PhD diss., Universidade de São Paulo, 2010, 103–6.

79. Eduardo Gabriel, "A expansão internacional do catolicismo carismática brasileiro," *Análise Social* XLIV, no. 1 (2009): 198–200.

80. Eduardo Gabriel, "Catolicismo carismático brasileiro em Portugal," Ph.D. diss., Universidade de São Paulo, 2010, 12–4, 92–3, 104–11, 115–7, 130.

81. Gabriel, "A expansão," 201. Jansenism was a Catholic theological movement of the seventeenth and eighteenth centuries that emphasized Augustinian themes such as human depravity and divine sovereignty in a manner similar to Calvinism.

82. Gabriel, "Catolicismo carismático brasileiro," 18, 115–21, 125–6.

## CONCLUSION

1. Hernando Salazar, "Avivamiento: una iglesia singular," BBC Mundo, May 2, 2007, http://news.bbc.co.uk/hi/spanish/specials/2007/en_nombre_de_la_fe/newsid_6611000/6611617.stm.

2. Avivamiento Bogotá, Youtube" http://www.youtube.com/user/AVIVAMIENTO-BOGOTA.

3. Avivamiento Bogotá, "Avivamiento: Ecuador en Fuego—Pastores Ricardo y Paty Rodriguez," January 29, 2010, http://www.youtube.com/watch?v = DsKR4jkVp3w&list=FLMSLAq9ogxwZBjVt-2olJQw&index=77&feature = plpp_video.

4. Gabriel García Marquez, *One Hundred Years of Solitude* (New York: Harper & Row 1970).

5. Mario Vargas Llosa, "The Latin American Novel Today: Introduction," *Books Abroad* 44, No. 1 (Winter, 1970): 12.

6. Vargas Llosa, "The Latin American Novel Today: Introduction," 12.

7. Mario Vargas Llosa, " 'In the Past One Wrote to Gain Immortality: Today Nobody Believes in Eternity': An Interview with Mario Vargas Llosa," *World Literature Today* 76, No. 1 (Winter, 2002): 67.

8. Perhaps Vargas Llosa's views confirm the damage done by the absence of Catholic-Protestant dialogue and cooperation, which made it difficult to see any "Christianity," just squabbling sects with no common "master key for perceiving reality." Ecumenism is treated later in the chapter.

9. Sheldon Annis, "The Production of Christians: Catholics and Protestants in a Guatemalan Town," in Virginia Garrard-Burnett, ed., *On Earth as it is in Heaven:*

*Religion in Modern Latin America* (Wilmington, DE: Scholarly Resources, 2000), 197–200.

10. Francisco Javier Errázuriz Ossa et al., "Documento de Santiago. Acuerdo sobre el Bautismo," May 19, 1999, Conferencia Episcopal de Chile, http://documentos. iglesia.cl/; Jeffrey Gros, "Some Reflections on Ecumenism in Chile," *International Review of Mission* 97, no. 384 (April 2008): 61.

11. Gros, "Some Reflections," 62.

12. Richard John Neuhaus, "The Public Square: Evangelicals and Catholics to the South of Us," *First Things*, November 1999.

13. Neuhaus, "The Public Square."

14. Pedro Moreno, "Evangelical Churches," in Paul Sigmund, ed., *Religious Freedom and Evangelization in Latin America: The Challenge of Religious Pluralism* (Maryknoll, NY: Orbis, 1999), 57.

15. Edward Cleary, "The Catholic Church," in Paul Sigmund, ed., *Religious Freedom and Evangelization in Latin America: The Challenge of Religious Pluralism* (Maryknoll, NY: Orbis, 1999), 23–6.

16. Pontifical Council for Promoting Christian Unity and the Lutheran World Federation, "Joint Declaration on the Doctrine of Justification," October 31, 1999, Evangelical Lutheran Church in America, http://archive.elca.org/ecumenical/ecumenicaldialogue/romancatholic/jddj/index.html.

17. Benedict XVI, "Saint Paul (13): The Doctrine of Justification: from Works to Faith," General Audience, November 19, 2008, http://www.vatican.va/holy_father/benedict_xvi/audiences/2008/documents/hf_ben-xvi_aud_20081119_en.html.

18. Daniel Carroll Rodas, "El diálogo entre evangélicos y católicos: Asuntos en torno a la evangelización. Una perspectiva evangélica desde América Latina," *Kairos* 30 (January 2002): 92.

19. Thomas Rausch, "Catholics and Pentecostals: Troubled History, New Initiatives," *Theological Studies* 71 (2010): 936.

20. Antonio Aranda, "Iglesia Católica y confesiones cristianas frente a las sectas en América latina," *Scripta Theologica* 25, no. 3 (1993): 946. In fact, the Spanish word "secta" has a more negative connotation than the English word "sect."

21. Rausch, "Catholics and Pentecostals," 938.

22. Milton Acosta, "Power Pentecostalisms: The 'non-Catholic' Latin American Church Is Going Full Steam Ahead—but Are We on the Right Track?," *Christianity Today* (August 2009): 40–2.

23. David Roldán, "Dilemmas in the Evangelical Movement and Its Theology: Argentinean Perspective," *Evangelical Review of Theology* 34, no. 4 (2010): 302.

24. Pontifical Council for Promoting Christian Unity, *On Becoming a Christian: Insights from Scripture and the Patristic Writings, With Some Contemporary Reflections*, 2006, http://www.vatican.va/roman_curia/pontifical_councils/chrstuni/eccl-comm-docs/rc_pc_chrstuni_doc_20060101_becoming-a-christian_en.html.

25. Rodney Stark and Buster Smith, "Pluralism and the Churching of Latin America," *Latin American Politics and Society* 54, no. 2 (2012): 35–50.

26. *Unitatis Redintegratio*, Second Vatican Council, November 21, 1964, http://www.vatican.va/archive/hist_councils/ii_vatican_council/documents/vat-ii_decree_19641121_unitatis-redintegratio_en.html.

27. Aranda, "Iglesia Católica y confesiones cristianas," 955.

28. John Paul II, *Ut Unim Sint*, May 25, 1995, The Holy See, http://www.vatican.va/holy_father/john_paul_ii/encyclicals/documents/hf_jp-ii_enc_25051995_ut-unum-sint_en.html.

29. Solidarity emphasizes "total gratuity, forgiveness and reconciliation" to the extent that "One's neighbour must therefore be loved, even if an enemy, with the same love with which the Lord loves him or her." Subsidiarity affirms that "societies of a superior order must adopt attitudes of help . . . with respect to lower-order societies" so that "intermediate social entities can properly perform the functions that fall to them without being required to hand them over unjustly to other social entities of a higher level, by which they would end up being absorbed and substituted, in the end seeing themselves denied their dignity and essential place." Pontifical Council for Peace and Justice, *Compendium of the Social Doctrine of the Church* 186, 196, June 29, 2004, http://www.vatican.va/roman_curia/pontifical_councils/justpeace/documents/rc_pc_justpeace_doc_20060526_compendio-dott-soc_en.html#a.%20Meaning%20and%20value; Leo XIII, *Rerum Novarum*, May 15, 1891, Holy See, http://www.vatican.va/holy_father/leo_xiii/encyclicals/documents/hf_l-xiii_enc_15051891_rerum-novarum_en.html; John Paul II, *Centisimus Annus*, May 1, 1991, Holy See, http://www.vatican.va/holy_father/john_paul_ii/encyclicals/documents/hf_jp-ii_enc_01051991_centesimus-annus_en.html; Benedict XVI, *Caritas in Veritate*, June 29, 2009, Holy See, http://www.vatican.va/holy_father/benedict_xvi/encyclicals/documents/hf_ben-xvi_enc_20090629_caritas-in-veritate_en.html.

30. Lamin Sanneh, *Translating the Message: The Missionary Impact on Culture* (Maryknoll, NY: Orbis, 1989); Lamin Sanneh, *Encountering the West: Christianity and the Global Cultural Process: The African Dimension* (Maryknoll, NY: Orbis, 1993); Lamin Sanneh, *Disciples of All Nations: Pillars of World Christianity* (Oxford: Oxford University Press, 2008); Andrew Walls, *The Missionary Movement in Christian History: Studies in the Transmission of Faith* (Maryknoll, NY: Orbis, 1996).

31. Sanneh, Translating the Message, 29.

32. William Bivin, "Mother Tongue Translations and Contextualization in Latin America," *International Bulletin of Missionary Research* 34, no. 2 (April 2010): 72.

33. *Ad Gentes*, Second Vatican Council, 1965, http://www.vatican.va/archive/hist_councils/ii_vatican_council/documents/vat-ii_decree_19651207_ad-gentes_en.html.

34. Paul VI, *Evangelii Nuntiandi*, 1975, http://www.vatican.va/holy_father/paul_vi/apost_exhortations/documents/hf_p-vi_exh_19751208_evangelii-nuntiandi_en.html

35. Todd Hartch, *Missionaries of the State: The Summer Institute of Linguistics, State Formation, and Indigenous Mexico, 1935–1985* (Tuscaloosa: University of Alabama Press, 2006), 1–7.
36. A good first step would be the translation of Lamin Sanneh's works into Spanish and Portuguese.

# Index